Celebrating the Eucharist

CELEBRATING
THE EUCHARIST

A Practical Ceremonial Guide
for Clergy and Other Liturgical Ministers

Patrick Malloy

CHURCH PUBLISHING
an imprint of
Church Publishing Incorporated, New York

Library of Congress Cataloging-in-Publication Data

Malloy, Patrick.
Celebrating the Eucharist : a practical ceremonial guide for clergy and other liturgical ministers / Patrick Malloy.
        p.   cm.
ISBN 978-0-89869-562-5 (pbk.)
1. Lord's Supper—Celebration. 2. Lord's Supper—Episcopal Church. 3. Lord's Supper (Liturgy). 4. Lord's Supper—Lay administration—Episcopal Church—Handbooks, manuals, etc. I. Title.
BX5949.C5M35 2007
264'.03036—dc22

                                        2007040412

Printed in the United States of America.

Illustrations by Dorothy Thompson Perez
Cover design by Jennifer Glosser
Interior design by Vicki K. Black

Church Publishing, Incorporated
445 Fifth Avenue
New York, New York 10016

www.churchpublishing.com

07   08   09   10   11   12   13   10 9 8 7 6 5 4 3 2 1

CONTENTS

II. THE SUNDAY EUCHARIST

PREFACE

Church Publishing asked me to write a eucharistic customary for the Episcopal Church: a step-by-step, how-to book for ministers, lay and ordained, and for the assembly. I wrote something else. Since the Reformation, one group of Anglicans and then another have claimed to know the authentic way to celebrate the Eucharist. I did not want to jump into that fray.

Besides, at this point in the development of the Western liturgy, too much is in flux for anyone to presume to say a definitive word. Officially authorized liturgical materials are multiplying and liturgical spaces are configured in ever-evolving arrangements. Episcopalians (as well as most other groups of Christians) are diverse in ways unthinkable when the current Prayer Book became *the* Prayer Book in 1979. Rite 13, *Quinceañara*, cremains, divorce rituals, discontinuing life support: while same-sex blessings may make the headlines, they are but one of the contemporary realities the framers of the 1979 Prayer Book could not have imagined in the context of common prayer. The other major denominations, too, find themselves living in a brave new liturgical world, even if they are not featured on the evening news as often as we are.

The scholars and pastors who coordinated the experiments and compiled the findings that led to the 1979 Book of Common Prayer were not naïve. They knew they were creating a book of prayer to form a church that would live in an inconceivable world. Some clever person said that the crates of Prayer Books dropped at the doors of nearly every Episcopal Church in 1979 were full of time bombs. Almost thirty years later, they are still ticking in a church unawares.

Immersed in the rich stew that finally boiled over at Vatican II, the learned and wise editors of the Book of Common Prayer imagined a church where baptism, not ordination, was the threshold into full membership. Where the voice of God might come from people who never before had the right to speak. Where the face of God might look like a person no cradle Episcopalian had ever seen up close. Where the will of God might dawn first on someone other than the priests. Today, we are living into a future the framers of the Prayer Book glimpsed in the fog of the future: too far off and too clouded for them to know exactly what it was, but intimated nonetheless.

People once wrangled over the language of the Prayer Book as much as we wrangle over blessings for same-sex unions. Some still do. But language is the least of it. The 1979 Book of Common Prayer was not a new skin to hold old wine, a new way of saying old things. It marked, some would argue, a revolution. The skin and the wine were both new. The revolution began before Prayer Book revision did, but when the 1979 Prayer Book flew off the presses and hit the pews, it mapped out a path that would carry the revolution into the future. This Book of Common Prayer was indeed a time bomb, and it keeps on ticking.

The liturgy is serious business. It is not about dressing up and parading around, saying peculiar words and doing odd things. It is a confrontation with God that changes lives. And changed lives change the world. Annie Dillard famously wrote that Sunday congregations are like children with chemistry sets mixing up batches of TNT. They are blind to the power they hold in their hands.

This book comes out of pastoral experience as much as it comes out of academic study. For six years, the people of Grace Church in Allentown, Pennsylvania, have realized that they were dealing with explosives, and they have handled them carefully. They have worked to celebrate the Sunday Eucharist with as much authenticity as they can muster, recognizing what is at stake. The rectorship has been mine, but the liturgy has been ours. Literally dozens of people, and sometimes the entire parish, have prayerfully considered how to make what we do on Sunday reflect as fully as possible what we as Episcopal Christians believe. At the same time, we have worked to make what we do during the week true to what we do on Sunday. Whether we have decided to tweak some minor detail or to rip the whole thing apart and start over, we have decided it together.

The first two chapters set out in general terms how ritual works and, in particular, how it works in church. Most of the examples are from the Episcopal tradition, but hardly all. With rare exceptions, the references throughout the book are to the liturgical texts themselves and to some of the primary commentaries on them. The next chapter sets out principles for how a community might sift through all of those details as it finds its own way. The remaining chapters in Part I consider from theological, historical, and social scientific perspectives the building blocks of the eucharistic rite: postures and gestures, buildings, objects, time, and the ministries. An outline of what is at the core of the eucharistic liturgy provides a matrix for focusing on what is essential and not being distracted by the endless details that can draw the intellect, heart, and imagination away from the essence, which is nothing less than the presence of Christ.

Part II on the Sunday Eucharist is the "how-to" that Church Publishing wanted in the first place. Those chapters do not describe *the* way to do it; rather, they set out *one* way, sprinkled liberally with options that, in a particular pastoral setting, might be far better. Only rarely do I intend to say that to do it any other way would be a mistake. And, since a picture truly is worth many words, a collection of brief streaming videos illustrating what is described in this book will be posted at the Church Publishing website, http://www.churchpublishing.org/celebratingtheeucharist.

The how-to chapters are as much descriptive as prescriptive. They outline, for the most part, what happens on Sunday morning at Grace Church and many Episcopal churches like it. The earlier and later chapters are not disconnected, however; the liturgy we celebrate and the theory that informs it feed into one another. In nearly every instance, it is difficult to say which came first. Seminarians often complain that their course work has nothing to do with life in the trenches, that the theory does not prepare them for "real life." This is an attempt to bridge the gap and to show that, actually, it does.

◆ ◆ ◆ ◆ ◆ ◆ ◆

It was Paul Marshall, the Bishop of Bethlehem, who introduced me to the people of Grace Church even before I was a priest. When Bishop Marshall and I met almost seven years ago, he sensed what he believed to be God's will and he set out to do it. Knowing full well the risk he was taking, still he moved ahead, heedless of the cost. Then, six years ago today, Bishop Marshall ordained me a priest. He gave me the greatest gift I will ever receive. Never before had I known such grace. I could never thank him sufficiently for opening before me the way into my life.

I am grateful, too, to the wonderful people of Grace Church, whose love for the liturgy is matched only by their love for the poor, and who recognize God in the procession moving toward our food bank as much as in the procession moving toward the Table of Christ's Body and Blood. I have worshipped in many of the most renowned liturgical communities in the United States and have been a member of some of them, yet never have I experienced the joy, witnessed the honesty, or felt so keenly the presence of God as when we gather around the altar in our little church. They often say that ministers are given more than those to whom they minister. I know now that it is true.

29 September 2007
The Feast of St. Michael and All Angels

PART I

PRAYING
AND
BELIEVING

Chapter 1

ACTIONS SPEAK LOUDER THAN WORDS

In October 2006, the government of North Korea conducted an underground nuclear test in direct defiance of a United Nations resolution. As the nations of the world, individually and in council, renounced this apparently hostile act, the government of North Korea led the populace through a series of elaborate, highly sensual, and carefully choreographed rites. These were secular liturgies. By day, thousands of soldiers marched in perfect goosestep before monumental portraits of the president, Kim Jong-il. By night, hundreds of thousands of marchers who had been rehearsed for months arrayed themselves, each holding a blazing torch, in perfect formation across the North Korean countryside. None of this was spontaneous. It was highly liturgical.

These demonstrations, like all political demonstrations, were meant to have a twofold effect: to *express* something and to *impress* something. The North Korean rituals were designed to express the supposed pride of the people in their government and its nuclear achievement and, at the same time, to instill in the people pride for their government and its nuclear achievement. These two effects were not separate in time, but simultaneous. The set of claims that was being expressed by the populace and the set of claims that was being instilled in the populace were identical, and the medium by which they were expressed and instilled was a singular medium. The dynamic was perfectly symbiotic. As the rite was enacted, one can assume, the Koreans' pride swelled, and as the Koreans' pride swelled, the rites gained a fervor that no amount of rehearsal could ever have fomented. To say which came first, the rite or the pride, is as senseless as to rule in favor of the chicken or the egg. The ritual expression of pride and the pride itself arose together in one seamless movement.

This same symbiotic dynamic is operative in the Christian liturgy. The relationship between common prayer and common belief is dynamic. The title of Leonel Mitchell's famous book *Praying Shapes Believing* is true. The converse is also true: Believing shapes praying. And so, as on that day in North Korea, the liturgy both expresses and instills a set of beliefs and, more importantly, a worldview that most of the time is not even conscious to the participants.

The first Book of Common Prayer was created precisely because the medieval rites it replaced did not embody the emergent and officially sanctioned beliefs of the English Church. In other words, the medieval rites expressed what had become an unacceptable worldview and they instilled it in the people. The reformers knew that reformed theology would never take root among people who were enacting unreformed rites. And so the rites were changed. The result was a collection of liturgies that both expressed and taught a worldview.

The liturgies Christians celebrate today have the same dynamic effect. That is why it is worth spending so much time and reading so many words exploring what takes just over an hour in a congregation's busy week. Nothing is more important to the life of a community than what happens during that one hour on Sunday. At the most pragmatic level, the Sunday liturgy is the only time in the regular life of a community when everyone gathers. From Sunday to Sunday, individual members of the community and subgroups within the community live out their particular vocations within the baptismal vocation. On Sunday, however, the Body of Christ—precisely as the Body, precisely as the community of the baptized in all of its diversity—experiences itself in its totality. In this way, the Sunday Eucharist is a pivotal moment, both in the church's expression of what it is and in being formed into what it is.

Here is a concrete example of how this dynamic can come into play with real consequences in the life of a real parish. If the Sunday liturgy is largely a clerical affair done by the priest for the people, so that the people are mere responders or observers rather than key actors, the chances that the parish will grow into a group of integrated, self-starting, empowered ministers is greatly decreased. The liturgy will have expressed a worldview and simultaneously instilled a belief that "Father knows best," or "The priest has all the power," or "Our job as baptized people is to wait for the clergy to speak so that we will know how to respond," or "We lay people know how to take care of the nuts and bolts of this operation but when it comes to God, that's better left to the professionals." There will always be a small group of people in any congregation who, because of theological education, personal history, or one-on-one relationships with the clergy, will be able to overcome the messages such a liturgy expresses and impresses. But the liturgy is precisely common prayer, expressing and creating a common life. For the majority of the worshipping community, the liturgy's message is not easily resisted.

There will also always be those in any Sunday assembly who are not members of the church, but seekers who have come hoping to find something that will give their lives meaning and direction. They are true participants, but they usually keep a safe distance, often literally, from the rest of the group. The Sunday Eucharist paints a picture for them of what the church is—or, more truly, what the church aspires to be. It is not the only place they could explore the church. They could visit the parish soup kitchen, for example, and see the church as a force for social change and compassion. They could sit in on a midweek reading group and experience the church as a community of learning and exploration. They could observe the children's Sunday school and see the church as an agency that cares for the vulnerable and includes everyone, regardless of age. At the Sunday Eucharist, though, all of what the seeker might see in any of those venues is on display at one moment, and more. What the seeker sees will not be perfect, because no community is perfect, but the seeker sees what this imperfect community is striving to become, what it imagines when it pictures life in the reign of God.

The Sunday assembly of the church, then, is the most important moment in the church's relationship with itself and in its relationship with the world. Done well, ministering at the Sunday Eucharist facilitates the church's seeing and experiencing itself as the Body it is growing into, and, at the same time, showing the world an image of how human beings live when God's kingdom comes on earth as it is in heaven. The liturgy, in other words, is both formative and evangelical. Experiencing itself at its best, the community will be inspired to conversion. Showing itself at its best, the community will inspire others to conversion. In the liturgical dynamic, then, formation and evangelism are fused. Sunday is the day when the church "comes home," and Sunday is the day when the church invites seekers to "come and see."

For Anglican Christians, the liturgy, especially the Eucharist, is the central moment in the weekly life of the community. The liturgy is like a lens through which Anglicans view the world. Pressed to encapsulate what they believe, Anglicans do not usually turn to doctrinal formulae or the writings of founding theologians. They turn to the liturgy. Often they quote a simplified version of the dictum of Prosper of Aquitaine, *Lex orandi legem credendi statuat*, that is, the law of prayer establishes the law of belief. Common prayer establishes common belief. It is equally true, as we have seen, that common belief establishes common prayer. How Anglicans pray and how they believe are mirror images of one another.

The liturgy is not static and timeless, embodying eternal truths for the ages. It is organic. It both shapes the church's perceptions and is shaped by the church's perceptions. It is the crucible where the past and the present meet for Anglicans, and where they are melded into a new thing, continuous with the past and yet divergent from it in significant ways. This dynamic relationship between theology and liturgy is not enacted at the upper levels of church government, but in the parishes. The academy and the various authoritative national bodies are key in monitoring, sifting, and judging what is happening in local parishes, but the parishes are the crucible in which common prayer is being forged—and increasingly so. If this were not true, parish liturgical ministers would not matter much. Moreover, books like this would not be necessary. Liturgical communities could simply be told precisely what to do by some appointed authority, and the last word would have been said. In fact, however, the interaction between liturgy and belief happens within the liturgy as it is celebrated. It is essentially a grassroots, parochial phenomenon. The dynamic is not set in motion at the printing press.

While Anglicans define themselves in terms of liturgical prayer more than most other Christian traditions do, the *lex orandi, lex credendi, lex orandi* dynamic is universal, at work in every Christian tradition, even those that would deny they are liturgical. It is at work even in traditions that disdain the very word. Even communities claiming to worship in complete spontaneity actually use stock phrases and repeat certain behaviors, perhaps unaware that they are doing so. It is an anthropological and sociological fact that if ritual patterns do not evolve in a group, the group will not survive. People internalize and then externalize the rules and patterns of their community, even if they think they are following no rules or patterns. Non-liturgical Christians actually have a liturgy, even if they call it by another name.

At the other end of the spectrum from "non-liturgical" Christians are those who (like Anglicans) are intentionally and proudly liturgical. The Lutheran, Roman Catholic, Orthodox, and, increasingly, some mainline Protestant churches are consciously "liturgical." They pray according to an *ordo*, a pattern of worshipping that is inscribed in officially disseminated books. They look to the texts of their liturgical books, as they might to the texts of Scripture or the writings of their founding theologians, to define what their particular tradition holds to be true. More than texts come into play, however, in the liturgy. The liturgy is not the script that directs it; the liturgy is the actual event.

At some level, those who shape the liturgy and those who willingly participate in it instinctively know that the liturgy's words are hardly the whole of the *lex orandi*. They know that the architectural setting, the physical artifacts, and the bodily acts of the liturgy bear at least as much meaning and have at least as strong an impact as the liturgy's words. Riots spilled from English churches into the streets when the nineteenth-century Oxford Movement and, more directly, the concurrent Cambridge Movement set about reforming the church's buildings, sacred objects, and gestures. Instinctively the people knew that a new theological mindset was emerging and that it was being promulgated through visual, tactile, kinesthetic, and even olfactory channels. All of this was undeniably happening even though not a word of the Prayer Book had been changed. Parliament debated, Anglicans hurled anathemas back and forth, and Christians judged one another worthy of hell, not because anyone was playing with texts, but because they were toying with liturgical ceremonial.

All of this—Gothic arches; altars fenced with rails and screens; altar candles and mass vestments; unleavened bread and incense; priests facing eastward from the west side rather than priests facing southward from the narrow north side—all of this signaled that a fundamental theological shift was underway. Some people were willing to fight for it and just as many were willing to fight against it. No matter which side they found themselves on, however, they knew that the essential character of common prayer was being radically changed, even though not a letter was being added to or subtracted from in the Prayer Book. True, some Tractarians and Anglo-Catholics did insert brief texts into the Prayer Book liturgies, but those texts were not the focus of the battles. The battles were about what was being done and where it was being done and with what it was being done, not about what was being said. Everywhere in the Anglican Communion, regardless of which edition of the Prayer Book the particular national church was using, changing the artifacts and the choreography of the liturgy brought our forebearers to blows.

Our ancestors instinctively saw what we often miss, though like us perhaps they did not know exactly what they were seeing. Meaning is conveyed not only by the words on a page, or even by the speaking of those words aloud. The meaning and the impact of the liturgy come primarily from the interplay of the setting, the objects, the sensual triggers, and, of course, the texts, but hardly the texts alone. The words, printed or spoken, may in fact be secondary. As Gordon Lathrop, professor of liturgy at the Lutheran Theological Seminary at Philadelphia, has pointed out, liturgical meaning occurs in the juxtaposition of one thing against another. The texts are only one of the many things that the liturgy sets in juxtaposition. What we *do* in the liturgy, not only what we *say*, expresses what we believe. What we believe finds expression not only in what we say in the liturgy, but in what we do. As we pray, so shall we believe, and as we believe, so shall we pray. The pageants of Germany's Third Reich could not have changed anyone who was not willing to be changed. But surely many of those who were initially resistant to the Nazis' program were gradually convinced to at least consider it by the compelling ritual displays of Nazi identity. The rites made the message not only palatable but irresistible. The combination of a strong, meaning-laden ritual and a group of participants open to transformation gave birth to conversion.

Week by week a community celebrates the liturgy. Week by week the liturgy with its subtle messages assaults and shapes the community. The chance that nothing will change in the people or in the liturgy is slim. No less than the rites of the Third Reich or the rites of Twelve-Step programs or the rites celebrated in North Korea in 2006, the liturgy is geared toward change and will produce change, even when the change is not welcome or recognized. Almost always, the change that occurs as a result of a liturgical event—whether change in the participants or change in the rites—is so infinitesimal that it goes unnoticed. Only over time, and long stretches of time, does it become obvious that a transformation has been underway, and by then it is too late to undo it.

The changes that take place in the liturgy reverberate beyond that crucial hour on Sunday. The liturgy is a kind of "rehearsal." In and through it the church, using the medium of ritual, behaves as it aspires always to behave, but in a very stylized and controlled way. The exchange of the Peace, for example, is seldom an actual event of reconciliation between enemies, but is a stylized gesture that rehearses the community in reaching out with love to whomever is near. By this very act of "rehearsing," the church can grow, if only by the smallest increments, into being what it aspires to be.

Practice makes perfect—or rather, practice moves the church further along the road to a perfection that it can never attain.

Baptism makes the church into the Body of Christ. The Eucharist forms the church for living out what it already and truly is. The Eucharist is the ongoing aspect of the sacraments of initiation since it continues what baptism begins: the incorporation of the church into Christ. This is not merely a theological assertion but a practical, psychological, sociological assertion. The liturgy changes the church.

The core force in the liturgy, of course, is grace. Grace motivates participation in the liturgy in the first place, and, within the liturgy, grace is again present. Grace—a relationship with God, whether conscious or not—is both the precondition and the offer of the liturgy. Without grace, the Christian liturgy is hollow, and fruitful participation in it is impossible. The liturgy, like everything good in life, is an instance of grace. Grace, however, does not operate apart from human action. It operates *through* it. Everything that brought the seeker or the believer to the door of the church is grace, and everything within the liturgy that moves the seeker or the believer further into the saving action of God-in-Christ is grace. None of it is purely human—yet all of it is thoroughly human. The personal invitation to a friend to come along some Sunday, the offhanded comment about how much you love your parish, even the ad in the Yellow Pages that brings a seeker to the door are all at once human actions and instruments of divine grace.

The same is true within the liturgy itself. The brilliant sermon, the moving anthem, the glistening windows are all at once the flowering of human action and the pouring forth of divine grace. The graceful moment in the liturgy that opens the human heart or the human mind, that triggers the human imagination, that compels the human response, is precisely a grace-filled moment. Even the sting of standing in solidarity before God with others whose theology is not like our own or whose personalities rub us the wrong way: that, too, is grace. The entire liturgical action is sacramental, not only the consecrated Bread and Wine. In all the concrete realities of human life that are put in motion in the Eucharist—human bodies, human words, human gestures, human objects, human insights, human emotions, human food and drink—the Divine Reality is present and available. Grace permeates the entire liturgical event. Everything leading up to the Communion is not prerequisite mumbo-jumbo for making grace-filled Food and Drink. In every moment, in every action, in every object, there is grace made present in what is most basic and ordinary.

Every member of the assembly, no matter who they are or what their function in the liturgy, is an instance of grace-made-flesh. Grace is made present in a unique way through the action of the lector, the acolyte, the deacon, the sacristan, the soloist, and all the other ministers of the liturgy. Often overlooked but the most basic of all is the grace made present through the many actions of the assembly in its entirely. The priest is likewise a concrete and specific instance of humanity through which grace is made real. For Anglicans, as clerical as it may seem, we believe the grace that is made present through the human action of the presiding priest is unique.

There is a great danger in overemphasizing the importance or the "power" of the presiding priest. No less dangerous, however, is treating the role lightly. Little children in the assembly sometimes run up to me, throw their arms around my legs, and call me Jesus. It is funny, but it is not a joke. The eucharistic presider stands in the midst of the assembly as a symbol of Christ. The presider is both a symbol of the Mystical Body of Christ and a symbol of the Glorified Body of Christ. The presider models the stance of the church before God, and the stance of God-in-Christ toward the church.

Selflessness, humility, reverence, courage, transparency, love: These are the attitudes of the glorified Christ before the world, and, likewise, they are the attitudes the church, the Body of Christ, aspires to embody before its Savior. Liturgical ministers, whether ordained or not, are icons of both. Narcissism, self-importance, pious pretense, minced words, defensiveness, and haughty disdain have no place in a worthy liturgical minister. Clearly, all liturgical ministers exercise significant power in the church, yet the presiding priest, especially if he or she is also the preacher, is uniquely powerful in determining whether the liturgy embodies the church's highest ideals and whether it does so with such intensity and vigor that it can hardly be resisted. Robert Hovda, the twentieth-century American Roman Catholic pastoral liturgist who perhaps more than any other single person annunciated for all the churches a new yet ancient vision of what it is to preside over common worship, said it best. Liturgical presiders must strive to be "strong, loving, and wise." The entire story is in those few words.

All those who prepare any rite—the visionaries, the designers, the technicians—are crucial to the rite's eventual ability to elicit openness, vulnerability, trust, surrender, and, finally, incorporation into what the rite signifies. But more than all of them, those who actually enact the rite determine whether the rite will do what it was meant to do. Good planning is no substitute for good execution. This is not a how-to book for liturgical ministers. Grace is not the same as magic, and liturgy is not casting spells. This is a book about how human beings who are chosen to preside over and in various ways to lead and encourage the church's common prayer can use all that they are—the fullness of their humanity—in the service of God's manifestation in the world. So even when we explore how a priest might elevate the eucharistic Bread or how an acolyte might hold the hands during prayer or how a thurifer might swing a thurible, beneath it all is a more basic question: How can a liturgical minister use what is human and worldly and concrete so that a community can be open to the grace that God is offering and, receiving what is freely offered, go forth to embody Christ in the world?

Chapter 2

RUBRICS AND CUSTOMARIES

Recently, during a rehearsal just before a liturgy, a priest asked me if he should cense the cross along with the bread, wine, and monetary gifts at the Offertory. Who is to say? Whose rules apply? The rubrics in the Book of Common Prayer mention incense only once but even then the text does not say what to do with it (see Consecration of a Church, BCP 576). Since we were pressed for time and the liturgy was about to begin, I turned to the most complete and most widely applied set of Western liturgical rules, the rubrics of the Roman Rite. I told him that the Vatican II Roman Rite had not included the censing of the cross, but that the 2003 revision of it does. He said he really didn't care about the Roman Rite but, in the end, he did cense it. Had he chosen well or poorly? Who is to say?

I don't know why he decided to cense the cross. Maybe he had clear liturgical, anthropological, or theological principles in mind. Maybe he simply decided to do what he had seen before. "We have always done it this way" is, after all, the basis for more liturgical decisions than most of us want to admit. Maybe he wanted to cense the cross as an act of personal devotion. Maybe he did it for purely aesthetic reasons or for dramatic effect. I don't know. If there had been time to reason it through, we could have searched for principles guiding the decision whether to cense the cross—or to cense anything else, for that matter. But there was no time, and so I gave him an answer based upon the simplest set of rules in my arsenal.

Episcopalians are not bound by the Roman rubrics, of course, or any rubrics but our own. The problem is, we have precious few. The Book of Common Prayer is vague, and intentionally so, about what exactly we are supposed to do when we do the liturgy.

During the drafting of the current American Prayer Book, and the period of parish-based experimentation and testing that was carried out as the drafts were refined, the Standing Liturgical Commission steadily gathered reactions from "the field." Notes on the drafts and reports on the experiments were collected in a series of numbered booklets called *Prayer Book Studies*, booklets that appeared throughout the period of revision. *Prayer Book Studies IV* concerned the Eucharist. It was circulated widely, and the Commission collected and distilled reactions. Then, in *Prayer Book Studies XVII*, the commissioners described their quite conscious decision, in view of the responses they had received, to keep rubrics to a minimum.

> The rubrics in *Prayer Book Studies IV* exhibited a very marked trend toward fixing ceremonial, especially that of the postures of celebrant and people. Many welcomed this as a move toward clarifying confusion. Others resented it as an unnecessary intrusion upon and limitation of what should remain free and open to local custom and choice....
>
> The Commission has tried to face the problem objectively and has come to the unanimous conclusion that the Prayer Book tradition of openness with regard to ceremonial should be continued. This opinion is not merely a concession to the difficulty of achieving any basic norm of practice in a Church such as ours, with its deep-seated dislike of authoritarian uniformity in matters that are essentially "indifferent." It stems from our conviction that the present age is one of liturgical change and experiment, which is affecting all of Christendom. Despite the difficulties and inconveniences for many worshippers, we believe that new experiments and trial usages will in the long run help us to establish patterns of worship more meaningful in the modern age, and give us a flexibility in the present ecumenical ferment of liturgical renewal. An attempt to "freeze" ceremonial at the present time might cut us off from valuable insights and possibilities of development, as they are working out within the exchanges of our Anglican tradition and of fellow Christians of other communions.[1]

And so gaps were left where rubrics might have been. Liturgy, though, like nature, abhors a vacuum. The Jesuit liturgist and Orientalist Robert Taft has said that the "soft spots" in the liturgy—the moments where something has to happen besides the reading of a text—tend to accumulate provisional material and, in time, that material becomes set. The Prayer Book liturgies are full of soft spots, and they invariably are filled in with ceremonial. Then what has been added becomes "hard." The soft spots are solidified.

Forget for a moment that you have ever celebrated the Eucharist in an Episcopal Church. Erase from your memory "how it's done." Then pick up a Prayer Book and see with fresh eyes what actions the text actually mandates, lists as options, and forbids. You will not find much. And so people create rubrics and import them, and in time these behaviors, although they were once innovations, become quasi-canonical. Everyone, or

1. *Prayer Book Studies XVII* (New York: Church Pension Fund, 1966), 24f.

nearly everyone, forgets that it was ever done another way. They may even come to believe that it *may not* be done another way. They come to think that any other way would be less than "godly and decent." Since 1549, when the Preface to the first Book of Common Prayer saw the light of day, no committed Anglican has wanted to fall short when it comes to godliness and decency in church.

I began a class for aspiring priests and deacons recently by asking them to list, without opening the 1979 Book of Common Prayer, the rubrics at the very beginning of the Rite II Eucharist. They were sure that a procession of the ministers was mandatory, and that the Prayer Book listed the order in which they were to come down the aisle. The version of the rubrics on page 355 that was imprinted on their brains included the words "vested choir" and "crucifer and torches." They clearly remembered a directive that the congregation was to stand as the procession entered. They could also see the words "prelude" and "opening hymn," and they knew there was a directive that something was to be reverenced, although they argued about what it was. Was it the cross, the Table, or the Sacrament reserved in the aumbry? They were not sure about that, but about everything else they were very sure, and they all agreed.

In fact, almost none of these directives is in the Prayer Book. The Rite II Eucharist begins with an optional "hymn, psalm, or anthem." Then, with the people standing, the presider says the Opening Acclamation. That's it. Everything else the aspiring clerics could see so plainly in their mental edition of the Prayer Book is not in the paper-and-ink edition of the Prayer Book authorized in 1979. The accretions they listed are not aberrations, but neither are they are in the Prayer Book. This simply shows that, in putting the Prayer Book in motion, people necessarily insert "rubrics," that is to say, directives for what is to be done. Often, in time, they then assume that the directives are actually printed there under the authority of the General Convention. Sometimes people write these rules down for themselves or their parishes. Usually they do not. Whether or not they write down what they decide to do, they *do* decide, and they must. If they did not, Episcopalians would come together on Sunday morning and not even know how to get started.

Soon, many of my students will be ordained to the diaconate and priesthood, and some will take charge of congregations. The canons of the Episcopal Church give rectors singular control over how the liturgy is celebrated in the parish. Disabused of the illusion that the Prayer Book gives explicit directions for how the liturgy is to begin, they will realize that the community itself must decide how it will begin: how it will assemble, in what order it will assemble, with what musical accompaniment it will assemble, and all the rest. And that is just the beginning. After these first minutes, the service will often last for well over an hour. The underlying decision this parish and its rector will have to make about their worship is: *How do we decide?* The truth is, all priests have to lead congregations through those decisions. Even leaving things as they always have been is to make a decision about how the liturgy will unfold. "The way we've always done it" is a choice. It is not an obligation.

There are at least three options for making liturgical decisions: making it up as you go, adopting some other tradition's patterns, or embracing a set of principles that will allow the community itself reasonably to decide. The first option usually results in chaos. The second can provide interesting alternatives that can expand one's experience, but when those practices are adopted wholesale and arbitrarily, without careful thought for their place within an Episcopal congregation, they can constrain like a straight jacket. Only the third option provides a lasting and sensible way of making liturgical decisions. Anyone charged with preparing, leading, or serving the assembly during the liturgy needs to have a principled way of deciding what actions to insert, or not to insert, into the endless "soft spots" in the liturgies of the Book of Common Prayer. And for those principles truly to shape the worship of a particular congregation, they need to be understood and embraced by all (or most) of the members, and not remain the private and mysterious preferences of the presiding priest.

The Book of Common Prayer is not the only liturgical script that is largely silent about ritual behavior. As the first (and many would say the preeminent) English-language liturgy, the Prayer Book has influenced other Christians who worship in English. Their books, too, are generally vague about how the liturgy is to be done. The admirable *Book of Common Worship* of the Presbyterian Church (1993), for example, gives only this directive for beginning the Service for the Lord's Day: "All may stand as the minister(s) and other worship leaders enter." The 1978 *Lutheran Book of Worship* says only, "Stand.... The entrance hymn or Psalm is sung.... The minister greets the congregation."[2] *Evangelical Lutheran Worship* (2006), the successor to the *Lutheran Book of Worship*, is only slightly more directive. One of the options for how to begin the Communion service says, "The assembly stands. All may make the sign of the cross, the sign that is marked at baptism, as the presiding minister begins" (ELW, 94). Compare these spare instructions to the introductory rubrics of the Roman Mass:

> After the people have assembled, the priest and the ministers go to the altar while the entrance song is being sung. When the priest comes to the altar, he makes the customary reverence with the ministers, kisses the altar and (if incense is used) incenses it. Then, with the ministers, he goes to the chair. After the entrance song, the priest and the faithful remain standing and make the sign of the cross....

Even further details are given in the *General Instruction of the Roman Missal*, the official customary that guides the celebration of the Eucharist in the Roman Catholic Church, which fills in the gaps and removes the ambiguity from phrases like "the customary reverence." It spells it all out, so that little is left to chance. And as time goes on and the reformed Roman liturgy of the 1960s is itself reformed, less and less is left to chance. The extreme specificity of the Roman Rite can be constraining and can pose serious challenges to a local community trying to make the liturgy its own. That is one end of

---

2. To augment these spare directions, Augsburg Publishing House issued a *Manual on the Liturgy: Lutheran Book of Worship*. It was not, however, an official publication of the Lutheran bodies that authorized the *Book of Worship*.

the rubrical spectrum. At the other end are rites that offer almost no directions. They pose equally serious challenges to the communities who want to celebrate them in a "godly and decent" way. Like all challenges, it can be a pit waiting to be fallen into or an opportunity waiting to be seized.

When Archbishop Thomas Cranmer and his collaborators compiled the first editions of the Prayer Book, they drew most strongly from the liturgical books of the Sarum usage, the Roman liturgy as it was celebrated in the Diocese of Salisbury (or *Sarum* in Latin). The books of the Sarum usage, like other medieval liturgical books, were highly rubricized. Rubrics were printed within the rites themselves in red ink (and from this took the name "rubrics"), in prefaces to the liturgical books, and in official, supplemental books of directions called "customaries." The rubrics directed not the *words* to be said during the liturgy, but the *actions* to be performed. Almost exclusively, the directions were meant for the clergy. The medieval books had little if anything to say about what the rest of the people did since they were not seen as important, much less essential, for the performance of the rites. The reformers, however, were convinced that these rubrics fostered superstition and scrupulosity within rites that had become like magic acts rather than expressions of faith in a God who freely saves. The reformers objected to liturgies that (they believed) encouraged a fear that salvation required not simply acceptance of the gift of grace in Jesus Christ, but the fastidious performance of arcane rituals. The common phrase "hocus pocus" is a corruption of the Latin liturgical phrase *Hoc est enim, corpus meum*: "This is my Body." "Hocus pocus" is how the priests' mumbling prayer sounded to the people. The liturgy had become a complex system of "magic words" paired with "magic gestures." The reformers, especially the more radical, went after the rubrics of the medieval liturgy root and branch.

Cranmer and his associates also slashed at the rubrics, but not so unrelentingly as many of their continental counterparts. The English reformers suppressed most but not all the gestures; Cranmer retained only what he could defend on the basis of antiquity or practical need. For many Anglicans, it was not enough. The more Protestant-leaning threatened to leave the church unless even the few remaining gestures were removed; eventually, they did leave. The Puritans objected especially to the wearing of the surplice and cope, kneeling for Communion, the giving of a ring in marriage, and signing the forehead with the cross in Baptism. They saw these acts as remnants of a corrupt religion that was not real Christianity, and they could not abide them.

These liturgical struggles were the backdrop for the Elizabethan Settlement, the attempt of Queen Elizabeth I to create liturgical forms that were tolerable to all but the most Protestant- and Roman-leaning members of the church. The 1559 Book of Common Prayer, promulgated during her reign, is recognized by some as a marvel of liturgical compromise and inclusivity, and by others as a triumph of ambivalence. What is beyond question is that the liturgy was palatable enough to most of her subjects that they were at least able to go to church on Sunday without feeling they were violating their consciences. Part of what made these liturgies successful was their ability to be put in motion in a number of ways without compromising what the Prayer Book intended. With regularity since the issuing of the 1559 Book of Common Prayer, Anglicans have taken liberties, not so much with what they *say* during the liturgy, but with what they *do*. Some have been slavishly obedient to the rubrics, few as they are; others have introduced behaviors beyond the rubrics, claiming that what is not forbidden is allowed; some, on the basis of principle, have ignored some of the few rubrics there are. Much of what some Anglicans added to the Prayer Book ritual were the very ceremonies the reformers detested.

The English reformers probably never imagined the level of liturgical complexity that the rites of the Prayer Book could accrue, and that eventually would become commonplace in Anglican churches. Since the Reformation, scores of complete guidebooks, some of which have become Anglican classics, have been written for how actually to celebrate the Prayer Book rites. These unofficial ceremonials are books of rubrics that *could* be in the Prayer Book, if there actually were such extensive rubrics in the Prayer Book. Each ceremonial is different, undergirded by a specific set of principles and assumptions, but few of those principles are ever explicitly laid out. Usually, ceremonials simply say what is to be done as if it were law, but never say why.

As we have seen earlier, when the directives of these ceremonials are put into motion in the liturgy, they not only assert a particular theology and worldview, but are a means of conveying it. All ritual accretions both express and impress beliefs, from the wearing of preaching tabs to signing the body with the cross at the naming of the Trinity to bowing before the altar or the reserved Sacrament. All of the innumerable ritual behaviors that Anglicans perform every day display a set of theological beliefs, and at the same time subtly and gradually propagate them. The absence of these ritual gestures—and especially the explicit conscientious refusal to include them—also makes a theological statement and imparts a theological worldview. This is the Anglican claim that belief and liturgy mirror one another in a circular, mutually determinative relationship, and that more than the words of the Prayer Book are involved in "how we pray." "How we pray" is the actual liturgy, which necessarily includes elements beyond what is on the printed page. Anglicans have always known this, and so have carefully attended to what people were actually *doing* when they went to church, not just to what they were saying.

Ceremonials, whether for the entire Prayer Book or only for specific rites in it, proliferated especially during the time of the nineteenth-century Catholic Revival. It was an era when scholars, first from Oxford and then from Cambridge, became fascinated with what the English Reformation had consciously abandoned. They believed that as a result of what had been lost, the church had grown devotionally tepid and theologically rationalistic, and they longed for what they imagined was the intense religious devotion and mysticism of the Middle Ages. They believed that restoring something of the medieval liturgy was the surest way to restore the intensity of medieval piety. To that end, they spelled out in detail how the liturgy was to be done, based upon how they understood its medieval antecedents had been done. Later, in the industrial slums of England, priests working with the destitute moved well beyond the ritual behavior and artifacts that had been discarded at the Reformation, and appropriated what they saw as the authentic organic development of the medieval rites: the post-Reformation Roman Catholic liturgy. Even beyond the liturgy, they taught and encouraged Anglicans to emulate Roman Catholic devotional customs. This included Italianate extra-liturgical accretions that did not even exist when the Church of England and the Church of Rome parted ways. This ritual elaboration of the Book of Common Prayer was the pinnacle of what has come to be known as the Anglo-Catholic Movement. It is ironic that many of the gestures introduced in the nineteenth century and now seen as integral to Anglican liturgy were vigorously suppressed by Cranmer and his colleagues. Even more remarkable, many of the customs were imported from the Counter-Reformation Roman Catholic Church, which was in the process of denouncing Anglican orders as "absolutely null and utterly void."

The Oxford, Cambridge, and Anglo-Catholic Movements were not the only revolutions that grew from the soil of nineteenth-century religious dissatisfaction. The equally important Liturgical Movement, a pastoral and academic revolution that simultaneously sent Anglican and Roman Catholic scholars and pastors on a quest for liturgical authenticity in light of the practices and theology of the early church, would change how Anglicans, Roman Catholics, and members of every other mainline Christian tradition understood and celebrated the liturgy. The Liturgical Movement shared with the Oxford, Cambridge, and Anglo-Catholic Movements a pastoral concern for ordinary believers and a sense that the solution for many of Christianity's modern shortcomings was to be found in the past. The proponents of the Liturgical Movement, however, reached further back in history than the Middle Ages. Thanks to advances in archeology and textual scholarship, they were able to engage in an extensive *retour aux source* that romanticized the patristic era. By settling on an era well *before* the theological disputes that gave birth to the Reformation, the Liturgical Movement pointed to common ground where nearly every Christian tradition could stand in good conscience. The liturgies of the earliest centuries, and especially those of the fourth century, when the formal public liturgy of the Western church first emerged and accrued much of the dignity of the imperial court, became the model that most mainline Christian traditions began to emulate.

After more than one hundred years of research, fermentation, and experimentation, the late twentieth century saw the creation of new liturgies that drew heavily on the historical, liturgical, and theological evidence that the Liturgical Movement had unearthed and explored. These rites were formed and studied with the tools of historians, anthropologists, sociologists, psychologists, linguists, and specialists in liturgy, as the churches attempted to draw upon what was most ancient and most modern, what was most enduring and what was newly emerging.

Setting aside the question of whether the liturgical tradition of the early church deserves such emulation, it is clear that these new liturgies bear a striking resemblance;

some are essentially indistinguishable, despite crossing denominational lines. Along with the similarity in the rites themselves, a common ecumenical liturgical vision has emerged. The polemics of the Reformation are not resolved, but they have generally receded behind a shared theology and a shared understanding of how liturgy is to be enacted and why. More than at any time since the Reformation, in the twenty-first century it is now possible to discern a Western normative liturgical pattern.

The liturgies of the many new revisions of the Book of Common Prayer in the churches of the Anglican Communion, most still sparse in rubrics, can be enacted in any number of ways. For those who lead worship in these Anglican churches the questions remain: How do we do these rites? Who is to say? Whose rules apply? At this juncture in the history of the Western church, we usually do not look for answers in a past era that has been dubbed "golden," whether the medieval or the patristic. We do not turn, either, to the Reformation age when the first Prayer Books were created, an age of discord and theological upheaval during which much of what was said and done was reactive, not creative. We look instead to the ecumenical consensus that has steadily emerged during the past fifty years. It is a dynamic consensus, forged as new liturgies have been shaped in the light of ancient ones, as communities have put them into motion, and as scholars have reflected on the actual experience of the church at prayer. The principles upon which this book is based come from this period of emergence, from the many and varied answers all of the Christian traditions have given in council, in classroom, and in church on Sunday. It is to these principles we now turn.

Chapter 3

PRINCIPLES FOR MAKING LITURGICAL DECISIONS

PRINCIPLE 1
The entire assembly celebrates the liturgy.

The 1979 Book of Common Prayer consistently refers to the priest who presides over the Eucharist as "the celebrant." In 1979, this represented the recovery of an ancient term. It replaced the two words "priest" and "minister" that were used in the 1928 Book of Common Prayer, the immediate predecessor of the current Prayer Book. The term "celebrant" was similarly adopted by many other churches, both of the Anglican Communion and from other traditions, in the liturgical books that emerged in that same era.

Since those early days when new liturgical texts were being issued, however, virtually every significant piece of writing on the liturgy has used the word "president" or a derivative term to refer to the minister who leads the service. This is consistent with the most ancient usage. For example, Justin Martyr, who in the second century recorded our earliest extant description of what Christians did on Sunday, speaks of "the president of the assembly." In the United States, where the word "president" carries obvious cultural nuances that clash with the church's understanding of the role of the one who presides over the liturgy, the neologism "presider" is the accepted term. *Evangelical Lutheran Worship*, the official liturgical book of the Evangelical Lutheran Church in America issued in 2006, has adopted the term "presiding minister." In the Church of England, recent liturgical books use "president."

Substituting "presider" for "celebrant" is not a semantic trifle. It bespeaks a mindset that affects how the liturgy unfolds and what impact it can have in the life of a community. If the priest is understood to be *the* celebrant, then others in the assembly may perceive themselves to be observers, or, at best, assistants to the one who is "up front." The ecclesiology of the Book of Common Prayer is that in the entire life of the church, including the liturgy, all those who are baptized are active, not passive, members of the Body of Christ. A key to inviting the entire assembly into assuming its active role in the church's life is to allow it to assume its active role in the liturgy. For this to happen, the presider must conceive of herself or himself as a member of the assembly who is presiding over the actions of the whole, not an isolated actor celebrating in view of or in place of the assembly, whose only task is to observe, assist, and passively receive.

PRINCIPLE 2
Liturgical acts are not things to be done during prayer, but are themselves prayer.

If you have ever gently touched the cheek of someone you love, or laid your hand upon the head of a fevered child, you know what love-in-action is. The gesture itself is loving. One might say that the gesture itself is the love being given. People instinctively know when an embrace or a touch is genuine, when it is love incarnate. They sense that the person touching them is somehow wholly present in the action. People instinctively know, by contrast, when a gesture is fraudulent or detached. The person is absent from the action. This is what we mean when we say that someone is "going through the motions." When a person is being authentic, we might say that she is "present in the motions." In the liturgy, every motion can be prayer if the actor is present in it. Walking can be prayer, sitting can be prayer, opening the arms in the *orans* (the praying position) can be prayer.

There is the bow that is made because it is supposed to be made, and there is the bow that is made because it is an instinctual or deep-rooted response to the presence of the living God. In such a bow, the eyes are drawn to the floor and the head bends toward the waist because the idea of being stiff-necked before God is unthinkable. A person at prayer does not always feel the emotions that would lead to such an authentic gesture. But the believer, trusting in the presence of God even when God seems absent, retains an attitude of reverence and wonder even when the immediate feelings are lacking. In Twelve-Step programs, recovering addicts encourage one another to "fake it 'til you make it." At times in the liturgy, the feelings that ideally would accord with the gesture will escape us. That is when the gesture must emerge from a deeper and more enduring place: from a carefully nurtured attitude.

Other Anglican churches, such as those in Africa, many youth gatherings, and congregations that are part of the charismatic renewal movement, have a great deal to teach the church about embodied prayer. Although most Episcopalians are not entirely comfortable embracing an exuberant style of praying and singing, dancing and swaying with one's whole body in the liturgy, we do in fact pray with our bodies throughout the liturgy. We pray as we stand, kneel, sit, or bow, and we can incorporate the principles of bodily prayer learned from other expressions into even the most formal liturgy.

To pray with one's body requires imagination. What are we doing when we are walking down the aisle? Is it just getting from here to there, or is it a snapshot of the march to the kingdom of God, an entrance of unworthy but readily accepted servants into the presence of the Body of Christ? A procession made up of people who have engaged their imaginations so they can pray with their bodies and who have made the simple act of walking a prayer can become a revelation for the entire assembly of a deeper truth about what God is doing in its midst.

Likewise, the *orans* position is not merely the aping of an ancient posture but can be a way of opening oneself in trust before God, making oneself vulnerable and undefended, taking one's heart in one's hands and then offering it with all that it holds to the One who fashioned it. In the *orans*, the person at prayer may feel the God within stretching toward the God who dwells in inaccessible light: deep calling unto deep.

When the presider, the other liturgical ministers, and all the members of the assembly pray with the body and do not merely do prescribed bodily gestures while praying with the voice, an authenticity shines forth that both expresses and impresses upon the church its most deeply held convictions about who it is before God.

PRINCIPLE 3
The church at prayer is Christ in his Body at prayer.

The church is holy, not because it is perfect or even good, but because it is the Body of Christ by baptism. Paul wrote that we do not know how to pray, but it is the Spirit in us that prays. It is that Spirit, poured into us in baptism, that makes us the Body of Christ. In us and through us, Christ cries out, "Abba, Father!"

In the liturgy, the church enters consciously and intentionally into the prayer that Christ offers ceaselessly before God. The liturgy, then, is not a matter of some people watching others do sacred things, but of the entire assembly being caught up in a sacred and eternal event. While the liturgy is sometimes considered a window into heaven, it is more than that. It is an *actual participation* in the liturgy of heaven. "Joining our voices with angels and archangels" is the least of it. We are giving our voices and our bodies to Christ so that he might pray his eternal prayer before God "on earth as it is in heaven."

This requires of the assembly, and especially of the liturgical ministers, a simultaneous awe before what is happening in and through it, and a confidence and strength worthy of what is happening in and through it. The church is a communion of saved sinners. It is the very Body of Christ, but it is made up of people who are ordinary and flawed. When the church is able to hold in tension humility and strength, it comes close to knowing itself for what it most deeply is. Ministers who are both humble and strong model for the rest of the church what it means to be the Body of Christ. It is a way of behaving that is born of a sense of who one is: *simil iustus et peccator,* at once saved and sinful. You cannot don that awareness with the vestments. Such self-awareness comes only through the willingness daily to live the life of Christ, crucified and risen.

PRINCIPLE 4
Christianity and Christian worship is earthy, not esoteric.

The scandal of Christianity is the belief that in Jesus, the formless and eternal God became flesh in a particular time and place. It is an astonishing claim with astonishing implications for everything that exists. The ecumenical International Consultation on English Texts (ICET) version of the *Te Deum* says, "You did not shun the Virgin's womb." The wonder of the incarnation is that the most earthly and earthy of realities are not only tolerated by God but are chosen and embraced by God as vehicles of grace.

The Eucharist is not about a sanitized or other-worldly event, and so it is not a sanitized or other-worldly event. What the world saw in Christ was not layered over his humanity or buried under his humanity. It was integral to his humanity: relational, warm, courageous, vulnerable, loving, and driven, it seems, to reach out to the socially alienated and the religiously hated. When the church rejected Docetism, it rejected the belief that God only *seemed* to be human in Christ. It affirmed that God was in fact present in the very humanity of Christ.

In what was most human in Jesus, the world saw what was divine. In the liturgy, the presence of Christ is revealed in the same way: in what is most human and earthy and basic. In human touch and oil lavished on; in bread broken and wine poured, in a meal eaten and drunk; in water washing over the one being made new; and in every other use the church makes of the things of the earth, God-in-Christ acts and is manifest. There is no need to make the "stuff" of the liturgy sterile or "holy" for God to use it as a vehicle of grace. The message of the incarnation is that in the very ordinariness of things God reveals the Divine Self.

In the Eucharist, Christ becomes present through the action of the church around bread and wine, two of the most basic elements of most human cultures. One of the greatest insights of the modern liturgical renewal is that the revelatory power of the objects and gestures of the liturgy comes from how fully the church allows their earthy and human qualities to shine forth. The bread of the Eucharist, for example, when it is real bread that can be torn and shared, can trigger deep insights that pressed Communion wafers cannot. Let me refer again to my students, the aspiring priests and deacons. The week after we discovered how little the Prayer Book rubrics actually say, we celebrated the Eucharist together using flatbread instead of hosts. For almost all of them, it was the first time they had ever used anything but wafers. During the fraction, the presider tore the one loaf into enough pieces for the entire group and then said the invitation.

After the liturgy, as we discussed what had impressed us during the celebration, many said that they were struck almost to the point of shock that we, though many, are one Body, for we all share in the one Bread. The notion was not new to them, of course, but the deep, personal experience of it was. What had been a purely intellectual notion had become a visceral, emotional certainty. The gesture of using earthy bread, and deliberately tearing it, at a measured pace, into enough pieces for everyone had a formative impact.

Other students commented—building upon the initial insight—that as the Bread was torn, they were put in mind of the broken body of Jesus. Others said their thoughts turned to those who have no bread to eat, who do not merit a piece of the earth's bounty. Someone said that it occurred to her that what was on the altar was a mirror image of we who were around it. St. Augustine, of course, said the same thing sixteen hundred years earlier. That depth of insight came from the reverent but unpretentious handling of the most earthy, simple, and human of things. If the presider had taken a host, quickly snapped it, and set the two pieces on top of a pile of perfect and completely separate hosts, there is hardly a chance that the fraction would have opened the hearts of those students to such rich religious feeling or such deep theological insight, or to such an engagement with some of the core biblical images associated with the Eucharist.

Incising a cross into the bread would have not made it any more "holy," nor would it have led to more profound insights. The power in the liturgical symbols is in the strength and integrity of the symbols themselves. The scandal of Christianity is that in humanity there was divinity, and in the earthly there is the heavenly.

PRINCIPLE 5
The essential elements should always be highlighted, not hidden or dwarfed.

The most important things on the Lord's Table are the bread and the wine. In many congregations, however, the bookstand is the visually dominant item. By virtue of its size and, in some cases, its ornamentation, it demands attention. Next to it, a shallow dish of paper-thin wafers does not stand a chance. What are the essential things when the church celebrates the Eucharist? Which actions are key, which are secondary, and which are purely utilitarian? Which objects are indispensable and bear the greatest theological weight? These questions apply not only to what is placed upon the altar, but to every object and every action in the liturgy.

No less a proponent of full and careful liturgy than Percy Dearmer wrote, "The evil in all religious customs, throughout history, has been the piling up of trivial details; and both wisdom and learning are constantly needed to prevent the perpetuation of individual follies."[3] The problem with "the piling up of trivial details" is that they dwarf and strangle the essential things.

Dearmer was not arguing for a Puritan aesthetic. Some liturgical details are anything but trivial, since they draw attention to the core of what God is doing in and through the assembly's action. Still, Dearmer was right. The liturgy does tend to collect bits of culture and traces of piety as the years roll by, and many of them, especially as they accumulate, pull the imagination, the emotions, and the intellect away for the heart of the matter. The Western churches today are seeking a balance between a liturgy laden with distracting clutter and a liturgy that denies that God reveals the Divine Self in created matter. The pastoral task is to distinguish the "trivial" from the enriching in liturgical objects, texts, and actions.

---

3. Percy Dearmer, *The Parson's Handbook* (London: Grant Richards, 1899), 227.

PRINCIPLE 6

When neither the rubrics nor the canons dictate what to do and reason does not provide a solution, the Roman Rite is a good place to start.

Some liturgical decisions can be made on the basis of theology, the social sciences, historical precedent, and the practical situation of the assembly, such as the configuration of its liturgical space or the number of ministers available. Some decisions, however, simply cannot be reasoned through.

For example, the Book of Common Prayer does not mention or have guidelines for how to perform the lavabo—the ritual washing of the presider's hands. How should it be done and what, if anything, should be said? A congregation could logically decide whether to do the lavabo at all, and even how. But what the presider should say, if anything, is not a matter of logic. The Roman Rite prescribes that the presider quietly recite Psalm 51:2. Why not? Why struggle to come up with something else?

The Roman Rite does not deserve consideration because the Roman Catholic Church and its liturgies are in any way superior to others. It is, however, the largest of the Christian denominations and its liturgical books are the most rubricated. The Roman Rite is normative in the West, not because it is superior, but because it is so widely celebrated and its rules are so complete. That is why, for example, the Roman color scheme has become, with only minor variations, universal. There is no logical reason, really, why green vestments should be worn during the weeks after the Epiphany and Pentecost except that it is the Roman custom and, therefore, it is remarkably widespread. When traditions that did not previously have a liturgical color scheme have adopted one, even unofficially, they have looked to Rome. It is the logical place to look.

This creates uniformity across denominational lines. It sets up a touchstone for all the churches. Of course, when the theology or the heritage of a particular church provides guidelines, the Roman rubrics should not take precedence. But when the particular tradition provides no guidance, Rome is a good place to search for answers.

Consistency across denominational lines has been an articulated goal of the liturgical renewal. In 1964, during the fertile days when all the major denominations that worship in English were revising their liturgical books, a commission was established to produce shared translations of common liturgical texts like the *Sanctus* and the dialogue "The Lord be with you. And also with you." The work of this body, the International Consultation on English Texts (ICET), ensured ecumenical consistency and made it possible for Christians of different traditions to worship easily together and to share musical settings for common texts. Many of the "Mass settings" in the *Hymnal 1982* are also used by other denominations. Some were composed for the Episcopal Church and borrowed by others. Some traveled the other direction.

Ironically, the Roman Catholic Church is about to abandon some of those agreed-upon texts and adopt more literal translations of the Latin originals. Many English-speaking Roman Catholics are resisting the change, and for good reason. Not only will it render useless a great deal of music written in the last forty years and cause upheaval in Roman Catholic parishes, it will also drive a wedge between Roman Catholic and other Christian liturgical traditions. In other words, it will move Rome out of what we have referred to as the Western ecumenical consensus. The consensus is the product of enormous effort and compromise on all fronts, and to have the largest constituent body abandon an important part of it, some would argue, is tragic.

Both the adopting of common texts and now the potential abandoning of common texts is instructive. It shows the value of seeking common ground and the damage that is done by leaving it. Still, Rome remains the most influential, holding the most ground and providing a place from which to seek commonality. Except in areas where Roman customs embody a foreign theology or culture, or are an explicit rejection of shared customs, they provide a common base, as the ICET texts do, for ecumenical convergence.

PRINCIPLE 7
Less is generally more.

A lot happens in the eucharistic liturgy. Those who do it every week may not realize just how much goes on. Visitors do. Even the core involves a great many words, objects, and gestures. The human mind can only attend to so much. At some point, known more by instinct than science, the mind can absorb no more. Not only does the brain (and, therefore, the heart and the soul) fail to take in what is added beyond the "breaking point," it fails to grasp anything. The circuit, as it were, shorts. The liturgy feels like a jumble, even if each of its constituent parts is, in itself, a gem.

In its entirety and in each of its segments, a rite can bear only so much before it becomes clogged. I have been to Easter liturgies that began with all the verses of the wonderful hymn, "Hail thee, festival day," and then, after only the Opening Acclamation, moved directly to a sung *Gloria*. Then, after each of the readings came all the verses of another metrical hymn. As the liturgy went on, so did the music. The rite was overload. Not just the last hymn was burdensome, but the memory even of the first hymn became unpleasant. There was simply too much music, and so all of the music seemed like too much. Less would have been more.

As the liturgical planning team considers each optional element, it must consider it within the context of the liturgical unit in which it will be embedded, and the complete liturgy. Many liturgical texts, objects, gestures, and musical elements have a great deal to commend them, but as they accumulate, they choke one another.

Although we are concerned here with the Sunday Eucharist, funerals are a common event when the accumulation of "meaningful" or "moving" items renders all of them meaningless and stultifying. The liturgical team working with the family to plan the funeral must move gently but with a clear vision of what the liturgy can bear. Often, if everything the family mentioned or even explicitly requested were done during the liturgy, the family and the rest of the assembly would find themselves drowning in a liturgical flood. By carefully partnering with the family to select a limited number of liturgically functional items, the ministers, in the long run, will provide a far more pastorally helpful liturgy.

The Sunday Eucharist is the same. Too much, even of good things, is still too much. Liturgical decisions should be made so that the overall structure of the rite is not obfuscated by the constituent elements, and the various elements do not accumulate until they strangle one another.

PRINCIPLE 8
*It is far more fruitful to ask what the liturgy and its components do
than to ask what they mean.*

When people come up against an unknown language or a secret code, they ask what it means. They do not experience it; they decipher it. When people come up against a thing of mystery and beauty, they wait to see what it will do to them, what impact it will have. They do not decipher it; they experience it.

Think of approaching a striking piece of art in a foreign museum. It draws you in and does something to you. Perhaps it delights you or disturbs you; it makes you smile or makes you frown. It confronts you with the brevity of human life or the boundlessness of the human spirit. It attracts you or repels you. It lifts you into hope or it drives you into despair. The art does many things to you, and as you change, your experience of the art may change. You might look at it from different angles; you could take it in quickly or sit before it for hours. Every time you see the artwork it does something else. To ask what the art *means* is to ask the wrong question. The right question is: What does this art *do* to me?

Think now of reading the placard next to the art. It is written in a language you do not know, perhaps in characters you cannot even pronounce. What does it mean? What is behind this code? Suppose the language is utterly distinct from English: Chinese, for example. Whether you look at the placard from various angles or only one, linger over it or catch just a quick glance, return to it many times or see it only once will not matter. You cannot force the characters to give up their meaning. They will remain opaque to you: a solid veil.

Imagine now that a docent wanders in and speaks to you about the art. Does that settle it? Has the docent exhausted the art's potential so that you need look no more, ponder no longer, return never again? Can the art *do* no more to you? Now imagine that the docent translates the placard for you: tells you what it means. Now you know the name of this piece of art, who crafted it and when, and how it came to be in this museum. Assuming that the docent has translated accurately, can the placard *mean* something else? Does the art actually have an endless number of names so that, if you come back again, another docent could list a few more? Will the artist suddenly have changed, or the date, or the donor?

The liturgy is like the art, not the placard.

In celebrating the liturgy, preparing it, or reflecting upon it, the question is not about meaning. It is about impact. It is about what the liturgy might do, can do, is doing, and did. It is not what a particular gesture, object, or the entire rite means. This is a matter of sacramental and liturgical theology. In the liturgy and in the sacraments, God acts. God does something in and through the assembly's action. The correct category, then, for considering the liturgy is *doing*, not *meaning*.

A planning team, as they make every choice, should ask what that element will potentially *do*. They should ask if this element (as far as they can imagine) will help to reveal what God is doing. What might singing a particular hymn do? What might using a particular object do? What might moving in a particular way do? What might selecting a particular lector do? What might the collection, arrangement, and juxtaposition of particular elements do? To give a rather facile example, if a team realizes that the liturgy they are sketching will last for over two hours, the fruitful question is not what this liturgy or any of its constituent elements will mean. The fruitful question is what it might do. It might well create boredom, frustration, resentment, and anything but a disposition in the worshippers that would allow them to sense the movement of God.

What is the opening of the liturgy meant to do? The Liturgy of the Word? The Holy Communion? The concluding rites? Will a particular element or the accumulation of elements do something that will support what a part of the liturgy or the liturgy as a whole is meant to do? Will it highlight what God is, indeed, doing? These are the sorts of questions that should guide liturgical planning.

announcements → How can/will announcements be offered that are in keeping c̄ the Spirit of Godly worship? How does God desire to encounter His people thru the "announcements" form?

PRINCIPLE 9

The liturgy must be scaled to the assembly celebrating it and congruent with their culture.

In preparation for the 2003 General Convention, the Standing Commission on Liturgy and Music was charged with taking stock of the state of the liturgy in the entire church. I was a member of the subcommittee that undertook that project. One of the facts we distilled from the large body of data we amassed was that most Episcopalians worship in large congregations but most Episcopal congregations are small. What that means is that we have a number of very, very large parishes that account for the majority of Episcopalians. The rest of us are scattered in relatively small congregations.

The Commission recognized that Episcopalians in many, if not most, of those small congregations use the large congregations as their model. They imagine they have to do it the way the huge congregations do it or they are not doing it well, so they try to imitate what these large congregations do. That tactic is bound to fail. First of all, what happens in large congregations is not always worthy of emulation! Even when it is, though, small congregations do not have the people, the buildings, the money, and often the culture for that kind of liturgy. And so they end up with a liturgy that limps along because it is trying to be something it cannot. By trying to do what they cannot do, and therefore doing it poorly, they miss the opportunity to do what they can do, and therefore doing it well.

Clergy often compound the problem by trying to recreate seminary chapel services. They imagine that what they did in seminary is *the* way to do it. The liturgical assembly in a seminary, however, is radically different from the average Sunday congregation. The preoccupations of seminary life, the focus on theological education, the seminarians' personal familiarity with one another, and even the proximity of their living quarters to the chapel do not reflect the lives and interests of most Episcopalians. Furthermore, because most seminarians aspire to the priesthood, the lay-clerical chasm may not seem wide to them or unbridgeable. Indeed, they fully expect to bridge it. They are less likely than most lay people to be caught in the trap of thinking that they are liturgical outsiders and, therefore, of seeing the liturgy as something priests do and others observe. It can be dangerous to assume that what is entirely integral and authentic in a seminary will be functional in a parish.

The liturgy in our large congregations and seminaries is often impressive. But small congregations can do great things too, and can celebrate a liturgy that is just as reverent and beautiful, and just as authentically Anglican. The task for each parish is to figure out how.

PRINCIPLE 10

Musical elements integral to the liturgy take precedence over music inserted into it,
and all the music in the liturgy should be coherent with it.

Some of the integral elements of the liturgy—those that are essential parts of it—are inherently musical. Musical efforts should be directed first of all to them. The *Gloria*, for example, can be "sung or said," but the same rubric calls it a "hymn." Hymns are sung. The *Sanctus*, similarly, is specifically called a hymn for singing, not a poem for reciting, in the segment of the Eucharistic Prayer that leads into it: "Therefore we praise you, joining our voices with Angels and Archangels and with all the company of heaven, who for ever *sing this hymn* to proclaim the glory of your Name" (BCP 362). The fraction anthem is preceded by the same rubric that allows singing or saying but it, too, is inherently musical: it is an anthem. Elements that are both integral to the rite and inherently musical should always be sung if anything is to be sung.

In small gatherings or groups who simply cannot sing, of course, saying the texts may be necessary. In most parishes on Sunday morning, however, the assembly is large enough and musical enough that singing is possible. They should give these required and inherently musical elements, not hymns or choir anthems, the first musical attention.

Other integral elements of the rite, while not preceded by a rubric indicating that they are to be "sung or said," are acclamations. That suggests music. Music is the logical mode for rendering these texts so that they are experienced as what they are. The "Amen" at the conclusion of the Eucharistic Prayer, for example, is a high point of the rite. It is a crescendo that demands more than weak recitation. Similarly, the brief Memorial Acclamations integral to most forms of the Great Thanksgiving should not be recited when auxiliary and optional elements are rendered musically. Acclamations, precisely because they are acclamations, should be sung. It is a matter of form following function. If the function is to acclaim, then the form is to sing (or shout).

The Prayer Book allows that other music may be inserted into the rite. Among these optional pieces, some by virtue of their genre should be sung, not recited. Psalms, for example, are poems written for singing. Reciting a psalm, it has been said, is like reciting a national anthem or the words to "Happy Birthday to You." Musical efforts should be directed toward the psalm before any of it is diverted to elements that are less integral to the rite or less inherently musical.

When music accompanies a liturgical action, it should cohere in intent and coincide in duration with the action. When, for example, an entrance hymn accompanies the entrance procession, the two should unify, orient, and invigorate the assembly for what lies ahead. The hymn should begin as the procession begins, and should be long enough to continue until the procession is complete, but should not extend much beyond it.

Music for the Communion procession should similarly be chosen to reflect and express the meaning of what is happening, and should equal it in length. Because the Communion is one action (the assembly receiving the Sacrament), not a collection of acts (the individual members of the assembly privately receiving the Sacrament) the music should suggest singularity. It should begin immediately after the invitation to Communion (when the Prayer Book directs that the procession is to begin) and continue until the procession is completed and all have received the Sacrament. Moreover, since the assembly must walk and sing at the same time, responsorial psalms or *ostinato* refrains like those from the monastic community at Taizé are more functional than hymns. The entire assembly—those moving to the Lord's Table and those who have returned from it—can sing in unison, again expressing musically what the rite intends: the communion of the members with Christ and, thereby, their communion with one another.

When an element of the rite is rendered musically, other liturgical principles and guidelines regarding the text still apply. For example, a sung greeting-and-response is still a dialogue. The presider looks at the assembly throughout the exchange. The presider must be familiar enough with the musical setting that there is no need to focus on the book instead of the group being addressed. (See "Looking" in chapter 8, "Postures and Gestures.")

When a single person or a group performs music within the liturgy, the rest of the assembly does not become an audience. The entire assembly is always an actor. Liturgical musicians are not entertainers in the model of rock stars any more than preachers are entertainers in the model of stand-up comedians or motivational speakers. The liturgy is common prayer in its entirety. If processions are analogous to parades, as I suggest in the chapter on the opening rites, they should be structured so that the assembly can watch actively, not passively. Ideally, the movement should draw the people in so that they experience themselves in it, almost as if they were part of it. Similarly, music within the liturgy that is performed by designated ministers rather than by the entire group should not seem to members of the assembly to be something that is being "done to them." Rather, the assembly should, by listening, be drawn into the music so that what they are hearing both expresses what is within them and impresses something upon them. If the assembly is to experience performance-style music as their own, the liturgical musicians must conceive of themselves not as providers doing something to the assembly, but as integral members of the assembly acting within it.

People do not enter the church on Sunday and immediately applaud the altar guild for ironing the linens or cheer the ministers of hospitality because they are distributing leaflets. The liturgical ministers remain members of the Body. While all the members should be grateful for the service of the ministers, the ministers should not be seen as outsiders or providers. Liturgical musicians are exactly the same as the other ministers.

They deserve the community's gratitude, not its applause. Because musicians in the culture are precisely providers in nearly every case, liturgical musicians are often viewed through that lens. In fact, however, liturgical musicians are more analogous to acolytes, lectors, and the people who take the collection than they are to stage performers.

Chapter 4

LITURGICAL SPACE

E veryone knows an Episcopal church when they see one. The telltale clues begin on the corner, with the blue and white sign. It points you to a Gothic-revival building with the trademark red doors. The room for worship is cruciform, with a tomb-like stone altar at the far end, often elevated in a narrow space called the chancel, about one-fourth the length of the rest of the space. The room is full of pews facing the altar, except in the chancel, where they face one another across a central aisle. The area immediately in front of the altar is segregated from the rest of the room by a low wooden rail. Perched on the edge of the chancel is a lectern topped by a large brass eagle, and opposite it, an elevated pulpit.

The predominance of this kind of building is a tribute to the tenacity of the Cambridge Movement of the nineteenth century. The Cambridge Movement was an attempt to reform the church by reforming its buildings. Taking the medieval English parish church as the ideal, the proponents of the Cambridge Movement banded together as the Cambridge Camden Society and,

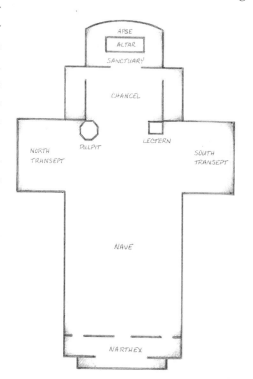

with remarkable efficiency, catalogued, sketched, and charted every detail of what they considered the best examples of English medieval church architecture. Primarily through their journal *The Ecclesiologist*, these reformers circulated their ideas throughout the Anglican Communion, and as the taste for the Gothic style spread, other Christian bodies were swept up in the rage as well. New Anglican churches, with few exceptions, were built in the Gothic style. Older churches that had been built in other styles were layered over with Gothic design elements so that the buildings took on as much of a Gothic feel as possible. Even buildings that simply could not be disguised as Gothic had their furnishings rearranged in the medieval style.

Centuries before, the first Anglicans in the American colonies had also built Gothic-style buildings, no doubt because that is what they remembered from England. But by the time of the American Revolution, even the English in England were building churches in other architectural styles and placing the furnishings in quite different configurations. These new buildings, many of which were needed after so many older churches were destroyed in the London fire of 1666, were an attempt to create spaces that were more congruent with the liturgies of the Book of Common Prayer than the medieval buildings could ever have been. The churches of Christopher Wren (1632–1723) and Nicholas Hawksmoor (1661–1736) are spectacular examples of post-Reformation churches built to give the entire assembly visual and aural access to everything that happens during the liturgy, as the Book of Common Prayer seemed to envision.

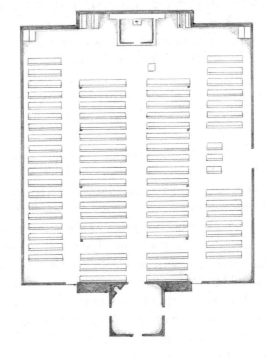

As the colonies evolved their own culture, and as the United States gained its independence and expanded in population and territory, American architects also set about creating buildings tailor-made for common prayer. They worked with their drafting tools in one hand and the Prayer Book in the other to create buildings that were just as reformed as the liturgy that would be celebrated in them. Some of those churches escaped neo-Gothic remodeling and remain essentially unchanged today. St. Peter's Church in Philadelphia (1761), for example, has the pulpit at one end and the altar at the other. (See views of the church at http://www.stpetersphila.org.) The pews face both directions so worshippers can reorient themselves as the action shifts from place to place. At St. Andrew's in Charleston, South Carolina (1706), the altar stands only feet from the front pews. Above it are tablets inscribed with the Decalogue, the Lord's Prayer, and the Apostles' Creed. The pulpit is halfway between the doors and the altar, bringing it as close as possible to the greatest number of worshippers in order to maximize the audibility of the preacher. Christ Church in Duanesburg, New York (1793) is a clapboard building with clear windows, box pews, and whitewashed walls. The pulpit and altar stand side by side. They almost touch the front pews, just as at St. Andrew's in Charleston. The pulpit in this church towers above the plain wooden altar, however, and in place of the Decalogue, Lord's Prayer, and Apostles' Creed, there are memorial monuments on the wall behind the altar. Many churches built in the American colonies were daring breaks from the medieval model. Gradually, however, the neo-Gothic buildings encouraged by the Cambridge Camden Society supplanted such experiments.

What is most interesting is that the Gothic buildings that multiplied throughout the Anglican Communion beginning in the nineteenth century were not conceived with the Book of Common Prayer in mind. They were designed for the pre-Reformation liturgy. The Gothic style was resurrected as a reaction to what many perceived as the failures of the church in the nineteenth century to live up to gospel (and Prayer Book) ideals. The members of the Cambridge Camden Society saw the medieval time as the golden age of Christian piety, and believed that the restoration of the architectural style that both expressed and fostered that piety was an essential step toward a renewed church.

The members of the Cambridge Camden Society sought to foster the holiness of the church by creating buildings that expressed the transcendence of God. Christianity, because it affirms that God is Other and yet One-Like-Us, necessarily lives in the tension between transcendence and immanence. The tension that tried the Anglicans of the nineteenth century is the same tension that faces the church today, and it is not really about architecture. How can Christians live authentically in the tension that is inevitably present in a religion that claims that God is both transcendent and immanent? How can Christians worship, standing as they do between the seemingly contradictory beliefs that God is beyond naming and yet has a human name, Jesus? What is the "right" worship of a God who is both absent in glory and present in the Spirit?

The members of the Cambridge Camden Society believed that that balance had tipped so far away from an appreciation of the otherness of God that it had triggered a lack of any reverence at all before the Holy. They tried to correct the imbalance, in part, by setting the liturgical stage differently. The movement reached its zenith not in the more affluent circles of English society, but in the slums. It was there, in Dickensian squalor, that those sympathetic to the Cambridge Movement saw the greatest need to give worshippers an experience of something utterly beyond their sad and ordinary lives—beyond them, and yet present for them, right there in their own neighborhoods, poor as they were. And so, while the Cambridge Movement sought to highlight the holiness of God, it did not lose sight of the intersection of the Holy and the most ordinary, even miserable, of human things and conditions.

This vibrant moment in the history of Anglican church architecture and liturgical style, however, did not settle forever how to integrate the two Christian perceptions of God in a single building. As beautiful as most Gothic-revival Anglican churches certainly are, many are not congruent with the theology and ecclesiology of the current Book of Common Prayer, or with the liturgical consensus of the modern Western church as a whole. When the original medieval English Gothic churches were built—the ones that were duplicated in whole or in part by Anglicans all over the world centuries later—the operative theology and ecclesiology of the church differed significantly from the vision of the contemporary church and its liturgy. In medieval England:

◆ The monastic life was considered the ideal, and therefore monastic-style church buildings were copied even in parish churches that were not used by monastic communities.

◆ When lay people actually worshipped with monastic communities, they were relegated to a visitors' area and were separated from the monks or nuns (who were the ones enacting the liturgy) by a screen. This, too, was replicated in many parish churches, putting the clergy on one side of the screen and the laity on the other.

◆ The most common liturgical activity in the monasteries was not the Eucharist but the Daily Office, and the part of the room used by the monastic community was arranged precisely to facilitate the antiphonal singing of psalms. This arrangement was duplicated in the parishes.

◆ When the Eucharist was celebrated in medieval monastic or parish churches, few worshippers, if any, beyond the presider received Communion. The rooms were not designed to facilitate the reception of Communion; rather, the intent was to frame what was believed to be a miracle: the transformation of bread and wine into Christ's Body and Blood, and the offering, in liturgical form, of the sacrifice of the cross.

◆ The liturgy was understood as the action of an ordained class on behalf of and in place of non-ordained Christians.

◆ Even in parish churches, the primary role of lay people during the liturgy was to carry out their own private devotions while they watched the clergy do the "official" liturgy.

Medieval English churches were perfect for expressing and fostering a medieval notion of the church. The buildings and the activities that took place in them were well suited to one another. The buildings were not a hindrance to the intended action, but contributed to it. Conversely, the action that occurred in the building had dictated how the space had been designed in the first place. The *lex orandi* and the *lex credendi* were in harmony. These buildings were statements in stone about the nature of the church: a strictly hierarchical organization that was defined by the priesthood. The church was seen as an outgrowth of the priesthood, not the other way around.

But medieval church buildings captured more than a notion of the great chasm between the lay and clerical castes. They also captured a sense that the liturgy was an event that demanded awe. This sense of awe and reverence, along with a renewed sense of the sacredness of the priesthood, was what the nineteenth-century reformers wanted to recapture through restoring the style of the medieval buildings. Something very good was certainly accomplished by these reformers, but it is hard to deny that they undid something of what earlier reformers, the leaders of the English Reformation of the sixteenth century, aimed to do.

Buildings like St. Peter's in Philadelphia were actually closer to the ideals of Archbishop Cranmer and the rubrics of the 1552 Book of Common Prayer than the neo-Gothic buildings that are now so closely identified with Anglicanism. Cranmer wanted to bring the people closer to the liturgical action and, while not lessening a sense of reverence during worship, to shatter the notion that some parts of the building were holier than others. Since the medieval monastic-style buildings were all he had to work with, he made do by dictating arrangements that would make the rooms more congruent with the new liturgy. For example, the rubrics of the 1552 Communion Service dictated that the tomb-like altar be ignored and that the Eucharist be celebrated at a simple table in the chancel, between the choir pews. The priest and those who intended to receive Communion were to gather around it. This was a make-shift solution that was instituted not because it was ideal, but because Cranmer realized that the reformed liturgy needed a reformed space and it was not reasonable to rebuild all the parish churches in England. He realized that *lex orandi* included more than just the words, but encompassed a host of nonverbal elements like architecture. Through the rubrics of the Prayer Book he tried to devise ways to bring the *lex orandi* in line with the new, reformed *lex credendi*.

The question for the church today is not what Archbishop Cranmer intended at the time of his liturgical reformation, but what the current Book of Common Prayer intends. The question is how to create liturgical spaces that are not hindrances to the enactment of common prayer, nor merely neutral shells, but are congruent and supportive of the *lex orandi* and therefore of the *lex credendi*.

In 1994, the Church Building Fund issued a short but theologically dense document called *The Church for Common Prayer*. As then Presiding Bishop Edward Browning wrote in the foreword, the document was developed "in consultation with the Standing Commission on Church Music, the Standing Liturgical Commission, the Association of Diocesan Liturgy and Music Commissions, and Associated Parishes. Each Commission or Association has endorsed the document." Although the document was not presented to the General Convention and so is not binding on the church, it nonetheless reflects not only the demands of currently authorized liturgies, but also the thinking of contemporary liturgists, ecclesiologists, and other theologians across denominational lines.

LITURGICAL SPACE | 37

The first sentence of the document is its key: "The People of God, the basic symbol of Christ in the world, is the criterion against which design issues are measured." The word "symbol" here is nuanced. It does not mean, on the one hand, a mere reminder; nor, on the other hand, does it mean a perfect embodiment. Rather, it means that the church, by the baptism of its members, is the normative way in which Christ carries on his mission in the world. Teresa of Avila is credited with saying what seems to be a cliché but is nonetheless true. "Christ has no body now but yours, no hands but yours, no feet on earth but yours." To say that the church is the basic symbol of Christ in the world is to say that the church in all of its diversity, when it is true to its mission, is the visible witness to Christ's ongoing presence and action in the world, and one of the chief means by which it is achieved.

The liturgy, including but not limited to the sacraments and sacramental rites, happens only through the agency of the church. They are actions of Christ, but they happen only in and through the action of the church. Christ acts as the church acts. Christ acts in the church's acting. In that sense, the church is the basic symbol of Christ in the world.

While this book is not about church renovation or design, it cannot ignore liturgical space. What can happen among people depends to a large degree on the space in which they gather and the objects they use within that space. This is obvious to everyone who has ever seriously considered how to set up a space for any event, and how to arrange the people in it. The impact of spatial arrangements upon what takes place is a human fact, not a religious oddity. This interplay is not lost on most people—just look at the modern shopping mall. Every element of the space is constructed to facilitate and encourage the activity for which the space is intended. Shoppers do not go to the mall unwillingly: they expect to be coaxed into buying something. Those who design malls know this and build to facilitate it. Likewise, worshippers come to church willingly, hoping to be persuaded to believe. They show up on Sunday looking for "something more." Most of them do not want to be bulldozed, but all of them are hoping to find something that they can claim as the answer to at least some of the pressing questions of their lives. The liturgical space is part of how that transaction is facilitated. It is part of how the church discovers for itself and invites seekers into an encounter with the living God. The church must undertake its project with the same care that we as a society invest in buildings of public interest.

A liturgical setting that is congruent with the current Book of Common Prayer would foster three beliefs in the assembly. First, it would foster a sense that they had truly assembled, that they had come together in more than a superficial way. Second, it would encourage a conviction that in their coming together, God in Christ is present and active among them. And third, it would urge them to go forth in mission because of what they have encountered. The goal is not merely to foster "togetherness," nor to foster a sense that God in Christ by the power of the Holy Spirit is present and active, nor to compel mission. All of these are laudable goals in themselves, but they are not isolated from one another. The liturgy's goal is to foster all three at once, and to foster a sense that the three insights and urges are not merely simultaneous but are integrated as a whole. The group is unified by the presence of the Spirit, the Spirit is present and expressed because the group has assembled, and the experience of being part of a Spirit-filled assembly leaves a worshipper compelled to act.

The question for liturgical ministers is how to use and arrange whatever building they have inherited so that the assembly can experience and respond to the grace that is surely offered. Through the human activities of the group—moving, reading, singing, listening, remembering, begging, regretting, eating, drinking, washing, anointing, and a host of other activities—the Holy is truly present. The Prayer Book Catechism describes the sacraments, not as reminders of a grace that has been given, but a *means* by which Christ actually gives grace. How can the liturgical space enable the assembly to receive the grace that is offered in the liturgy?

ENACTING THE LITURGY IN VARIOUS SPACES

Most liturgical communities have inherited spaces that, given current liturgical principles, pose great challenges. The most common space in the American Episcopal Church, due to the great success of the neo-Gothic revival, is a cruciform room, or a simple rectangular one, with a chancel and altar at the east end. (For purposes of comparison, the convention is always to refer to the wall where the altar stands as "the east wall," no matter what actual direction it faces.) In the 1960s and 1970s, largely in response to the liturgical reforms in the Roman Catholic Church occasioned by the Second Vatican Council, the altars in most (but not all) of these building were pulled far enough away from the east wall to allow a priest to stand behind it and face the rest of the assembly across it. In some buildings, the altar was pulled far enough away from the wall to allow the clergy and some of the other liturgical ministers to sit behind the altar as well, but only a few feet from it. A smaller number of churches brought the altar much farther into the room so that it became visually detached from the east wall and stood free in the room. In cruciform churches, the altar was often brought into the crossing: the intersection of the two "beams" of the cross.

THE ALTAR AGAINST THE EAST WALL

In churches with the altar against the east wall and a chancel with choir pews, the clergy and other ministers should sit either in the same seating as the choir or in chairs aligned with the pews. Since the altar is one of the primary foci of the liturgical space, it is never appropriate for the presider and the assisting ministers to sit in front of it. The altar has traditionally been seen as a symbol of Christ standing in the midst of the assembly, and it is the community's common table, belonging to the entire assembly. To turn it into a

backdrop for chairs does not give it the dignity the liturgy accords it. The only time when it is appropriate to place a seat in front of the Lord's Table is for some rites conducted by a bishop. Even then, it is best that the bishop not preside from in front of the altar, but move there only when necessary and to sit, if possible, on a stool that does not block the altar. (A folding seat called a "faldstool" is commonly used for this purpose.) If the bishop's custom is to administer confirmation or to perform some of the rites associated with ordination (such as the giving of the Bible and other symbols of ordination) while seated, this would normally take place in front of the altar. If possible, however, this should be done far enough from the altar—at the edge of the chancel, perhaps—for the altar to be visually unencumbered.

The greatest challenge of a space with the altar attached to the east wall (so that the presider sits perpendicular to the altar or aligned with the choir pews) is that the presider can seem not to be presiding during most of the rite. The presider can disappear into the back rows of choir pews or be hidden in a chair beyond the choir. The presider's role is public and communal. It is to facilitate, using both words and bodily actions, the community's liturgy, and to model for the community intentional liturgical participation. This becomes impossible when the presider cannot be seen. Without a good sound system, this arrangement can also interfere with the ability of the rest of the assembly to hear the presider. In our consideration of the various parts of the liturgy, we will explore how to compensate for these problems.

THE ALTAR PULLED SLIGHTLY FROM THE EAST WALL

When the altar is only a few feet from the east wall, the same seating arrangements apply as when it is fast against the wall. This altar placement, however, creates significant challenges, especially during the Great Thanksgiving. The express purpose of creating a space for the presider to stand behind the altar was to allow the assembly to see what the presider was doing during the Great Thanksgiving. This was laudable, on the surface, since it increased one aspect of how the assembly can participate: by witnessing and attending to liturgical actions. The problems this arrangement presents, however, can outweigh its benefits. The presider standing behind the altar can become like an actor on a stage, and the assembly can become simply an audience. In virtually every other instance in our culture where a room is arranged this way, a complex dichotomy is set up between the person facing one way and the group facing the other: think of a courtroom, a classroom, a theater. In each case, the person facing the group holds power, talent, or knowledge to which the rest of the group must listen, attend, and perhaps even submit. The group can become dependent and passive, while the one person facing them remains powerful and active. The arrangement can set one person up as the actor, and the rest as the acted-upon.

It certainly makes sense for the presider to face the members of the assembly and to look at them when addressing them (as with ritual greetings such as "The Lord be with you"), when proclaiming Scripture or giving an exhortation (as in the liturgy for Ash Wednesday), or when preaching. The Great Thanksgiving, however, is not addressed to the assembly but to God. To face the assembly during the prayer is at cross purposes with what the action is meant to do. The *lex orandi* clashes with the *lex credendi*.

Archeological and textual evidence make it clear that in early Christian church buildings, altars did stand a great distance from the east wall. During the last century, as this fact became widely known, it was assumed that the purpose was to allow the assembly to see what the priest was doing as they faced him across the table. Subsequent study, however, shows that the presider did not face the assembly across the table but stood facing east, along with the rest of the group. Some members of the assembly might have been to the presider's sides, some behind him, and some even in front of him. It did not matter. Everyone faced east to pray. Clearly, visibility was not the goal of how the room was arranged. The impetus was mystical, not visual, since the east was seen as the region of God and the west was considered the region of Satan. The arrangement of the space bespoke a church all facing the same way, looking toward God with its back to evil.

Well before the 1960s (no doubt for many cultural and theological reasons, and surely because altars were situated so far from the majority of the assembly, and because the priest stood at the altar while everyone else knelt), the perception arose that the priest, when facing an altar attached to the east wall, was not united to the assembly in its act of prayer but was praying alone with his back to the people. It seemed, and logically so, that he was celebrating while they were watching and waiting to receive the fruits of what the priest had done. To combat this view, which was increasingly at odds with the accepted theology (the *lex credendi*), the old altars were moved or new ones were set up a few feet forward. This well-intentioned shift may have had an impact, however, that is the opposite of what it intended.

◆ It suggests that the Eucharist is something done by the priest and observed by the rest of the assembly.

◆ It visually polarizes the assembly into the ordained (behind the Table) and the un-ordained (in front of the Table).

◆ It encourages the presider to treat the Eucharistic Prayer not as a prayer, but as a script for reenacting the Last Supper. (This is especially evident when the presider looks up from the Altar Book during the Institution Narrative and addresses the words to the assembly as if impersonating Jesus, rather than praying to God in the name of the assembly.)

Nonetheless, in almost every parish it would be pastorally unadvisable (if not physically impossible) for the presider to resume the "eastward position" during the Eucharistic Prayer, that is, to face the same direction as the rest of the assembly. No doubt, this would be perceived as the priest turning the back on the people. Still, given the principles we have set out, especially that the liturgy is celebrated by the entire assembly under the presidency of a priest, and not by the priest on behalf of or in the view of the rest of the assembly, great care must be taken during the Eucharistic Prayer in churches that are arranged as most contemporary churches are. This will be dealt with in more detail in the ritual considerations for the Eucharistic Prayer.

THE ALTAR PULLED SLIGHTLY FROM THE WALL WITH SEATING BEHIND

This arrangement has the advantage of positioning the presider in a place that clearly denotes presidency: at all times the presider, with the deacon and other ministers, is visible and, all things being equal, audible. It also carries all of the problems of the previously considered arrangement, and adds a further pitfall. When the ministers sit very close to the altar, they truly appear to "own" it. It seems to be the ministers' altar, not the assembly's or even Christ's. This arrangement can also look like the presider is sitting at a table chairing a business meeting; even worse, from the pews it can look as if the ministers' heads are detached and sitting on the altar. James White, one of the great American Methodist liturgical historians of the past century, often said that no sooner had Protestants managed to get their ugly, oversized minister's chairs from behind the altar and pulpit than Vatican II came along and the Roman Catholics bought them in thrift shops and installed them in their churches. Some Episcopalians were in line right behind the Romans. For the clergy to sit alone or with assisting ministers behind the

Lord's Table without creating undesirable effects requires that a significant distance stand between the chairs and the Table.

OTHER SPATIAL ARRANGEMENTS

Many churches, even neo-Gothic churches with deep chancels, have altered their buildings differently and with greater success to bring them into congruence with the current Book of Common Prayer. The National Cathedral in Washington, D.C., Grace Cathedral in San Francisco, and many other cathedrals and parish churches have successfully installed an altar at the crossing: the central area of a cruciform church where the vertical and horizontal beams of the cross intersect. No matter on what side of the altar the presider stands, the other members of the assembly are gathered around

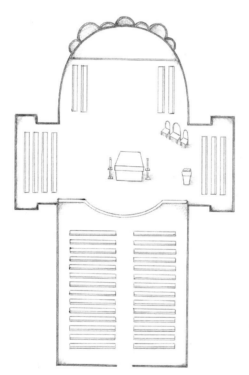

equally on all sides. This is especially evident if the altar is proportioned more like a cube than a sarcophagus. It conveys that the liturgy is the action of the entire assembly under the leadership of an ordained priest. Because the altar has ample space around it, the presider can be seated in any number of places in the room to suggest authority but not dominance. For example, the presider and the assisting ministers can sit directly behind the altar but quite a distance from it. They might be seated midway into the chancel. They might also be seated on the diagonal at the far rear of the altar's platform, at some distance from it so that the altar remains in its own space, as in the illustration. Or they could be stationed in the front row of the seating in one of the transepts (the arms of the cross). All of these arrangements can make it clear that the presider and the other ministers have particular roles of leadership in the liturgy, but that they are first and foremost members of the assembly of the baptized.

This kind of arrangement bespeaks the presence of God in and through the assembly and its action, and so gives the immanence of God its due. But care must be taken not to lose the sense of God's transcendence. Traditionally, domes and towers, canopies and baldachins (like the baldachin over the altar in St. Paul's Cathedral, London) suggest that there is more happening in the people's action than what they alone could create. Special lighting, especially the infusion of natural light from windows above the altar, can have this effect. The way the altar is adorned and the dignity with which the various ministers approach it will also balance the emphasis on God's immanence—God's presence in and through the assembly and its actions—with elements evocative of a sense of God's transcendence—God's presence in inaccessible light.

St. Luke in the Fields, New York City, is a fine example of how this arrangement can be used successfully in a non-cruciform church. The clergy and other assisting ministers are seated directly behind the altar, some other ministers are seated along the sides of the altar, and the rest of the assembly faces forward. St. Luke's design is successful for four reasons. First, the altar stands very far from the seats of the clergy and is actually closer to the front pews. This overcomes the sense that the clergy "own" the altar. Second, an elegant balustrade surrounds the entire altar area with stylized angels atop the corners. This functions like a canopy, dome, or overhead window to set off the area around the altar and to balance the sense of God's immanence with signs of God's transcendence. Third, the altar itself is a substantial, well-proportioned, and beautiful piece of furniture. All four sides are equally elegant, making the altar neither a prop (like those that are hollow in the back and are, in effect, theatrical deceptions) nor something that dignifies one order of the assembly (the ordained behind it or the non-ordained in front of it) more than any other. Fourth, the pulpit, from which all three readings are proclaimed and from which the sermon is preached, is outside the balustrade and is far more related to the seating for the assembly as a whole than to the seating for the officiating ordained members. This means that during the Liturgy of the Word, the clergy are not even on the focal axis. All of these features, taken together, make St. Luke's arrangement a very successful renovation of an early nineteenth-century building. It has been made congruent with the liturgy of the current American Prayer Book, but it has lost nothing of its architectural and artistic integrity. (For photographs of this unique space, go to http://www.stlukeinthefields.org.)

NEW CONSTRUCTIONS AND OTHER ARRANGEMENTS

Many newly constructed churches place the altar and other liturgical foci—the reading desk (increasingly referred to as the "ambo") and sometimes the font—in the center of the room. The seating for the assembly can be arranged around this center in an arc, a circle, or a squared-off U. In such an arrangement, the presider and the other ministers can be seated in a designated area of the front row of one of the arms of the U or in the opening of the U, so that the assembly surrounds the altar and other liturgical focal points. This places the ministers in a specifically designated position from which they can readily facilitate and coordinate the liturgy, while not making them the celebrants and the rest of the assembly, the observers.

The document *The Church for Common Prayer* advocates the use of moveable furniture and platforms. While furnishings that are portable to the point of being flimsy or seemingly temporary risk diminishing the dignity of the liturgy, furniture that is solid and beautiful yet moveable allows for different spatial arrangements depending on the occasion (Sunday Eucharist, Evensong, funeral) or the season (Advent, Lent, Easter). In

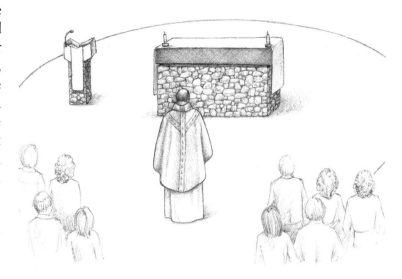

a flexible space, the assembly can be gathered in one part of the room for the Liturgy of the Word, perhaps in a semicircle around the ambo, with the presider sitting at the end of the arc. Then, at the Offertory, they can move to another area where the Lord's Table is set, and gather around it. Even in a fully flexible arrangement, the community might choose as a permanent custom or a seasonal variation to stand together—ministers and all—on the same side of the altar, symbolically facing God together. A flexible space makes possible what no fixed space can.

Perhaps the most famous recently constructed worship space in the Episcopal Church, purposely built for the liturgy that is celebrated in it, is the Church of St. Gregory of Nyssa in San Francisco. The liturgical space is actually two rooms: one for the Liturgy of the Word, and one for the Liturgy of the Eucharist. The assembly at St. Gregory's is best known for its liturgical dancing. Every member of the community, not just a designated few, dance twice during each Eucharist. The dance is simple and strictly choreographed. It is how the assembly moves from the room where it gathers for the Word liturgy into the room where it celebrates the Table liturgy. For the Word, the assembly sits in "choir," or in an antiphonal arrangement, with half of the community facing the other half across a central aisle. The ministers, including the presider, sit at the head of the aisle, with the ambo at the other end. For the Eucharist, the community encircles the altar, which stands in the middle of the second liturgical room.

The liturgy at St. Gregory's, while having its own integrity, is not remotely reflective of the liturgies celebrated in most of the Episcopal parishes in the United States. Still, the principles it embodies are those we have identified as the basis for liturgical spaces that are congruent with the Book of Common Prayer. Another church that, like St. Gregory's, has received significant architectural recognition is Trinity Church, Toledo. Trinity is closer to what one would expect an Episcopal church to be, but many of the design elements incorporated at St. Gregory's are also at Trinity: the emphasis on the key liturgical centers, the ability of the members of the community to see one another, the ample space around the altar so that it stands unencumbered, and a pulpit that gives the Word and the Eucharist equal dignity. Because the entire liturgical space at Trinity is so open, it leaves many possibilities for the placement of the ministers so that they can assume a position of leadership that does not imply dominance.

St. Gregory's is a new construction and Trinity underwent an extensive and costly renovation. Similar results can be obtained, however, even in churches that do not have extensive building budgets. At Grace Church in Allentown, Pennsylvania, a middle-class parish in the heart of a decayed inner-city neighborhood, the parish at an annual meeting agreed with the comment of one of the members that the arrangement of the liturgical space was contrary to what the community believed it was doing when it celebrated the liturgy. In particular, the speaker pointed out that while the community believed that the liturgy was a common action, the arrangement of the furniture suggested that it was the priest's action carried out in the view of the rest of the assembly. A committee was formed to study recent renovations and to devise a plan that would not require funding.

The committee suggested, after some months of study and inquiry with members of the parish, to rearrange all the pews so that they faced one another the length of the room. This turned the entire church into a "choir." The ambo stands at one end, and the presider sits at the other, facing it. The deacon and other ministers sit near the presider in the same pews as the rest of the assembly. In this way, the presider and the assisting ministers can be seen to have specific roles in the assembly and are situated to command attention when it is called for. During most of the Word liturgy, however, the assembly does not face the vested ministers.

The altar stands in the liturgical east end, behind the ambo and at a significant distance from the wall. The entire assembly gathers around the altar at the Offertory and remains there until everyone has received Communion, and then returns to the pews for the postcommunion rites.

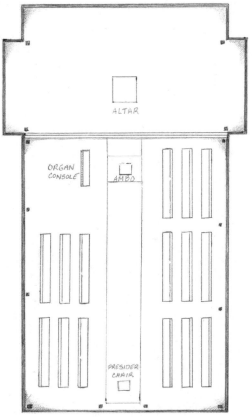

No two liturgical spaces are exactly alike. The responsibility of designers and liturgical ministers is to arrange the space and to act within it so that essential liturgical principles are honored. In each section of the actual exploration of how to enact the rite, differently configured liturgical spaces will be considered. Where might the presider stand for the Opening Acclamation, the Collect for Purity, the offertory sentence, the dismissal?

Various options will be explored. In the end, however, it will be for the particular community and its leadership to discern how it can most authentically use the space it has, with all its possibilities and limitations, so that the *lex orandi* and the *lex credendi* are coherent and expressed as fully as possible and, therefore, have a formative impact on the assembly.

Chapter 5

VESTURE AND VESSELS

Vesture, vessels, and other liturgical objects, like church architecture and the arrangement of the furniture, bear meaning and have an impact upon the assembly. The Book of Common Prayer mentions only five vestments: the alb, surplice, rochet, stole, and tippet. It also refers to other vestments distinctive of the orders of diaconate, presbyterate, and episcopate, but it does not name them.

Vestments were a point of contention in Anglicanism from the time of the Reformation. The Ornaments Rubric, inserted in the 1559 Elizabethan Prayer Book, prescribed the use of the ornaments—and that would include the vestments—that had been in use in the "second year of the reign of Edward the Sixth." This rubric is retained in the 1662 edition of the Book of Common Prayer, still the official Prayer Book of the Church of England and many churches of the Anglican Communion.

It is still not clear what the Ornaments Rubric intended, since "the second year of the reign of Edward the Sixth" was marked by shifting liturgical styles and preferences. Furthermore, the vestments that were worn, as well as the color scheme, varied from diocese to diocese and even from parish to parish. Consequently, Anglican eucharistic vesture was not consistent from place to place or person to person even after the Ornaments Rubric was put into effect. The variety of Anglican vesture after the Reformation is striking, if not startling. Eventually, however, as the Anglican liturgical tradition took shape and evolved, most clergy tended to wear choir dress even for the Eucharist (cassock, surplice, and tippet); later, with the Catholic Revival, colored stoles were adopted in place of the tippet, and eventually full eucharistic vestments were used.

Today, a consensus has emerged among Episcopalians, Lutherans, and Roman Catholics about the appropriate vestments for the celebration of the Eucharist and, with only two possible variations, about the system of liturgical colors. More liturgically minded members of other denominations also wear exactly the same vestments and follow the same color scheme: United Methodists, for example, and even Presbyterians.

Advent	Purple or Blue
Christmas Day / Season	White
Season after the Epiphany	Green
Lent	Purple or Unbleached
Passion Sunday	Red
Maundy Thursday	White
Good Friday	Red
Easter Vigil / Day / Season	White
Feast of Pentecost	Red
Season after Pentecost	Green

The 2001 General Convention of the Episcopal Church mandated the Standing Commission on Liturgy and Music to undertake "a thorough process of data collection involving the whole church to be reported to the 74th General Convention." Seven thousand congregations were asked to report on their liturgical practices, and 1,143 responded—a high percentage by the standards of statistical sampling. Of those, almost 900 reported that the presider regularly wears full eucharistic vestments (alb, stole, and chasuble) when presiding at the Eucharist, and about 250 reported that this custom is observed "sometimes." Only 50 congregations out of 1,143 reported that the presider never wears full eucharistic vestments. The norm in the Episcopal Church is for the presider to wear the alb, with a stole and a chasuble in the appropriate liturgical color.

THE ALB

The alb is the basic, universal garment for all liturgical ministers. It is not specific to any order. The alb has its origins in the standard undergarment of the Roman Empire, but soon took on a specifically Christian significance as the white robe in which the newly baptized were vested. It is the forerunner of the white baptismal dresses that in many churches are still the norm, and is thus the appropriate liturgical vestment for all baptized persons.

Before we consider the alb, a note should be said about the cassock, which is often confused with the alb; in some places the two garments are (mistakenly) used interchangeably. The cassock, which for centuries functioned as the normal liturgical undergarment, is in fact not a liturgical garment at all. It began as the common street dress of the clergy, and some still wear it outside the liturgy, especially for solemn functions. When clergy who are dressed in a cassock participate in the Eucharist but not as the presider, they put a loose alb—a surplice—over the cassock. The word "surplice" comes from Latin, and means "over the fur." The surplice began, essentially, as a very ample and floor-length alb that was cut full enough to slip over the bulky fur-lined cassocks clergy wore in the winter. It gradually was cut back, however, sometimes clinging close to the body and reaching only to the waist. Such a diminutive surplice is sometimes called a "cotta," and today is worn almost exclusively by acolytes and choristers in Anglican and Protestant churches, although some Roman clergy wear cottas as a matter of course.

At the Eucharist, the alb is the basic garment for all liturgical ministers. This includes acolytes and members of the choir. In fact, however, vested choirs have traditionally worn cassocks and surplices, not albs. In parishes where the cassock and surplice are retained for some ministers, the surplice should be significantly large so it, and not the cassock, appears to be the actual liturgical vestment. So-called choir gowns, especially those that incorporate a scapular (part of a monastic habit) or a stole (a vestment for the ordained) are a recent innovation and are rarely used in Episcopal churches since they have no relationship to the current ecumenical consensus and have no precedent in the Anglican tradition.

The word "alb" is from the Latin *albus:* white. A vestment of any other color is not an alb. Some manufacturers produce albs in flaxen colors, closer to beige than white.

Natural linen is flaxen since it is, in fact, made from flax, and in earlier times it could not easily be bleached to pure white without damaging the fibers. This may be the reason for the production of flax-colored albs today: not because it is impossible to bleach the cloth (which today is rarely linen) but to imitate vestments of an earlier time. In any case, no vestment that is any darker than flax is an alb, although some manufacturers produce garments of every imaginable color and call them albs.

The alb is part a symbolic program that extends through the entire liturgical life of a Christian. It begins with the vesting of the newly baptized in a white robe and ends with the draping of the earthly remains with a white pall. All three—baptismal gown, alb, and pall—are, in effect, the same garment. They identify the vested person as one of those who, as the Book of Revelation puts it, "have washed their robes and made them white in the blood of the Lamb" (Rev. 7:14). This baptismal symbolism is further rein-forced by the use of the paschal candle at both baptisms (BCP 313) and funerals (BCP 467). The connection between the funeral pall and the baptismal garment is entirely clear in the funeral rite in *Enriching Our Worship 3*, which begins in one form with vesting the coffin with a white pall, sprinkling it with water, and reading the great baptismal passage from Romans, also read at the Easter Vigil: "Do you not know that all of us who have been baptized into Christ Jesus were baptized into his death?" (6:3).

Some albs are gathered at the waist with a cincture, while others are not. Some are double-breasted and are put on like a coat, while others must be dropped over the head. (The latter is the more ancient design, but that does not make it superior; these varia-tions are simply a matter of taste and expediency.) Most albs today are tailored to fit close to the neck so they completely cover the street clothes. This is as it should be, since in the liturgy the minister takes on a ritual *persona* that envelops the individuality of the person without obliterating it. The alb should cover clerical collars worn by priests and deacons. These are part of clerical street clothing, and should be covered by the vestments. If the alb does not rise far enough up the neck to completely vest the minister, an amice may be worn. An amice is a large square of cloth with long strings attached to two corners. It matches the alb, and is folded around the neck like a scarf, then tied in place. The alb fits over the amice.

EUCHARISTIC VESTMENTS

THE CHASUBLE

The essential presidential eucharistic vestment is the chas-uble, a poncho-like garment of the appropriate liturgical color. It originated as the ordinary outer garment of Roman citizens, the *paenula*. In its ancient form, the garment was essentially a semicircle of fabric, folded in half, and seamed from the bottom almost to the top. The result was a cone of fabric with an opening for the head. When the arms were dropped to the sides, the *paenula* fell to the feet all the way around. To use the hands, the wearer had to gather the garment up on the arms into the crooks of the elbows. This created folds across the front so that the grace and dignity of

the garment was achieved not by anything that was sewn onto it, but by the quality of the fabric itself and the way it interacted with the body of the person wearing it.

By the seventh century, the garment was called a *casula*, from which comes the English word "chasuble." Chasubles intended specifically for liturgical presiders gradu-

ally came to be made of heavy and ornamented fabric. The thickness and weight made it virtually impossible for the priest to lift his arms and gather the *casula* in the crooks of his elbows. When, for example, he opened his arms into the *orans* position for prayer, the *casula* was too heavy and stiff to move freely and gracefully. In effect, the presider was trapped in his own clothing. Rather than return to more simple fabrics and eliminate the elaborate ornamentation that was becoming *de rigueur* for the liturgical garment, the sides were folded up. Eventually, artisans trimmed back the sides of the cone, so that it came only to the wrists of the presider. This restored mobility and dexterity, but altered the character of the vestment and the way it interacted with the presider as he moved.

The evolution of the chasuble continued apace, and in time the garment became so heavy, both in its base fabric and in the various designs and bandings that were appliquéd to it, that the priest could not even elevate the eucharistic Bread or Wine without having assisting ministers raise the weight of the vestment off his arms. In the Baroque period, rather than halt this elaboration, artisans reduced the size of the chasuble even further so that it reached, not the priest's wrists, but only his shoulders. The chasuble by this stage had become a shoulder-wide panel of fabric, stretching from the knees in the front, over the head, to the knees in the back. Finally, so that the garment would restrict the priest even less, the portion across the chest was trimmed back on both sides and the bottom of the front panel was widened, so that it resembled an hourglass.

Today, we refer to the four styles of chasubles, in the order of their evolution, as the conical, the Gothic, the Roman, and the fiddleback (so called because of the shape of its front). Except in some parishes that trace their roots to the early days of the Catholic Revival and some Roman parishes (or, more accurately, some Roman priests) who are working to rehabilitate the liturgy as it was celebrated before Vatican II, Roman and fiddleback chasubles have fallen into disuse. The conicle chasuble has seen a modest revival, perhaps surpassing the Roman and fiddleback, but it, too, is rare. Fabric artists and trained liturgists are largely responsible for creating conicle chasubles, not as mass-marketed items, but as unique pieces of art. It is the Gothic chasuble that has become the Western norm. Virtually none of the mainstream manufacturers of quality vestments in the United States produce anything but Gothic chasubles. These mass-produced vestments, even from well-regarded manufacturers, are generally far smaller than authentic Gothic chasubles, and thus they have far less visual impact than they might. Still, the essential shape of the Gothic chasuble is the most common in the Western church today.

What principles, regardless of the twists and turns in the evolution of this vestment, determine which form is preferable? If there is no golden age in other liturgical matters, then neither is there one in this. Is it, then, simply a matter of taste? The late Aidan Kavanagh, professor of liturgy at the Yale Divinity School, wrote, "The vestment is a garment, not a costume." He went on to say that vestments should be chosen not for what is applied to them, like crosses or other religious symbols, but for their intrinsic quality as human festival clothing. A garment whose meaning derives instead from signs sewn onto it is "a billboard whose purpose is to shout ideologies instead of clothing a creature in beauty." Robert Hovda quotes Kavanagh and then expands upon his comments:

> The chasuble is the principal Eucharistic vestment, the outer garment, the one whose design and form and texture helps to focus the action of the assembly and whose massive color relates to feast and season and festive celebration. The traditional pattern [that is, the conical]...produces horizontal folds when the arms of the presider are raised. Newer patterns with even more ample use of cloth produce vertical folds. In either case, the chasuble is the garment that covers the body entirely, from neck to foot....If the design of the chasuble is convenient for the most efficient movement and frail enough for comfort in the hottest climate, it is probably entirely unsuited for liturgical celebration. A chasuble sufficiently reduced in size and quality to meet these criteria (as happened in the medieval period and still characterizes most vestments sold and used) will lack the dignity and visual impact necessary for its corporate and celebrational function.[4]

The arguments of Kavanagh and Hovda can be summarized in these principles:

◆ The chasuble and all liturgical vesture must be conceived as *clothing*, not as a costume. As such, the standards that would apply to any formal clothing apply to vesture. The authenticity, texture, and drape of the fabric; its fit on the body of the wearer; and the harmony of its colors are the criteria that are foremost.

◆ Liturgical vesture is not primarily for singling out the one wearing it, but for expanding the experience of the assembly in which it is worn. The size, shape, and color should make it seem to the entire assembly a part of *their* liturgy—an element within the corporate event—and not a piece of the presider's private wardrobe.

◆ Vestments are not billboards meant to convey ideas or to shout ideologies, but are pieces of art meant to elicit a deep human response. Vesture, therefore, must be judged by the same standards as other art.

---

4. Robert Hovda, "The Vesting of Liturgical Ministers," *Worship* (March 1980).

◆ Liturgical vesture is a sign of the excess that is characteristic of life in the reign of God: an element of holy feasting in the midst of and in defiance of the injustices and struggles of life. It should be full and, as Hovda says, stretch "from neck to foot."

When people dress for a non-liturgical formal event, they instinctively know the basics. Some of the finer points are dictated by social convention, but the essentials are self-evident. Whether a man must wear patent leather shoes with a tuxedo might not be obvious, but he clearly should not wear ill-fitting or worn shoes. People also instinctively realize that they are making themselves part of a greater whole at a formal social event, and they choose their clothing in order to participate appropriately for the occasion, not only for themselves. When artists design vestments, artisans craft them, and ministers wear them, the principles are essentially the same as for designing, crafting, and wearing clothing for non-liturgical ritual events.

The chasuble is the appropriate vestment for the entire eucharistic liturgy, not just the second half. The Eucharist is one unified rite. The Liturgy of the Word is not the stepchild of the Liturgy of the Eucharist. The presider should wear the chasuble from the beginning of the liturgy to the end. The chasuble is sometimes seen as a vestment for performing sacrifice; that may be why Cranmer substituted the cope for it in the 1549 Prayer Book. Given the complexity and contentiousness of the notion of eucharistic sacrifice, however, and given that the relationship between the chasuble and sacrifice is an extremely arcane point, nothing is to be gained by putting on the chasuble only at the Offertory.

Moreover, on the face of it, this change of costume suggests that Christ is more present or more active in the second half of the liturgy than in the first. While the mode of Christ's presence may be different, neither contemporary sacramental theology nor the Reformation tradition would allow that Christ is less present in the proclaimed Word than in the shared Meal. The only time the chasuble might be donned after the beginning of the Eucharist is when an elaborate, especially an outdoor, procession is appended to the beginning, as on Palm Sunday. A cope is appropriate for the procession, as will be explained below, but should be exchanged for the chasuble immediately after the procession.

THE DALMATIC

The dalmatic is the principal eucharistic vestment of the deacon. Like the alb and the chasuble, the dalmatic began as non-liturgical clothing. Its name is derived from its place of origin: the dalmatic came to the West from Dalmatia—part of modern-day Croatia—in the third century. It was adopted first by the upper ranks of Roman society and government and was only gradually accepted by the general populace as something other than a fad. Unlike the *casula*, the dalmatic has wrist-length sleeves that are much wider than the sleeves of the alb over which it is worn. Like the chasuble, the dalmatic

began as an ample garment but was trimmed further and further back as it evolved. Just as the Roman and fiddleback chasubles developed into little more than scapulars (that is, panels of cloth stretching from *scapula* to *scapula*), the dalmatic eventually became only a wide panel of cloth stretching over the head from the front of the knees to the back, with vestigial sleeves at the shoulders. In its most reduced form, the dalmatic was essentially a Roman chasuble with a square of fabric hanging over the top of each arm.

In the medieval liturgy as it was celebrated in Rome and as it survived after the Council of Trent, the dalmatic was in most cases reserved to the deacon. In pre-Reformation England, the dalmatic was worn with less restriction than in Rome. In at least some places, acolytes, thurifers, cantors, and others wore it for solemn occasions. In others, the tunicle, a vestment very much like the dalmatic, was the outer vestment of subdeacons. It differed from the dalmatic only in the number and placement of its orpheries (the decorative bands of contrasting fabric).

The subdiaconate has not existed in the Anglican churches since the Reformation. When some nineteenth-century Anglo-Catholic parishes imported post-Reformation Roman Catholic ceremonial into the Book of Common Prayer liturgy, they commonly designated one of the acolytes as the "subdeacon" for Solemn Mass because the Tridentine rubrics required one. In fact, however, the office of subdeacon is not part of the Reformation heritage. Moreover, the subdiaconate was suppressed in the Roman Church in 1972. Especially now that Rome has suppressed it, it makes little sense to retain the role or even the term in any Episcopal church.

The diaconate, of course, was never suppressed in either the Anglican Communion or in the Roman Church. There have always been deacons in both traditions. In the age when the Tridentine Roman rubrics were imported into the Prayer Book Eucharist, however, the diaconate in both traditions was a transitional order that was entered near the end of seminary training, and few people outside the seminaries ever saw an actual deacon. For an Anglican parish to celebrate the Eucharist in the style of the Roman Solemn Mass, therefore, laymen or priests donned the dalmatic and "played" deacon, just as others put on the tunicle and "played" subdeacon. Today, deacons—both those who are transitional deacons and those for whom the diaconate is a unique and lifelong vocation—are present and active in Episcopal parishes. There is no defense for having someone who is not a deacon masquerade as one. Some argue that since every presbyter is first ordained a deacon, priests are also, in fact, deacons. Put another way, it is often said that there is a deacon within every priest. Regardless of whether one accepts a hierarchical view of ordained ministry or not, in the church's liturgy the orders of priesthood and diaconate are distinct and unique. Only deacons should wear dalmatics in the liturgy: neither priests nor non-ordained members of the assembly should be vested as such. It should also be noted that efforts continue to be made at all levels of church government to ordain those called to the priesthood directly, without being ordained as deacons first. This practice would ritualize the integrity and distinction of the two orders of diaconate and presbyterate, making it clear that the diaconate is not a station on the way to the priesthood, but is a distinct and complete order of ministry. Vesting a priest or anyone else as a deacon who is not in fact a deacon is inauthentic and moves counter to the evolving sense of the church.

THE STOLE

A stole is a narrow strip of fabric signifying ordination. It is worn around the neck. Bishops and priests wear the stole so that the two ends fall straight down over the chest and to the legs. Deacons wear it over the left shoulder and fastened or tied below the waist on the right side of the body, so that it lies diagonally across the chest and the back. In the Eastern church, the equivalent of the deacon's stole is the *orarion*. Also a narrow band of cloth, and also worn over the left shoulder, it is worn in one of two ways. Either it is allowed to fall straight down along the left side of the chest and back, or it is wrapped across the body and under the right arm in the fashion of a bandolero, so that it crosses the chest and back, with the ends still falling straight down the left side of the body. Some deacons in the Episcopal Church wear the *orarion* in place of the stole.

There is no Western precedent for this, nor is it the current practice in any Western church.

The stole apparently comes from scarves that were bestowed upon Roman civic officials as marks of rank. The function of stoles has not changed. Unlike the chasuble, dalmatic, and cope, the stole is not a festive vestment large enough to have a visual impact on the liturgical event, but is merely a sign that the person wearing it has been ordained. To wear the stole without the chasuble or dalmatic emphasizes the ecclesial order of the person but does little to embellish the assembly's liturgy visually.

For a short period in the 1970s, it became quite common to wear the stole over the chasuble or dalmatic. There is no precedent for this and, perhaps more to the point, it emphasizes order-as-rank over order-as-role in the community of the baptized. The stole, whether for deacons or presbyters, should always be worn under the principal garment.

In practice, even in places where the presider is always vested in stole and chasuble, the deacon often wears only the stole. This is almost certainly because most congregations cannot afford complete sets of vestments in every color for both the presider and the deacon. Instead of omitting the dalmatic completely, however, the deacon could wear a dalmatic of a neutral color with the stole in the appropriate color beneath, which would show above the collar and at the bottom of the dalmatic.

THE COPE

The cope is a floor-length cape, fastened at the neck. It is worn in the appropriate liturgical color. The cope shares a common ancestry with the Roman conical *casula*. Unlike the *casula*, however, that was sewn shut from the feet almost to the neck, the cope was sewn closed only at the neck. In time, the fashion became to fasten the two sides with a clasp called a morse so it could be opened and closed.

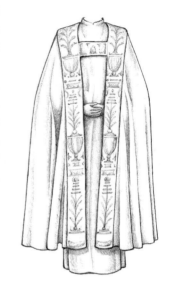

The cope is called a *pluviale* in Latin: a raincoat. It began as a purely functional garment that was adopted for liturgical use somewhere between the ninth and twelfth centuries. At that time, some houses of monks used it predominantly as a garment for the entire community on great feasts. In other monasteries, or on lesser feasts, it was worn by only certain liturgical ministers, especially cantors at both the Eucharist and the Daily Office.

Some Anglican bishops habitually substitute the cope for the chasuble. Many wear it over an alb when they are present at the Eucharist but are not presiding, in place of the rochet and chimere.

The cope can be used by any minister, lay or ordained, in non-eucharistic contexts, such as at weddings or solemn celebrations of the Daily Office. In a parish Eucharist, the cope is used only for solemn and, especially, outdoor processions that precede or follow the liturgy proper as, for example, a procession into the fields on the Rogation days, or to the cemetery for a burial immediately following the funeral. The *pluviale* began as a processional garment for outdoor use. In a parish Eucharist, it should echo its original purpose.

THE MEANING OF THE VESTMENTS

People often ask what the various vestments in the liturgy mean. Quite simply, the stole is the only vestment that functions primarily to convey meaning: that the wearer is ordained. The other vestments, like most of the elements of the liturgy, *do* something rather than *mean* something. They add festivity, solemnity, and dignity to the rite, but they do not mean anything per se. They are ritual clothing and have much more in common with formal wear or party clothes than they do with signs or, as Kavanagh says, billboards. Because people want the vestments to mean something, however, they have often found what they have sought.

The result is liturgical allegory: imposing a meaning on a liturgical event or artifact that is not inherent in the thing itself. The ninth-century liturgist Amalarius of Metz is recognized as one of the most prolific of all the liturgical allegorists. Amalarius devised elaborate schemas in which virtually every object and every action in the liturgy was given a hidden meaning, including the vestments. Series of prayers, based upon allegories, were composed to accompany the donning of each vestment. The amice, for example, which was put on the head like a kerchief and then pushed down around the neck, was usually allegorized as the helmet of salvation. The chasuble became the yoke of salvation, since it was put over the shoulders, and so forth.

If such allusions foster the devotion of the minister as he or she vests, they serve a good purpose. Pastorally, however, it is counterproductive to imply that the liturgy is made up of arcane codes. The liturgy is an experience of the Mystery, not a confrontation with a puzzle. In the actions of the worshipping community, a genuine encounter with God is possible. The liturgy is, in itself, an occasion of grace. It is not a stand-in for something else or a reminder of something that is not there. To suggest that the assembly should not first of all experience the essential characteristics of the objects and gestures of the liturgy but should think of something else instead (what other thing this object or this action really means) vitiates the evocative potential of the liturgy. It suggests that the liturgy is a reminder of another time and place, not an encounter with the Holy, revealed in created reality in the here-and-now.

VESSELS

FOR BREAD AND WINE

Containers for the bread and the wine are the only necessary vessels for celebrating the Eucharist. So that this sacrament might express the unity it signifies and effects (that it expresses and impresses), the Prayer Book mandates that only one vessel of bread be on the altar during the Great Thanksgiving. A separate vessel for the "priest's host" is absolutely contrary to the Prayer Book's understanding of the Eucharist.

A single large plate or bowl is suitable for holding hosts. If leavened or substantial unleavened bread is to be consecrated, a bowl is definitely required. All of the wine should likewise be in one chalice, or in a single flagon with one chalice poured from it.

A ciborium is a vessel for the eucharistic Bread, but unlike a paten or a bowl, it is fitted with a tight lid so that the fragments remaining after the liturgy can be covered and stored. Because leavened bread and most substantial unleavened bread cannot be stored without becoming stale or moldy, the ciborium is suitable only for hosts. Most ciboria sit on a stem and look like a chalice. Within the past fifty years, low, bowl-like ciboria have also been produced. This style of ciborium resembles a large pyx and is generally preferable because it makes it visually obvious during the Eucharistic Prayer that bread as well as wine has been set on the Lord's Table.

In extremely large gatherings, multiple vessels of bread and numerous flagons of wine are necessary, but every attempt should be made to have them visually convey the unifying effect of the Eucharist. They should, for example, match and be clustered on the altar, as if to suggest one vessel. In any case, there is never a need to place more than one chalice on the altar during the Great Thanksgiving.

If additional vessels are needed for the distribution of Communion, they are brought to the altar just before the Breaking of the Bread. The Sacrament is divided into them while the fraction anthem is being sung. If possible, these vessels, too, should match one another.

Since the eucharistic Bread and Wine are "the Gifts of God for the People of God" and a foretaste of the heavenly banquet, the vessels that hold them should both convey and elicit reverence for the Real Presence of Christ. How this is done will depend on the style of the liturgical space, the traditions of the congregation, and the standards of the culture.

Vessels should be judged by their artistic worth, their quality, and their functionality. A chalice with a very small cup or an unsteady base, for example, is not ideal for the Eucharist, no matter its cost or beauty. Some would say that only precious metal vessels are fit for the altar, because they are so highly valued and are unbreakable. Beautiful and dignified vessels of other materials, however, like fine crystal, should not be discounted outright. They can be true and beautiful art, as noteworthy as metal vessels. Standard, commercially produced glass vessels, however, can be inappropriate for the liturgy, since in general they are scaled to a dining room and not a church. In a large liturgical space, their small size and lack of mass can make them and what they contain seem negligible. Their diminutive size can also create a jarring visual impact, like dollhouse dishes on a full-sized table.

Simply because vessels are made for a liturgical purpose, they are not necessarily worthy of the liturgy. Mass-produced communionware can be ill-proportioned, gaudy, derivative, and unwieldy. Some glass Communion vessels are nothing but dining crystal with a cross etched into them. Everything used in the liturgy should be the finest available, and simply because they are featured in a catalog of religious goods does not make them fine.

Pottery vessels are sometimes used for both the bread and the wine, especially during Lent and in small gatherings. Pottery can be a true art form that reveals the earth from which it is made and the human hands that crafted it, and in that it is perfectly suitable for the celebration of the Lord's Supper. Some occasions, like Lenten services, and some venues, like homes or retreat houses, call for simplicity—but never lack of dignity or poor taste. Nothing banal, amateurish, or shoddy has a place in the liturgy, and pottery meant for the Lord's Table should be pottery worthy of an art gallery.

The use of baskets lined with corporals for the eucharistic Bread presents many problems. Unlike pottery, baskets, with rare exceptions, are not fine art. Moreover, especially if substantial or leavened bread is used in the liturgy, the breaking of the Bread will produce crumbs. While the Prayer Book does not encourage scrupulosity regarding the eucharistic Food and Drink, it is clear that the Holy Gifts should be treated with reverence and that whatever is left over should be consumed. Cloth-lined baskets full of fragments are contrary to the spirit of the Prayer Book, and do not facilitate the gathering and consuming of what remains after Communion.

In many Episcopal churches, the chalice sits veiled on the altar from the beginning of the liturgy. The removal of the veil is a visual signal that the liturgical focus has moved from the Word to the Table. This practice, like a great deal of what is taken as thoroughly Anglican, is actually an importation from medieval custom or the Tridentine Mass. It is more effective if nothing at all is placed on the altar until the Offertory, except the enthroned Gospel Book. The chalice and other vessels are placed on the Table only during the immediate preparation for the Great Thanksgiving. The act of setting them on the altar at that moment visually marks the transition in the liturgy, so that the chalice veil and its removal become unnecessary.

The elimination of the chalice veil and burse is advantageous for another reason. The removal and folding of the vestments that cover the chalice is often far more elaborate and visually striking than the essential action of filling the cup with wine. It is a triumph of the lesser over the greater and the incidental over the essential. Since the burse and veil are often left on the Lord's Table, they also create clutter and visually distract from the essential things: the bread, wine, and the monetary offerings.

A pall—a stiffened square of cloth—is often placed over the chalice on the Lord's Table. It is then removed and replaced at various points during the Great Thanksgiving and the rites leading up to Communion. The rationale is to keep insects that are attracted by the scent of the wine from falling into it. That could, indeed, happen. Still, people sit at dinner tables every day with uncovered glasses of wine in front of them, and flying insects seem not to be a problem. It is difficult to see why they would be more pesky in church. The placing and removing of the pall seems an unnecessary and potentially distracting addition and should be omitted except in conditions where insects could be expected to swarm, like outdoor celebrations.

THE FLAGON

In most pastoral settings, at least two chalices are required for the distribution of Communion. In general, it takes twice as long to receive Communion in the form of wine than in the form of bread, so two ministers of the cup should be paired with every minister of the Bread. The auxiliary cups are filled during the fraction anthem, just after the

Breaking of the Bread. The wine that is not in the single chalice during the Great Thanksgiving is consecrated in a flagon. Most flagons meant specifically for this liturgical purpose are pitcher-like vessels with a hinged lid, fashioned from precious metal. As with chalices, though, other worthy containers can be used. Even if only one chalice is needed for the distribution of Communion, the flagon from which it is filled at the Offertory should be worthy of the Lord's Supper.

THE WATER VESSEL

The Prayer Book says that is it customary to add some water to the wine in the chalice at the Offertory. "Customary" would suggest more than a permission and less than a mandate. In Roman secular culture, wine was always watered before it was drunk. After the quality of wine changed and the secular culture abandoned the custom, it was retained in the liturgy. Because it no longer seemed normal or made apparent sense to people, the action assumed an allegorical meaning, usually that Christ had two natures: human (water) and divine (wine). The Sarum usage saw it as an allusion to the blood (wine) and water that flowed from the side of the dead Christ. The custom is retained in the Prayer Book because it was nearly universal in the ancient and medieval liturgies.

The cruet for the water, even though it is not a principal or even a required vessel, should be of high quality and artistic value. Often, a cruet from an ordinary oil-and-vinegar set is used for this purpose. Putting a cross on top of the stopper does not increase the worthiness or dignity of the cruet. As with everything else associated with the Lord's Table, the cruet or pitcher for holding the water for the admixture should be worthy of the assembly's sacred action.

THE LAVABO BOWL AND TOWEL

The Book of Common Prayer does not mention, even as an option, the washing of the presider's hands after the offerings are set on the Lord's Table (and censed). The custom is common in the Episcopal Church today, however, and has ancient precedent. In both the East and the West, the presiding priest and, in some rites, the deacons who helped him to receive the offerings of the people washed their hands before the Eucharistic Prayer. In some rites, the priest washed his hands at least once more during the liturgy, and sometimes more. In most traditions, the presider also washed his hands in preparation for the liturgy, before vesting.

Some commentators emphasize that the *lavabo*, a Latin word meaning "I will wash," was essentially practical. Those who had received the various offerings of the people and thus soiled their hands needed to wash them before handling the food that had been set on the Lord's Table. Other commentators emphasize the symbolic nature of the various ablutions, since it was common in both Jewish and early Christian cultures to wash the hands before prayer. These commentators also point out that there would be no practical purpose for washing the presider's hands at multiple points in the rite—as, for example, was done in some rites after the *Sanctus* as well as after the reception of the offerings.

Today, the Roman Rite retains a single handwashing, between the reception of the offerings (and the censing) and the beginning of the Eucharistic Prayer. This reflects both a practical need (to clean the priest's hands before he handles the bread) and a symbolic one (since the priest is about to begin the central prayer of the entire rite). This is the logical place for the lavabo in the Prayer Book Eucharist as well. However, as in all other things, the decision to perform the lavabo and the arrangement of how it is to be done must first of all consider whether it will enhance or detract from the essential action that is taking place: the preparation of the food and drink and of the assembly for the praying of the Great Thanksgiving. The answer may differ from place to place and occasion to occasion. For example, if incense is used, the lavabo would happen during the censing of the assembly and would be veiled, as it were, by this action. In a small setting, on the contrary, it would be quite visible and would become a prominent element of the rite. Whether to perform the lavabo and how to do it must take into account a number of factors and how it will affect the core actions and objects.

Often, the same vessel of water that is used for the admixture is used for the lavabo, with a small bowl to catch the water. When the lavabo is done in this way, it is little more than the moistening of the priest's fingers. The use of a larger bowl of water into which the priest can dip the hands would be more authentic.

THE THURIBLE AND BRAZIER

In the liturgy, incense is burned in a thurible (a bowl on chains, which can be swung) or in a brazier (a bowl). Thuribles are of two sorts: four-chain and single-chain. Four-chain thuribles have three chains attached to the bowl and a fourth chain attached to a lid. The lid is raised with the fourth chain, so that charcoal and incense can be spooned into the bowl. Most single-chain thuribles have lids topped with a heat-proof knob. The lid is raised by grasping the knob and lifting the lid to a point on the chain where there is a large ring that stops it. Some single-chain thuribles, however, do not have moveable lids at all, but have large openings in the top that allow the charcoal and incense to be added directly to the bowl. Four-chain thuribles are used in both the Western and Eastern churches. The chains on Western-style thuribles are about thirty inches long. Eastern thuribles are shorter and often have bells attached to the chains. The techniques for using the two types differ, and will be discussed below.

Unlike thuribles, which disperse perfumed smoked by being swung, braziers are stationary. When they are crafted from a material that is not heat-resistant (like pottery, which will crack if exposed to the heat of the burning coals), they must be lined with sand. Charcoal is ignited in the brazier, and incense is spooned onto it. Braziers are used, for example, for burning incense in front of an icon, during an extended litany, or during the singing of Psalm 141 at Evensong or An Order of Worship for the Evening. Liturgical braziers are used far less than thuribles, but are becoming more common.

LITURGICAL BOOKS

Liturgical books do more than hold information. They convey impressions about the nature of the texts they contain. In this, they are no different from other books: leather bindings suggest durability and importance, while paper covers create the opposite impression. Liturgical books, depending on how they are bound and how they are handled, convey many things about how the assembly understands what it is doing. How provisional are the actions outlined in these books? How enduring are the stories? How weighty are the moral precepts? Did they come out of the lector's or the presider's own musings, or did they emanate from a source greater than the individual assembly, the particular place, and the current moment? Are these texts so current and timely that they are to be used only once and then thrown away, or are they ageless and meant to last?

In the liturgy, some elements are timely and some are ageless. Different kinds of books, therefore, have a place in the liturgical assembly. Some aspects of the liturgy must be entirely current if they are to be authentic, but some must be perceived as ageless if they are to have an impact. The book that contains the Scriptures, which the church long ago determined to be timeless, might be of one sort, while the book that contains the Prayers of the People, which should be freshly composed just before each liturgy, might be of another.

Whether books are meant to convey relative permanence or to suggest immediacy, however, both must be of good quality. Even materials that will be used only once can be beautifully produced using modern desktop publishing techniques. The Prayers of the People, for example, can be laid out in a carefully designed format, printed on good paper, and inserted into a leather or cloth-covered three-ring binder. This conveys that the assembly's prayer is serious (as shown by the high quality printing and the careful decoration of the binder), that this is a recurring and integral part of the rite (as shown by the repeated use of the same binder), but that this is about something entirely up-to-the-minute and relevant to the assembly (as shown by the use of a binder and a just-printed list of biddings).

As always, the same questions apply to the nature of ritual books as to every other area of the liturgy. What will the use of this object or the making of this gesture do in the assembly? What will it convey? What will it elicit? Will it support the essential aim of this part of the rite, or will it undermine it?

CONGREGATIONAL ORDERS OF WORSHIP

Nearly every Episcopal parish and most congregations of other traditions provide each member of the assembly with a printed order of worship created for the particular service or for all the services on a particular day. The importance of this leaflet cannot be under-estimated. Not only does it allow the regular members of the assembly to participate competently, it also conveys important information to visitors so that they, too, can move through the liturgy without feeling lost. They can relax and, one would hope, pray.

Congregational orders of worship, then, are important tools of evangelism and hospitality. They are a way graciously to invite people to share in the life of the church *at their own level of comfort*. If a well-crafted order of worship has been provided, the members of the parish do not have to look over visitors' shoulders and tell them what to do. Visitors will know what will happen next and can decide, person by person, what they are physically, psychologically, or spiritually comfortable in doing.

What makes for a "well-crafted" order of worship, however, is not self-evident. Some say that virtually every word that will be uttered and every note that will be sung should be printed, along with careful rubrics describing every action that will be done. Others say that, to ensure that Episcopalians are familiar with the Prayer Book and hymnals, only page references should be given so that the members of the assembly will be required to use the books provided in the pews. Many agree that, in any case, someone (usually the presider) should supplement the printed leaflet by announcing page numbers and giving postural directions throughout the liturgy.

Pastoral experience has shown me that the following principles and guidelines lead to the most effective congregational orders of worship, for both regular members of the assembly and visitors, no matter how limited or how extensive their liturgical experience may be.

1. Every word and every note that make up the assembly's corporate participation should be printed in the leaflet.

Long-time Episcopalians often admit that even though they have learned how to navigate their way through the Prayer Book, *The Hymnal 1982*, and whatever other hymnals a congregation may use (*Wonder, Love and Praise; Lift Every Voice and Sing; El Himnario; Enriching Our Music I; Enriching Our Music II; Voices Found*), all while holding the service leaflet, handling all the books sometimes distracts them from the liturgy and impedes their ability to pray. For visitors, all of these resources can be a frustrating paper maze and a source of embarrassment. Visitors report that they just cannot get it all straight, and they feel inept. A complete order of worship benefits long-time members and first-time guests.

The software package *The Rite Stuff* puts the entire collection of Episcopal liturgical material a mouse-click away. Scanners, which are now built into most photocopiers, make other material nearly as accessible for reproduction. As a matter of justice, since musical composers live on royalties and reputation, copyrighted material should be acknowledged and paid for. Guidelines for obtaining blanket and one-time permissions and the proper formats for citing copyrighted work are bundled into *The Rite Stuff* and are widely available online.

Undeniably, producing an all-inclusive order of worship requires the expenditure of money and the use of paper. It raises questions of stewardship, both of financial and natural resources. In view of the significant benefits this kind of booklet can have in the life of a congregation and its evangelical mission, however, these costs do not seem frivolous. Perhaps for the sake of having a complete service leaflet, other less productive spending could be cut from the budget. Likewise, other uses of expendable resources could be reconsidered. For example, can the parish use reusable china and cloth napkins instead of paper at the coffee hour? Can the newsletter be circulated electronically to people who have email? Can the parish office be more rigorous about recycling? There are many ways to conserve paper that would offset using it for a truly effective order of worship.

2. Words and notes that are not required for the assembly's participation should not be included in the order of worship.

Giving people texts that are not theirs to say creates insularity, as each individual buries the head in the booklet, reading along rather than listening to others and watching their actions. Printing material in the order of worship that is not proper to the assembly *as a whole* threatens to undermine the corporate nature of the event.

While the analogy is not perfect, think of what would happen in the theater if each member of the audience read from a complete script as the play went on. The experience of the play as real, immediate, and corporate would be greatly reduced. Its evocative power would be diminished. The visual impact of the event, which is at least as essential as the verbal and musical, would go unnoticed as people attended to words printed on a page instead of the set and the actions of the cast. (In the liturgy, of course, the entire assembly as the Body of Christ is "the cast.")

Theatergoers do not need the entire script, but what they do need is a general outline of what is happening and clear directions about what is expected of them. For example, they need to be reminded to turn off pagers and cell phones, and to pace themselves during the intermission so that they can make it back to their seats on time. That is what the playbill gives them. It does not tell them how many minutes the various actors have for costume changes nor does it print the piano accompaniment for the grand finale. That might be of interest to serious students of theater, but even they would not expect it in the playbill and, moreover, they would realize that the average person would be distracted by it. It would not contribute to making the play a lively, dynamic event.

A stage event that is more akin to the liturgy than a play, and is therefore perhaps more instructive, is the annual *Messiah* sing-along that many orchestras sponsor. Exactly as in the liturgy, the "assembly" as a whole enacts the event. The entire room becomes the stage. When it comes to printed material, the "performers" have all that is needed for their roles, but only that. The members of the alto section do not have the French horn score or the scores of the soloists, perhaps not even the scores of the other vocal sections. What they do have is an outline indicating the order in which the pieces will come, and including those bits of others' parts they need so they will not miss their cues. That, however, is all. A good congregational order of worship follows that model.

A booklet like that allows the assembly to look at the liturgy and experience it as an event; to listen to the Scriptures as a living proclamation, not a text on a page; to attend to the movements of their own hearts and minds as possible clues about the movement of God rather than to a word-by-word script; and to experience themselves as parts of a whole, not as units in a conglomerate of individuals. Then, when the time comes for them to act, detailed instructions are in front of them, along with the texts and the music. A printed order of worship that gives the assembly all it needs while not burying it in what only the designated ministers need contributes to a liturgy that feels alive (as opposed to feeling "canned") and that allows each person to attend to the entire liturgy using all the senses.

I have seen many orders of worship that provide the members of the assembly all they do *not* need, and very little of what they actually *do* need. These booklets include the full texts of the readings (something the assembly does not need, especially if the lectors are well trained), but makes them go to the Prayer Book to find the Psalm (which it does need). These booklets give the people the full text of the Prayers of the People, even though they need to have only the responses they repeat. It also means that the prayers were composed for a printing deadline, days before the liturgy. What of the real needs of the world that arose in the meantime? Printing the list of needs and names rather than simply the responses not only gives the assembly text they do not need, it misleads them about what these prayers are: genuine intercessions about concrete, right up-to-the-minute, socially and personally significant needs.

Often, such unhelpful orders of worship then force the members of the assembly to dive for Prayer Books to find the text for the Confession, something that is essential to their role: something they do, in fact, need for the ministry of the assembly. Such booklets give the assembly the full text of the Great Thanksgiving, something they do not need (and, moreover, something that distracts them from looking at the bread and wine and the core actions that occur around and with them). Yet, these booklets send the people hunting in one of the hymnals for the music for the *Sanctus* and, perhaps, the Memorial Acclamation (after they have figured out *which* hymnal). Then, after the Communion, they must page furiously through the Prayer Book to locate the postcommunion prayer, hoping to get in a few words before others in the assembly have finished reciting it. This is especially disruptive if the prayer is one that people generally do not know by heart (the prayer used at funerals, for example).

In general, orders of worship should provide the members of the assembly with *everything* they need to celebrate the rite with ease and vigor, yet not distract them with other material. The booklets should help the assembly to engage the rite with all the senses and to experience it as a vital, living encounter with God.

3. *The Prayer Book prints all congregational texts in sense lines, and orders of worship should follow the same convention.*
That is, the Prayer Book texts are laid out so that the end of each line signals a pause in recitation. This allows the assembly to pray in unison. In orders of worship, the same convention should be followed. Arranging texts in sense lines aids the assembly exactly as musical notation aids them. Setting out texts in sense lines ensures that the recitation is crisp and strong, and helps the worshippers feel more secure about how to express the text. This is a matter of hospitality and works toward the goal of making the assembly confident and competent.

Often people will stumble at the beginning of a unison text. For the presider to say, "All together now," or something similar, is artless and puts controlling words unnecessarily in the presider's mouth. To avoid this, a parish can establish a policy about when the assembly "jumps into" a text. A useful pattern, and the one with the most precedent, is for the leader to recite the first line (technically called the *incipit*), and then the other members of the assembly take up the second line. This creates a clean, orderly beginning and puts the assembly at ease. The pattern must be indicated in the order of worship, especially for the sake of visitors. For example, the postcommunion prayer might be printed this way:

incipit. leader

Presider:	Let us pray.
	Eternal God,
Assembly:	Heavenly Father,
	You have graciously accepted us as living members....

Providing detail like this is not a control tactic. On the contrary, it is meant to help the assembly to act independently.

4. *The rubrics are just as important as the texts and music. A functional order of worship provides the assembly with directions about their actions.*
For visitors, these directions are probably even more important than the texts and music. They also give members and regular churchgoers the tools to be fully functioning, self-confident worshippers who do not have to be told what to do at every turn. When the priest habitually tells the assembly what to do, a dependency is established that subtly conveys to the assembly the message that they are not the celebrants. And when the assembly believes that the priest, and not the assembly, celebrates the liturgy, it has repercussions in the life of the congregation far beyond the hour on Sunday.

Rubrics should be as complete as possible without being condescending. For example, many congregations in their order of worship assure all the members of the assembly that they are welcome to approach the Lord's Table at Communion, and explain how those who wish to seek a blessing instead of the Sacrament signal this to the presider. Notations like that are exceedingly helpful to visitors. They convey both important information (You are truly welcome) and important instructions (If you do it this way, you will look like a pro and the presider will know what you desire) without being patronizing. This is hospitality in print.

5. *Sometimes explanatory notes are useful, especially if something unusual is happening or if people are present who are unfamiliar with the liturgy.*
For example, at the beginning of an outline of worship for a funeral—an event that draws many people who are not familiar with the Episcopal liturgy—it would be helpful to print something like, "The presider sprinkles the coffin with water from the baptismal font, and a white pall, symbolic of the white garment in which Christians are clothed at Baptism, is spread over it." Visitors who do not know that the vessel of water is the baptismal font or that Christians are vested in white at Baptism would benefit from the note.

Explanatory notes become counterproductive, however, when they presume to spell out exactly what symbols mean. Such notes rob the symbols of their power to evoke responses at multiple levels in the human mind and heart. For example, even people who do not know what a baptismal font is do know what water is. They are well aware, at both conscious and preconscious levels, of the numberless functions and meanings of water. To tell the assembly precisely what water *means* would stand in the way of what water *does:* It elicits a multiplicity of insights and experiences, almost all of them relevant to the Christian understanding of baptism. To choose one meaning from all of these, or even a few, and spell them out in an order of worship robs the water of its ability to engage the worshippers at multiple levels. The same is true of every other symbol in the liturgy, be it verbal, aural, tactile, kinesthetic, or visual. Explain it too much, and you have explained it away. To borrow from Aidan Kavanagh's comment about the nature of ritual clothing, to explain a symbol is to convert it into a billboard: two-dimensional, flat, and purged of the mystery that is a window into the Mystery.

Chapter 6

THE
LITURGICAL YEAR

Most people come to church on Sunday hoping for an experience. They are not usually looking for information, and almost never for historical information. History lessons can be interesting and instructive, even inspiring and challenging, but they are not enough to get most people to church. In time, people may want to learn about the church's history, but it will not be what compelled them to come in the first place.

It is impossible to catalog all the reasons people do the countercultural thing and get up on Sunday morning for church. Some are searching for a community that will break through the often strangling isolation of modern society. Some are looking for partners in the fight for justice and right action. Some are seeking a values-based environment where their children, perhaps by osmosis, will learn how to live honorable lives. These are good reasons to go to church, but they can all be satisfied just as well in other places. Country clubs, social groups, political action committees, scouting troops, soccer teams, and a host of other vibrant and accessible programs would do. Why do people choose to come to church? Because the church promises what nothing else dares to promise: an encounter with God. It is not that the church is the *only* place God is present. God is no more present in a church on Sunday morning than in any of those other places. The church has no monopoly on God. But what we *do* have is an articulated intention to find God and a shared willingness to surrender to God. God can be found anywhere and in any group, but the church is where people are explicitly looking and willing to find God.

Nowhere is the church's intention to seek a deeper knowledge of God—to "find and be found" by God (BCP 386)—more clearly articulated than in the liturgy. In its ritual action, the church intentionally opens itself to an encounter with God. As the Catechism says, the sacraments are "given by Christ as sure and certain means by which we receive" spiritual grace (BCP 857). Grace is not a commodity. It is a relationship—"God's favor towards us, unearned and undeserved" (BCP 858). Bread and wine, water and oil, art and architecture, human touch and human speech, human faces and human bodies: all of these ordinary, earthly, and earthy things become the meeting place of God and the people of God. And among all the ordinary things that form the ground upon which the human and the divine meet is time.

The liturgical year, like liturgical space, is a context in which the eucharistic divine-human encounter unfolds. Just as the church building is the spatial structure where the church expresses and experiences its relationship with God, the liturgical year is the temporal structure. In time, God's people encounter the God who is beyond time, present in their very midst.

Unlike our ordinary calendars of days and weeks and years, the liturgical year is not a series of anniversaries or commemorations of events long past, but a structure for approaching the Eternal within the finite. Day by day, week by week, season by season, the liturgical year provides a series of lenses through which the church can see in tiny glimpses a reality and a relationship that no human being can grasp in its entirety. Even with one another, even in the most vulnerable and intimate of relationships, human beings eventually encounter the ultimate elusiveness of the other. No person can ever grasp the entirety of anyone else. How much less reducible is the relationship of humanity and God! The liturgical year is essentially a schema that, in the course of the year, holds before the assembly a series of small windows into the Divine Life active in the world and, in a particular way, active in the Body of Christ. Taken together, all of these glimpses meld into a larger picture—though still partial and imperfect—of the God believers know in Christ.

The first generation of Christians came to know the Divine Presence in their world by knowing Jesus in his historical incarnation. In subsequent generations, the liturgical year gradually evolved as an organized pattern meant to give latter-day Christians an echo of their ancestors' firsthand experience. The recorded stories of Jesus' life became the lens through which they could see what was, in fact, still happening before their eyes: the saving ministry of the Christ. Today, as the biblical accounts of Jesus' life are carefully strung together through the liturgical year, the life of the historical Jesus shows contemporary Christians what the Mystery is like, so that they will know it when they see it. Otherwise, it might pass before them unnoticed, or at least unnamed.

As the church moves through the liturgical year, it strives to see the saving action of God that was once present to the world in Jesus of Nazareth present today in the Spirit. Thus the liturgical year is not for remembering something that happened long ago, but for recognizing what is happening now. The liturgical year is not meant to give a history lesson, but to facilitate an experience.

The fifth-century Pope Leo the Great said that "what was present in the Savior" has passed into the "Mysteries," that is, into the sacraments, a category that was far more fluid in his day than now. In the life of the community, and especially in its official and liturgical acts, Jesus Christ is just as truly present as he was in his first-century historical manifestation, although in a different mode. The entire healing and reconciling ministry of Jesus is accessible today. We are at no disadvantage by being separated by millennia from the biblical events. In the course of the liturgical year, the contemporary church focuses from one angle and then from another on the presence and action of Jesus in the world and in the Christian community, using the life as the historical Jesus as its guide. And while it is impossible for humanity to grasp divinity, in the course of the entire liturgical year the church looks from as many angles as possible at the Living One in its midst.

The liturgical year is about *now*. It is not about *then*.

One of the great rediscoveries of the early twentieth-century Liturgical Movement was the notion of *anamnesis*, that is, a certain kind of remembering. The German Benedictine Odo Casel was singularly important in reintroducing this biblical notion of remembrance into theological, and especially, liturgical thought. The question that haunted him was how the events of Christ's historical life can be brought to bear on the lives of those who live after Christ's glorification. Casel believed that, through liturgical remembrance, contemporary Christians come into actual contact with the saving events that took place in the life of Christ, especially his Paschal Mystery: his passing from life to death to glory. Casel and others who built upon his work, which, in turn, was built upon patristic thought, did not arrive at anything definitive or even terribly clear about how this might happen. But they were clear that what Christians encounter in the liturgy is not grace in the sense of some spiritual commodity, but grace in the sense of a divine-human relationship. What confronts the liturgical assembly is not a force but a person. In the liturgy, the church meets Jesus Christ. And what he offers today is no less than what he offered his contemporaries. He offers an actual encounter that brings healing, reconciliation, salvation, wisdom, and everything else that he offered his first disciples and, through them, the world. As the landmark ecumenical document from the World Council of Churches, *Baptism, Eucharist and Ministry*, says, "Christ himself with all that he has accomplished for us and for all creation (in his incarnation, servanthood, ministry, teaching, suffering, resurrection, ascension and sending of the Spirit) is present in this [eucharistic] *anamnesis*, granting us communion with himself."[5]

---

5. *Baptism, Eucharist and Ministry*, Faith and Order Paper No. 111 (Geneva: World Council of Churches, 1982), Eucharist II.B.6.

ORIGINS AND DEVELOPMENT

The series of lenses the liturgical year provides for seeing the divine action did not emerge all at once as an intact system. In the beginning, there was only one Christian feast: the weekly Sunday. It did not commemorate anything in particular in the life of the historical Jesus. It was not (at least not in the sense that people often mean it) a "little Easter"; that is, it was not a celebration of the resurrection as an event. Rather, it celebrated the entire life, death, resurrection, and glorification of Jesus and its fruit: his living presence in the life of the church. Sunday was the weekly encounter of the members of the Body of Christ with one another and, therefore, with the One who lived through, with, and in them, and in the sacramental Food and Drink they shared.

The story of Emmaus can be read as an allegory of the weekly assembly of believers, who experience Christ in Word and Sacrament. In the entire liturgical event, Christ is truly present and active for the church—not in memory, but in actual fact. That his presence is elusive, as in the Emmaus story, is surely one of the reasons the liturgical year so often devolves into a series of commemorations of past events. The historical Jesus is far more manageable and easier to pin down than the Christ who is present-in-absence. It is easier to remember what Jesus *did* than to discern what he might be *doing*. The potential power of the liturgy is lost, however, when the church takes the easy way out. The goal of the Christian life is a personal relationship with Jesus, through which we intentionally and consciously encounter the Living One and are thereby changed. The liturgical year is a system, based upon the recorded events in the life of the historical Jesus, for negotiating that encounter. The liturgical year is a schema for encountering Jesus in the breaking of the bread (taken in its broadest sense: the entire liturgical event), not for remembering that once, long ago, people encountered God as they sat at table with him.

After the emergence of the weekly Sunday festival, Christians added to their calendar the feasts of local martyrs, celebrated on the anniversaries of their deaths. The martyrs themselves were not the focus of the feasts; rather, worshippers remembered Christ's continual self-offering made manifest in the martyrs. Recognizing the dying of Christ in the death of the martyr, and hence the glorification of Christ in the glorification of the martyr, the church experienced that the mission of Christ in the world was ongoing and concrete. Those who celebrated the martyrs' deaths were not implying that the Passover of Christ was less than a once-for-all, sufficient act. Rather, they were witnessing that Christ continued to live out the self-sacrificial pattern of his life, evident from the moment of his *kenotic* (self-emptying) incarnation, even in the contemporary church.

The martyrs were exemplars of what Christ was still doing. Christians celebrated the Eucharist at the tombs of the martyrs as a witness that they were in communion with the martyrs, since they were all in communion with Christ. In the liturgy, they knew themselves joined with "Angels and Archangels and with all the company of heaven" (BCP 362). The saints who have been added to the calendar ever since, and who are added at each General Convention, are reassuring signs of the ongoing ministry of Christ.

THE TRIDUUM

Next in the development of the liturgical year came the increasing imposition of Christian imagery onto the Jewish Passover until it was, in essence, no longer Jewish. Many of the classic images from the pre-Christian era remained, especially those of the Exodus and the Red Sea. In time, however, Jesus' Passover from life to death to glory became the focal paschal image for Christians. A thoroughly Christian *Pasch* evolved, so divergent from the Jewish Passover that it had become a different feast.

By the third century, the Christian Passover celebration (Easter) had become an annual baptismal celebration. The final preparation of the elect took place in a pre-paschal season, known today as Lent. The Prayer Book's invitation "to the observance of a holy Lent" in the Ash Wednesday liturgy explicitly notes the baptismal character of the season. In the paschal baptisms, the once-for-all dying and rising of Jesus was not merely commemorated as a past event but was experienced anew in the dying and rising of the newly baptized. "What was present in the Savior" had truly passed into the Mysteries. The epistle at the Great Vigil of Easter is from Romans: "Do you not know that all of us who have been baptized into Christ Jesus were baptized into his death?" (6:3). This biblical passage is the key to the entire vigil, since it brings into sharp relief the fact that the celebration is not about an event that is lost in the past, but a transformation that is accessible in the present. The church does not merely *remember* what happened at the time of its origins, it *experiences it anew* in ritual.

Just as the Jewish Passover held together in one celebration the various aspects of the Exodus event—slavery, plagues, flight, Red Sea, liberation—so the Christian Passover held together in one celebration the various aspects of the Paschal Mystery of Christ—betrayal, capture, trial, torture, journey to Calvary, death, burial, resurrection, glorification, presence in the Spirit. These were not celebrated at distinct liturgies on distinct days but were all held together in one "unitive feast," as liturgists say. In the fourth century, various aspects of the one reality began to be celebrated, not on one day, but over three days: Friday (marked from sundown on Thursday), Saturday, and Sunday. This extended three-day feast is called the Paschal Triduum.

It is crucial for pastoral ministers not to lose sight of the origins of these three days. They are essentially the pulling apart into three strands of what began as one event. They are not three days celebrating three distinct historical events, but one three-day-long event celebrating one saving dynamic. As James Farwell writes in his important book on the Triduum, "The liturgies of the Paschal Triduum are the point in Christian ritual practice where the readiness of Christian faith to face human suffering squarely, and to find God working in and through suffering, is simultaneously most in evidence and most easily obscured.... The resurrection is celebrated not as a moment 'after' suffering and separate from it, but as a mystery born in and of suffering."[6]

A responsible pastor cannot preach to real people who live real lives that the day will come when all their suffering will finally end, at least not short of death. Instead, a wise pastor will invite the church to trust that in the very midst of suffering, the transformative hand of God is often most active and most able to change lives. This is the message of the Triduum. When observed not as a sequence of historic commemorations (that began bad and ended well), but as a three-day celebration of the inextricably interwoven realities of suffering and salvation, of death and life, the Paschal Triduum forms the church for living the authentic Christian life. Since the Triduum is the annual ritual enactment (not reenactment) of the core Christian message in all its pastoral practicality—that even in the midst of death there is life—the Roman Catholic Church and the Evangelical Lutheran Church in America have set the Triduum apart as its own three-day season. The calendar in the recent *Evangelical Lutheran Worship* calls the season "The Three Days" (ELW 14). In many Episcopal congregations the Triduum is kept as a single three-day celebration, though unfortunately the current calendar of the Episcopal Church considers Good Friday and Holy Saturday part of Lent.

The Presbyterian *Book of Common Worship* expresses the unity of the Three Days by ending each of the services with a rubric indicating that the service *continues* the next day: at the end of the Maundy Thursday liturgy it notes that "the service continues on Good Friday" (BCW 279), and at the end of the Good Friday liturgy it states, "The service continues with the Easter Vigil, or on Easter Day" (BCW 291). This is a useful cue to the worshippers that the Three Days are actually one "day," and that the liturgies of the Triduum are actually one liturgy. Just before the publication of the *Book of Common Worship*, a church-appointed commission issued a volume on the liturgical year as the seventh of its Supplemental Liturgical Resources. Its treatment of the Triduum is compact but rich.

> The Triduum engages us from Thursday until Sunday in a unified act. What happens on Maundy Thursday, Good Friday, and the Easter Vigil forms a continuous dramatic story. These days are to be seen together rather than separately.... Because of the interrelationship of the three days, each service of the Triduum needs the others to tell the whole story. For example, resurrection is incomprehensible without Christ's self-giving in crucifixion and at the Lord's Supper. Therefore, Easter needs Good Friday and Maundy Thursday to be fully understood. The way to the triumph of Easter is through the Triduum.[7]

6. James Farwell, *This Is the Night: Suffering, Salvation, and the Liturgies of Holy Week* (New York: T & T Clark, 2005), 7.
7. *Liturgical Year: The Worship of God*, Supplemental Liturgical Resource 7 (Louisville: Westminster/ John Knox Press, 1992), 35.

Evangelical Lutheran Worship expresses it this way. "The services of Maundy Thursday, Good Friday, and the Vigil of Easter unfold in a single movement, as the church each year makes the passage with Christ through death into life" (ELW 247). This emphasizes not only the unity of the Three Days, but the *current* reality they celebrate. The church actually makes the passage with Christ—it does not merely recall his historical and long-past passage.

EASTER TO PENTECOST

As early as the second century, Easter began to be celebrated not as a day, but as a season. It coincided with the Jewish festival of Weeks, which lasts for fifty days and ends with the festival of the fiftieth day, Pentecost. The Fifty Days of Easter are, like the original Easter Day and the expanded Triduum "Day," a sort of protracted unitive feast. They are an extended period of paschal celebration, not a series of sequential commemorations. They are a prolongation of the Easter festival. The Feast of Pentecost marks the end of the Easter season. The Sundays after the fiftieth day are referred to as the Sundays after Pentecost, just as the season is called the Season after Pentecost, not the Season of Pentecost (BCP 32).

EPIPHANY/CHRISTMAS

The Epiphany/Christmas cycle was the last great development of the liturgical year, coming rather late—at the end of the fourth or beginning of the fifth century. This innovation marked a shift in the dominant conception of a Christian feast. The exact origins of the celebration of the incarnation and manifestation of God-in-Christ are disputed, but from its inception this group of observances had the flavor of an anniversary. While this cycle of feasts, like the rest of the year, did not fail to recognize that Christ's incarnation is a continuing and ongoing reality, it did rather quickly create a series of anniversary celebrations for the various events mentioned in the gospel accounts of Jesus' nativity and other records of the life of the young Jesus. By the mid-fourth century, a series of commemorative feasts was in place in the West. These were all centered on what today is called "Christmas," and set the precedent for thinking of all liturgical feasts principally as commemorative: reminders of Christ's past rather than encounters with Christ's present.

The Eastern churches had a similar feast: the origins of what we call the Epiphany. The Epiphany originally celebrated the reality that, in Christ, God was manifest. Its imagery drew on the many early epiphanies of God-in-Christ: birth, magi, shepherds, baptism, and Cana. Because the baptism of Jesus was a key image, the Epiphany became the second annual baptismal feast in the East and in areas of the West that were heavily influenced by the East, though not in Rome and the churches most strongly influenced by it. A preparatory season, like Lent, was put in place before the feast, during which the catechumens underwent their final preparation for baptism. Like Lent, it had a generally penitential tone.

In the northern part of Europe, in addition to the historical manifestations of God-in-Christ and baptismal imagery, a third thread was added: the eventual manifestation of Christ at the consummation of history. Unlike the earliest Christians, who prayed, "May grace come and this world pass away," expecting to share in Christ's glory, early medieval Christians lived in fear of an unfavorable judgment at the parousia. In the regions where the return of Christ became a focus of the Epiphany feast, the penitential and fearsome tenor of Advent was intensified.

The Advent that evolved in Rome took a different course. In Rome and the churches that were strongly influenced by it, including the English Church, a pre-Christmas season did emerge, but it was a time to make ready for the anniversary of the Lord's birth, not for baptisms. This season of Advent was not penitential in tone. Gradually, however, some penitential Advent customs migrated from the churches that were influenced by the East, just as the Roman customs seeped into them, leaving the Western Advent with a somewhat conflicted identity. The marks of the conflict endure even today. For example, in the current rubrics of the Prayer Book, the *Gloria* is not sung during Advent, just as it is not sung during Lent; however, Alleluia is sung in Advent, while in Lent it is not. Today, many parishes use blue vestments in Advent rather than purple (the common color for Lent) to distinguish these two seasons and, especially, to deemphasize the penitential quality of Advent.

While some claim that blue Advent vestments are authentically Anglican because they were the Sarum custom, they actually were not. Blue vestments were worn for the Sarum liturgy, but not in Advent. Still, blue Advent vestments do visually distinguish Advent and Lent, and are an emerging development of the Western tradition. (The Roman Church, incidentally, does not use blue vestments except by special permission in specific churches where there is ancient precedent, and on exceedingly rare occasions. It explicitly forbids them for Advent.)

The history of Advent is so complex that a case could be made to celebrate it in any number of ways: as a time of baptismal preparation, a period of penitence, or a joyful season of anticipatory preparation. The third option is clearly the Western ecumenical consensus, and so we will consider it the norm.

Why not all 3?

PASTORAL PRACTICALITIES

◆ Every Sunday is a feast and should be treated like one.

◆ What constitutes festivity varies from culture to culture, and even from congregation to congregation. The liturgical planning team and the ministers have the task of discerning what suggests festivity within their particular context.

◆ Every assembling of the church is about the Christ, present in the Spirit. There are no other liturgical themes. What are commonly called "themes" are better understood as angles of approach to the single mystery.

◆ A significant number of the "ordinary" Sundays occur in the summer, but summer is not a liturgical season. While modern means of transportation make it inevitable that members of the liturgical assembly will travel during the summer, a decrease in attendance is not an excuse to neglect the festivity of the weekly feast. The liturgical planning group, and especially the musicians, the presider, and the preacher must determine how to sustain the quality of the liturgy despite a smaller congregation and perhaps no choir. This may yield insights that will invigorate the rest of the year.

◆ The liturgical year begins on the First Sunday of Advent. On that day, the reading of the synoptic gospel assigned to that year begins: Matthew in Year A, Mark in Year B, and Luke in Year C. The commencement of the gospel should be brought to the attention of the assembly, perhaps homiletically, on Advent 1.

◆ Each of the gospels has its own internal logic and theology, and each Sunday's texts should be viewed, especially by the preacher, within the evangelist's overall program.

◆ On the "green Sundays," the assigned synoptic gospel is read in order from week to week. Some segments of the gospel are skipped over, however, or are used on feast days. This is called a "semicontinuous reading" of the gospel, as opposed to a "continuous reading," where no passages are skipped. The ordered reading of the gospel from Sunday to Sunday reflects the most ancient stratum of the liturgical year, when Sunday was the only feast. The two great cycles of Easter and Christmas are inserted into this basic structure. The Sundays after

Pentecost and after the Epiphany, on which the numbered propers are read, are the continuous thread of the year. They are not just filler between the seasons.

◆ The other readings on the "green Sundays" in the *Revised Common Lectionary* are also semicontinuous. A preacher could focus on the thread that they run from Sunday to Sunday.

◆ While a preacher must do a thorough exegesis of each text to learn what it meant in its own time, the preacher's ultimate task is to explore how God is still doing *now* what God was doing *then*. Exegetical material is for the sermon's foot-notes and seldom deserves a prominent place in the preached sermon. The sermon is not about the text. It is about the current presence and action of the God whose presence and action are attested to in the Scripture.

"Keep the main thing, the main thing"

THE EASTER CYCLE

The entire Easter cycle, from Ash Wednesday to Pentecost, focuses on the Baptismal Covenant and is directed toward the Great Vigil of Easter. Even the penitential aspect of Lent must be seen as the church's recognition that it has failed to express the grace God freely gave it in baptism. Lenten penitence is rooted in the church's sense that it has not lived up to undeserved and unearned baptismal grace, not that it must do better to deserve or earn that grace.

LENT

◆ If catechumens are to be baptized at the Easter Vigil, the community's prayer throughout Lent should focus on them. In observing and fostering the conversion of the catechumens, the entire community vicariously retraces its own steps toward the font. This identification with those to be baptized can be the impetus for radical reengagement, or engagement for the first time, with the Baptismal Covenant. *The Book of Occasional Services* provides a schema and texts. On Lent 1, the catechumens are presented by their sponsors and accepted by the church as candidates for Easter baptism. On Lent 3, 4, and 5, the candidates are called forth and prayed over, with the laying on of hands. These rites are traditionally called "the scrutinies." Since baptism knits a person into the church, Christ's Body, the rites should be arranged so that the entire assembly experiences itself as an actor, not a passive observer. *The Book of Occasional Services* directs that the candidates and their sponsors "come forward" for each rite. This does not necessarily mean that they move to the extreme east end of the room. They could move into the midst of the assembly for most of the rites and then, for the laying on of hands, move toward the presider. Placing the catechumens in the heart of the room, perhaps midway up the center aisle in a traditionally arranged neo-Gothic space, expresses and invites the involvement of the entire assembly in the formation, election, and initiation of the catechumens.

◆   The Tridentine rubrics directed that all sacred images in the church be veiled during the last two weeks of Lent. For many years after Vatican II the custom was abandoned, but it was explicitly permitted again in the United States beginning in 2002. Some Episcopal congregations follow this practice, while others have adopted the pre-Reformation Sarum custom of veiling images during the entire Lenten season. Today, the veils are often changed to accord with the color of the day: purple or unbleached fabric through most of Lent, then red on Passion Sunday, and so forth. This changing of the veils and the large blocks of color they create draw attention to the images, and may actually work against the intention of the custom. The goal is simplicity and visual emptiness, to foster an interior openness in the assembly and a longing for the glory of God. When images are veiled, it should be to minimize their impact, not heighten it. Images that are portable should be taken out of the church entirely, not veiled. In congregations where the presentation and veneration of the cross is part of the Good Friday liturgy, all crosses that cannot be removed should be veiled at least before the Triduum begins. Otherwise, the presentation of the cross on Good Friday will be redundant and without impact.

◆   In some churches, the baptismal font is kept filled with water during most of the year, or there are vessels of baptismal water at the doors. In remembrance of baptism, those who enter the room may touch the water and cross themselves. During Lent, the font and other vessels for water might be left empty or covered, in anticipation of the baptismal rituals at Easter. This parallels the removal or veiling of images.

Ash Wednesday

◆   On Ash Wednesday, the ashes are produced by burning palms from the previous Passion Sunday. During the service, the ashes are brought before the presider, who should lay a hand upon them or make the sign of the cross over them during the prayer of blessing (BCP 265). The assembly should be able to see the ashes during the blessing.

◆   The presider may invite other ministers (lay and ordained) to join in the imposition of ashes, if the size of the assembly requires it.

◆ In some congregations, a custom has emerged of mixing the ashes with oil so that they can be almost painted onto the forehead. The apparent goal is to make the cruciform shape more distinct, but it robs the ashes of their essential qualities: fragile, dry, earthy. The dryness of the ashes is a counterpoint to the water of baptism toward which the Lenten season moves. It is also reminiscent of the text of committal during the burial rite: "Earth to earth, ashes to ashes, dust to dust" (BCP 501). The ashes precisely *as ashes* are the primary sign on Ash Wednesday, not the cruciform shape in which they are imposed on the foreheads of those who come forward. Note that the Prayer Book does not even mention that a cross be traced with the ashes, only that they be placed on the forehead.

Laetare Sunday

◆ The Roman Rite allows rose-colored vestments as an option on the fourth Sunday of Lent, commonly called "Laetare Sunday." Since the Episcopal Church does not have an official liturgical color scheme, the practice is entirely at the discretion of the parish. The rose vestments signify the halfway point in the demanding penances of Lent—a sort of visual sigh of relief. If personal and communal penance and liturgical restraint has been encouraged and observed in the parish during the season, rose vestments would be reasonable. If not, they would have little meaning, and might even be distracting.

Passion Sunday

◆ The liturgy of Passion Sunday, commonly called Palm Sunday, is the joining together of two distinct liturgical traditions. Until the eighth century in the West the reading of the Passion Gospel was the distinctive and governing feature of the day. The tone was understandably ponderous. The festive procession with palms was grafted onto the beginning of this Passion-focused liturgy by stages. In the first stage, palms were simply carried in the entrance procession. In the second stage, the people carrying the palms were blessed. Finally, the palms themselves were blessed, so that an entire short liturgical rite had evolved. (Note, incidentally, that this feast in its original form is an example of how the liturgical year was *not* understood as a series of historical commemorations. If it were, the Passion Gospel would not have been proclaimed a full week before Easter. The palm procession, however, is an example of the increasing tendency toward historical commemoration and reenactment.)

◆ Clearly, there is a "seam" between the procession and the rest of the liturgy. Not merely their history but their entire focus and tone are different. The festive quality of the first section and the ponderous quality of the primary second section must be marked by a clear break and a definite shift in tone. The reader of the first lesson should not approach the lectern or begin the proclamation until the assembly is perfectly still. The reader should also understand the shift in focus and tone that begins with the first reading, and proclaim it accordingly.

◆   Passion Sunday differs from Good Friday insofar as Good Friday is actually a part of the Easter celebration. Passion Sunday has a more commemorative focus than Good Friday. On Good Friday, the Passion is held up as one aspect of the paschal dynamic, inseparable from and intertwined with the resurrection and glorification of Christ, and the presence of the Spirit in the church.

THE TRIDUUM

◆   The Triduum rites in the Book of Common Prayer are not distinct liturgies but are three segments of one continuous liturgy. Note that neither the Maundy Thursday liturgy (which is actually a Good Friday liturgy, since it is celebrated after sunset on Thursday) nor the Good Friday liturgy has a dismissal. That is, neither one actually ends. Rather, each one is like a movement in a symphony, and feeds into the next. To that end:

    ❖   Only one booklet should be prepared, if possible, containing the orders of worship for all three segments of the one Triduum liturgy.

    ❖   No postlude should follow the rite on Thursday or Friday, nor should a prelude come before the rite on Friday or the Great Vigil of Easter. The only prelude should come before the entire cycle begins on Thursday, and the only postlude should come after the entire cycle ends with the Vigil.

    ❖   Each of the three rites should include elements reminiscent of the others to emphasize the connection of the three. For example, the hymn "At the Name of Jesus" would keep Good Friday from devolving into a "funeral for Jesus" and would emphasize that Christian glory is precisely in Christian *kenosis* (self-emptying). Similarly, the hymn "Lift High the Cross," used at the Easter Vigil or on Easter Sunday, would express the Christian conviction that resurrection comes in the midst of death, not after it, and that the cross is a thing of resurrection glory, not deathly shame.

    ❖   Since the liturgies for the Triduum in the Prayer Book are of a piece, alternate devotional exercises, such as meditations on the Seven Last Words or celebrations of the Stations of the Cross on Good Friday, are not part of the Triduum liturgy. Because the three rites of the Triduum are properly conceived as one liturgy, other major rites cannot be interjected into them, especially ones that are merely commemorative, without damaging the flow and potential of the liturgy.

◆ Many seekers come to church on Easter morning, making it one of the most important opportunities for evangelism of the entire year. The principal Easter morning service should be advertised, and the parish should invest time, money, and personnel in the liturgy. At the same time, the religious formation team and the homilists must use Lent to prepare the regular liturgical assembly to celebrate all three of the Triduum liturgies and to see them *as a unit* as the parish Easter celebration. Even in advertisements in print and other media, the parish can note that the Great Vigil of Easter is the principal celebration of the feast.

THE GREAT FIFTY DAYS

◆ Since Easter lasts for fifty days, the energy and funds allotted for Easter should be budgeted to last for seven full weeks. As flowers die, for example, they should be replaced. The work of artists and musicians should be distributed throughout the seven weeks. In short, every liturgy during the Great Fifty Days should carry something of the intensity of the first day of the season.

◆ Explicitly Easter music—what one would expect to hear on Easter Sunday—should be used on each of the Sundays in Easter. Often, liturgy and music committees choose hymns to accord with the readings of the day, and rightly so. During Easter, however, at least some of the hymns and other music must be chosen in view of the overarching Easter feast of which the individual Sundays are a part.

◆ The baptismal emphasis of the Great Vigil stretches throughout the entire Easter season. The font can be filled every Sunday and surrounded by plants and flowers and, if it is not stationary, the font can be located in a prominent place. The paschal candle also might be adorned with flowers and should stand near the reading desk or, if there are two, near the pulpit. The Easter season, since it is so strongly baptismal, is an opportunity for exploring how to decorate the liturgical space with something other than the predictable two vases of flowers on the retable behind the altar.

◆ The paschal candle should be lighted before any members of the assembly arrive and extinguished only after the entire assembly has left the church. It is a symbol of the risen Christ and should not be seen unlit during the season, even when the other candles in the room are extinguished.

◆ The paschal candle is removed from prominence and no longer lighted only after the Day of Pentecost, that is, the last day of the paschal season. While for centuries it was extinguished, often with ceremony, on Ascension Day, this treated the liturgical year as a series of commemorations of past events rather than a celebration of present realities. Therefore, the flame that represented

Christ was made to disappear on Ascension Thursday as a reenactment of his disappearance on the fortieth day after the resurrection. Today, the entire Easter season is understood as a celebration of the risen Christ present here and alive now, it is not a reenactment. This ancient view is considered a more pastorally fruitful approach to the liturgical year.

◆ While the Prayer Book designates the Day of Pentecost, the last day of Easter, as one of the four days especially appropriate for Baptism, the penitential rites of the catechumenate are not appropriately celebrated during the season leading to Pentecost. *The Book of Occasional Services* is clear that the rites of the catechumenate are celebrated only in Lent and Advent, leading to adult baptisms at the Great Vigil and the Feast of the Baptism of Our Lord, respectively. If adults are to be baptized on Pentecost, other texts will be needed and, perhaps, an entirely different schema, for their immediate preparation.

THE NATIVITY CYCLE

The entire Christmas cycle, from Advent to the Feast of the Baptism of Our Lord, focuses on the earthly manifestation of God in Jesus. The cultural Christmas festivities begin long before December 25 but the liturgical Christmas celebrations do not. Christmas decorations and music are not introduced into the church until the first liturgy of Christmas Day.

ADVENT

◆ The Advent lectionary texts reflect the various strata of the history of the Western liturgical year. They speak of the manifestation of Christ in the parousia as well as his manifestation in the incarnation. The context in which these texts are proclaimed—the liturgical assembly—proclaims his constant manifestation in the Spirit.

◆ While Advent and Lent both call for restraint, Advent stresses anticipation rather than penitence.

◆ The Advent wreath is a domestic custom that has become very common in churches. Rites often accompany the lighting of the wreath before or during the Sunday Eucharist, although *The Book of Occasional Services* specifically excludes them (BOS 30). The wreath is a secondary symbol and should not be allowed to dominate the primary symbols, nor should lighting the candles overpower the primary actions of the assembly.

❖ When an Advent wreath is used, it is lighted before the liturgy begins. Various color schemes can be used for the candles. They may be all blue or all purple. One of the candles can be rose, depending on the color of the vestments used in the parish. Four white candles can also be used. The principal symbolism of the wreath is the dispelling of darkness as an additional candle is lighted each week, not the color of the candles.

"Jesus, The Light of The World"

CHRISTMAS

◆ Three sets of readings are provided for Christmas Day. If there are three services, the sets are used in order. Otherwise, any of the three sets may be used.

◆ Like the Advent wreath, the Christmas crèche is not integral to the liturgy but is, nonetheless, a cherished custom in most churches. The crèche is not set up until the first liturgy of Christmas. *The Book of Occasional Services* includes a rite for a "station" at the crèche on Christmas Day; that is, the entrance procession may pause for prayer at the crèche. Each of the elements of the rite may be used, but none must.

❖ Since the assembly should look at the crèche during the rite, it may not be helpful to use the versicle and response given in *The Book of Occasional Services*, which would force the assembly to look at the order of worship and away from the crèche. All of the figurines can be set in place before the rite, or the statue of the infant can be carried in procession and placed. Others can be brought in and placed as well. Because the crèche is not an integral part of the Christmas Eucharist, however, and the placing of numerous figurines could become a clumsy and protracted distraction that would overpower the essential elements, the station should be as simple as possible.

❖ In order not to emphasize the commemorative dimensions of the liturgical year, but rather its current, dynamic quality, figurines should not be added to the crèche throughout the season according to a supposed chronology in the gospel stories. Even more, they should not be made to move through the church closer and closer during the days of the Christmas season. For example, the figurines of the magi should not be set on a windowsill far from the crèche and then, day by day, moved closer as a sort of reenactment of their journey from the East.

❖ The crèche is thought to be a thirteenth-century invention of Francis of Assisi. Other representations of the incarnation and manifestation of God-in-Christ, both ancient and modern, are just as suitable. An icon of the Mother and Child, for example, captures in one image the humanity and divinity of Christ.

◆ In the Episcopal liturgical calendar, the Christmas season extends from Christmas Day through the Feast of the Epiphany: the twelve days of Christmas. Since the commemoration of Jesus' baptism in the Jordan was originally part of the unitive Epiphany celebration, the Feast of the Baptism of Our Lord (the First Sunday after the Epiphany) is often treated like part of the Christmas season, especially if there are baptisms on that day. In any case, as during the Easter season, the tone and decorations of Christmas Day are maintained throughout, but not beyond, the Christmas season, however it is defined in the particular congregation.

THE EPIPHANY

◆ Since in the Episcopal Church the Feast of the Epiphany on January 6 is not transferrable to a Sunday, in most years its celebration lies outside the scope of this book. It is important to note, however, that many parishes do make a concerted effort to mark the conclusion of the Christmas season with a festive midweek Epiphany celebration.

◆ If there are to be baptisms on the Feast of the Baptism of Our Lord (the First Sunday after the Epiphany), the enrollment of the candidates and the scrutinies follow the sermon and precede the Prayers of the People on the Sundays of Advent, just as in Lent.

Chapter 7

LITURGICAL MINISTRIES

Because of the widely held belief that religious services are done by professionals (clergy) on behalf of or in place of non-professionals (the baptized who are not ordained), we have emphasized that the Book of Common Prayer understands the liturgy as an action of the entire assembly. The liturgy mirrors and rehearses the life of the church: a community based in a baptismal equality in which, as the Catechism and the Baptismal Covenant make clear, all the members share in the ministry.

Still, that is not the whole story. Within the radical equality and shared ministry of the baptized community, there are a variety of gifts and needs. Ideally, in a process of mutual discernment, each individual's gifts and the community's needs find places of intersection, and through that coincidence the mission of the Lord Jesus effectively continues in the world today. There are different roles and different needs in the church, both in its "internal" life and in its mission to the world, and there are people with different gifts who are perfectly suited for some of these roles but who would do damage in others. The church is a community of radical equality, but not of anarchy.

The liturgy encompasses and expresses both aspects of what the church is: a community of equals and a community of differing gifts. As the church celebrates the liturgy, it both reflects and forms its own complex identity. In the liturgy the baptized community experiences the equality of its members as well as the variety of gifts its members bring. The liturgy not only demonstrates what the church is, but reinforces the church's self-understanding and its ability to live out practically what it knows itself to be.

In the Episcopal Church, the wide diversity of ministries can be categorized in a number of ways. One is to separate them into "lay" and "ordained" ministries. Given the polity of the Episcopal Church, as well as the ecumenical consensus that the ancient ordering of the Christian church into four orders is normative—the baptized who are not ordained, and the baptized who are ordained as bishops, priests, or deacons—there is no need to apologize for making a distinction between ordained and lay ministries. Still, neither the Episcopal Church nor any other church can ignore the danger these distinctions bring. The ordained have often been seen as superior to those who are not, or even holier simply by virtue of ordination. This is entirely contrary to the polity and ecclesiology of the Episcopal Church. The liturgy is authentic and faithful to the Prayer Book when it exemplifies a community of members who are equal in their very essence but who are, nonetheless, ordered and commissioned for specific tasks in service of the church's health and mission.

Within the order of the baptized who are not ordained, some are called to undertake ministries to which they are not permanently ordered. In a sense, since the liturgy is the work of the entire assembly, every member is a minister to the others, just as in the wider life of the church all the baptized are ministers. There are, however, particular ministries within the liturgy, apart from the ministries for which a person is set apart by ordination, that are integral. While these ministries and ministers may not exercise the same pervasive force in the liturgy as the ministry of the ordained clergy, they are just as integral to the rite. Likewise, in the life of the church the servant leadership of deacons, priests, and bishops is vital, yet it is only part of the ministry of the wider church. In the liturgy, the same balance and complementarity among the roles of the orders is expressed, but in ritual form.

THE LITURGY AND THE "REAL WORLD"

Liturgical ministries are not "roles" in the theatrical sense because the liturgy is not a stage production, no matter how similar various aspects may be. Liturgical ministries are acts of genuine service that reflect and "rehearse" the community's life of service outside the liturgy. Liturgical ministries, then, are most authentic when they are accurate reflections of what happens in the life of the community when it is not in church. This is what keeps the liturgy from being "an empty ritual." When liturgy and life mirror one another, the liturgy takes on an integrity and depth that makes it much more than simply going through the motions.

Acolytes are often said to "serve" at the liturgy. In fact, *all* the ministers serve the assembly and, in that, they serve God. To exercise any of the liturgical ministries authentically, a person must first be a servant in the life of the wider community. How each person serves will differ, but a person who does not serve the community and the world in the name of that community cannot authentically serve in the liturgy. A dichotomy between what the liturgical minister does ritually and what the person does in "real life" makes the liturgy a pretending game—and a "pretentious" one at that.

What exactly *is* the service that "servers at the altar" exercise in the assembly? What reflection might one find in their service to the church from their service to the world? In the weekday lives of choir members, soloists, and cantors, for example, what do we see that reflects their service within the liturgy? Is there something about singing in the liturgy that carries with it a more life-pervading demand than singing on stage ever would? What in the life of a liturgical musician makes the ministry more than a performance? For each of the liturgical ministries, authenticity demands an echo of the ministry in "real life." Or to look at it the other way, the gifts a person has been given and that he or she exercises within the wider community are pointers to the ministries that person should exercise in the liturgical assembly.

Similarly, the one who presides over the liturgy should also be the one who presides over the life of the community, or should be the delegate of the one who does. (In the Episcopal Church, all presiders are delegates—vicars—of the bishop, who is the true local pastor with the right liturgically to preside whenever present.) The qualities to which a presider aspires within the liturgy should be the qualities the person who presides over the congregation's life aspires to in the "real world": reverence, strength, humility, vision, generosity, self-control, orderliness, respect for others, a love for the Word, and an eye for the presence of God in created things, human lives, and the unfolding of history. When these are present in the "real life" of a person, then the act of presiding seems natural. More than merely carrying out ritual behaviors by rote or "going through the motions," such a liturgical presider is living out yet one more aspect of who he or she truly is before God and God's people.

Lectors, ideally, should love the Scriptures and, at least as much, delight in speaking by word and example of their faith and the church's mission. Since they proclaim the Good News in the assembly, they should also be evangelists—proclaimers of the Good News—when they are not standing at the ambo.

Eucharistic ministers (formerly called "chalice bearers") serve the community by administering the Sacrament that bonds the church to Christ and the members of the Body to one another. Outside the liturgical assembly, one would expect eucharistic ministers to be agents of unity in the church, who work by word and example to make the church one, even as the Bread is one. A eucharistic minister should also have a genuine reverence for the eucharistic Presence of Christ, and should without fail assemble with the church when it comes together weekly as a unified Body. In an earthier context, the person might also work day by day to feed the hungry. For some, this will mean welcoming others to their own homes for meals. For others, it will mean serving the poor in soup kitchens or food banks. Somehow, though, what is enacted ritually must be enacted "really" if the ritual is to have integrity.

The recruiting and formation of liturgical ministers offers an opportunity for a discernment of the gifts that exist in the congregation quite apart from the liturgy. While it is the canonical responsibility of the rector to coordinate the liturgy, when the process of discernment becomes a shared endeavor—like discernment for ordained ministry has become in the Episcopal Church—it gives the entire congregation an opportunity to become more aware of its needs and gifts and, in the process, to grow into a deeper sense of what it is doing when it celebrates the liturgy. The shared discernment of gifts and needs, both in the liturgy and in the wider life of the church, is an opportunity to explore how the liturgy is both a reflection of the church's life and a rehearsal for it.

If the life of the church is nothing less than the life of the Body of Christ in the world, then the liturgy is nothing less than the prayer of Christ in the world. Just as the common life of the church rather than the life of any individual member is the most complete manifestation of the life of Christ, so in the liturgy the common prayer of the assembly, and not the prayer of any individual member, is the most complete manifestation of the prayer of Christ. The liturgical ministers are entrusted with serving, leading, and facilitating the prayer of the Body so that it might experience and express the one prayer of Christ being prayed in it.

LITURGICAL MINISTERS
ASSIGNED BY THE RUBRICS OF THE PRAYER BOOK

THE CELEBRANT

The word "celebrant" is the 1979 Prayer Book's convention for referring to an ordained presider. When the bishop is present, the bishop, as the one who presides over the life of the local church, holds the right to preside over the liturgy. In the normal course of parochial life, the bishop delegates this role to the rector, who, in turn, can delegate it to assisting priests.

The presider's role is not to dominate or to overwhelm the assembly, but to set the pace and tone of the liturgy, to speak in the name of God to them, and to speak to God in the name of the community as a whole. While some schools of thought take this to mean that the presider alone approaches God while the assembly looks on, the assumption in this book is that the presider prays aloud the prayer of the entire community, which is the Body of Christ. The presider is not praying as a surrogate for the community, but as its spokesperson.

Because the presider is the link between the congregation and the bishop, who in turn is the link between the local church and entire church, the presider is also entrusted with speaking on behalf of the greater church and the church's tradition. The presider is entrusted not with preaching a gospel or enacting rites of his or her own devising, but with making available to the assembly the Christian tradition as this church has inherited it.

A note should be made here about concelebrants. The Roman Catholic Church, to create an alternative to the long-standing custom of private masses (that is, a priest celebrating the Eucharist alone or with only one attendant), instituted the practice of concelebration in the mid-twentieth century. This is not simply a liturgy in which more than one vested priest is present but one in which all or some of the additional priests are understood to co-consecrate the elements. The practice of concelebration has gained ground in the Episcopal Church and, although the word does not appear in the Prayer Book, the concept does.

At the time when the current Prayer Book was being compiled and refined, the idea of concelebration was in favor, since it expressed the unity of the presbyters with the bishop, who is the true pastor of the local church. It also showed the presbyters to be a "college," that is, a unified body of leaders, not a cluster of independent ministers as in a congregational church polity. In the Roman Church, in addition, it was a way to counter the long-standing but anomalous custom of every priest celebrating Mass every day, even if it meant doing the liturgy absolutely alone. The idea of priestly concelebration, however, is antithetical to the notion that the entire assembly is the celebrant of the liturgy, and all of the members are, therefore, concelebrants, presided over by a single ordained minister. The custom of concelebration unnecessarily clericalizes the liturgy and portrays an ecclesiology that is discordant with, if not antithetical to, the baptismal ecclesiology of the Prayer Book.

If vested priests other than the presider are present in the room or even at the Lord's Table, they are best understood as symbols of the way the community of the baptized is ordered, with some members permanently set apart for specific roles. The priests gathered in their collegial relationship around the bishop should not be seen as co-consecrators or concelebrants, except insofar as all the members of the assembly are concelebrants.

THE DEACON

The deacon has five principal roles in the Eucharist: to bid the people to act ("Let us confess our sins against God and our neighbor"; "Let us go forth . . ."); to proclaim the Gospel; to bid the Prayers of the People; to prepare the altar for the Liturgy of the Eucharist; and to be the presider's primary assistant, especially at the Lord's Table. There is symmetry between these liturgical tasks and the deacon's tasks in the larger life of the community. The Examination in the rite for the ordination of a deacon calls this order "a special ministry of servanthood." It elaborates that the deacon is to "serve all people, particularly the poor, the weak, the sick, and the lonely." The deacon-elect is further instructed "to study the Holy Scriptures, to seek nourishment from them, and to model your life upon them." Since deacons, in general, have "secular" employment to earn their livelihood, they are exhorted to be evangelists in their day-to-day surroundings, making "Christ and his redemptive love known, by word and example," in daily life, at work, and at worship. From their knowledge gained through daily work they are "to interpret to the Church the needs, concerns, and hopes of the world" (BCP 543).

None of these directives is liturgical, but each has an echo in the liturgy: the one who is charged with a ministry of servanthood in the world is the primary servant in the liturgy, making sure the things that make a liturgy run smoothly are done, so that the assembly can concentrate on their work of celebration. The one charged with studying and embodying the Scriptures is the one who, in the assembly, proclaims the Gospel. The one who in some sense straddles the distance between the church and the workplace and who is therefore charged to keep the church abreast of the concrete needs of the world is also the one in the liturgy who bids the congregation to pray for the world in its specific and concrete neediness during the Prayers of the People. What the deacon does in the liturgy both expresses what the deacon does in the greater life of the church, and ritually reinforces in the deacon the qualities of character that are demanded by diaconal ordination. Authenticity is achieved when what the deacon does in church and what the deacon does in and on behalf of the church in the wider community are mirror images of one another.

THE READER

The introductory rubrics for the Eucharist indicate that the norm is for laypersons to proclaim the readings before the Gospel. To have an ordained person exercise this role is not the norm. The rubric further allows that a layperson may lead the Prayers of the People. If a deacon is present, however, the deacon should share in the work of preparing, introducing, and leading the prayers, since deacons are ordained precisely to know the needs and concerns of the world and to bring them to the awareness of the church.

We noted above that those who read the Scriptures in the liturgy should, in the name of authenticity, love the Word of God and be genuine evangelists, in the manner appropriate to their circumstances. If they are to proclaim the Good News authentically in the midst of the assembly, in other words, they must also proclaim it authentically beyond the assembly. Equally important, however, is the demand that readers have the talents and skills for public speaking. For the assembly to hear the biblical proclamation as the Word of the Lord, the reader must be able to read aloud well. Only then will the assembly be able to "Hear what the Spirit is saying to God's People," as *Enriching Our Worship* puts it.

The skills for public reading—projection, pace, how to use a microphone—can be taught or honed to a certain extent, but some people simply do not have the ability to become effective public speakers. It is a delicate pastoral task to direct well-intentioned members of the community away from tasks for which they are not suited, and the ministry of reading in the liturgy seems to be particularly problematic in this regard, since many people assume that since they can in fact read aloud, they should be able to read the Scriptures in the liturgy. The Prayer Book is clear that the presider is responsible for appointing lay people to the ministry of reading, and so the difficult task of not appointing well-meaning people falls to the presider as well. A process of mutual discernment involving more than just the priest and the aspiring reader, in which the goal is to discover a "best fit" for ministry, is probably the kindest and gentlest way to approach this task. Usually, some liturgical ministry will come to light as the one for which the person is most suited. Nonetheless, some will not wish to give up on exercising this ministry, and a sensitive pastor must be prepared to be both honest and gentle, to care for the liturgical life of the community while caring for the feelings and self-respect of the aspiring minister.

In many congregations, the readers sit in the assembly and do not wear liturgical vesture. In others, the readers do vest, and have seats with the other vested ministers. This question of who should vest and where liturgical ministers (vested or not) sit is very significant. If, for example, only the presider vests, some would say that this emphasizes the ministry of the laity by showing that even "ordinary" people in "ordinary" clothes can carry out sacred functions. Others see the opposite: vesting only the priest diminishes the dignity of the laity and clericalizes the liturgy, since only clergy are "worthy" of formal liturgical vesture, and sets up an us/them dichotomy. To vest *all* the ministers, however, may create another harmful effect. It may suggest that liturgical roles are so distinct from the core role of being a member of the assembly that no ordinary person dressed in an ordinary way can do anything in the rite. In other words, an abundance of vested ministers can give the impression that the secular and the sacred are two completely distinct realms that dare not come close, and can also create a sort of quasi-clerical caste of lay ministers. A "middle of the road" solution might be to have only some ministers vest—perhaps those who are associated directly with the altar or who move in formal processions. In any case, every congregation should think through issues of who to vest and where ministers should be seated in the assembly. Each of the possible combinations can have a different impact and express a different understanding of what the church is, how it is ordered, and what it is doing when it gathers for the liturgy. At various points in the life of a congregation, a different emphasis or a different way of conveying balance may be necessary.

THE PRESENTERS OF THE OFFERINGS

Members of the congregation are to bring the bread and wine and the monetary collection to the deacon (or the presider or an assisting priest, if a deacon is not present), who then places them on the Lord's Table. The congregation is to stand as the offerings are placed on the altar, an obvious indication that these things are symbols of the self-offering of the people. The Prayer Book does not further define who the representatives of the community should be. Often, congregations delegate this ministry to those who want to participate in a liturgical ministry but who do not want to undertake anything needing the skill or investment of time that other ministries require. On special occasions, the representatives are often chosen because of their relationship to the congregation as a whole (the wardens at the patronal feast, for example) or the focus of the celebration (friends or family members at a funeral or baptism). In some places, the ushers or greeters are normally given this task.

Because the presenters are representing the congregation, and because the congregation joins itself to their action by an external gesture that signals an internal disposition, those chosen for this task should be members of the congregation who are at least active enough that they can reasonably be said to represent it. Also, while presenting the offerings of bread, wine, and money is not a complex task, the presenters must know specifically what they are to do so that confusion does not distract the assembly at this point and thus undermine its ability to participate in their symbolic offering. A clear explanation and perhaps a rehearsal is in order. To whom are the offerings presented? Is this done at the chancel step, across the altar, or behind the altar? Do the presenters return immediately to their places in the assembly or do they wait for some cue? Do they make a gesture of reverence to the Lord's Table or to the minister who receives the offering from them? All of this must be considered and explained in advance.

EUCHARISTIC MINISTERS

The ministers long referred to as "chalice bearers" are now called "eucharistic ministers." According to the canons, "A Eucharistic Minister is a lay person authorized to administer the Consecrated Elements at a Celebration of Holy Eucharist. A Eucharistic Minister should normally act under the direction of a Deacon, if any, or otherwise, the Member of the Clergy or other leader exercising oversight of the congregation or other community of faith" (III.4.6). Eucharistic ministers are to be drafted into service, the Prayer Book says, when the clergy are not numerous enough to administer the Sacrament.

It is important to note that the canon does not distinguish between the eucharistic Bread and the eucharistic Wine. These ministers are not chalice bearers but are ministers of both forms of the Eucharist. This alters the Additional Directions given in the Prayer Book, which do restrict the distribution of the eucharistic Bread to clerics (BCP 408). The new canon merely expands this permission so that any ordained or licensed Communion minister can offer either form, while the presider always offers the Bread.

The local bishop licenses eucharistic ministers at the request of the rector or another ecclesiastical authority in charge of the parish. The license is not permanent and is given for a period determined by the bishop. The license can be renewed at the bishop's discretion.

LITURGICAL MINISTERS NOT EXPLICITLY MENTIONED IN THE RUBRICS OF THE PRAYER BOOK

ACOLYTES

It may be surprising to many Episcopalians that the Book of Common Prayer does not mention acolytes. The word does not occur even once. This is not really unexpected, however, because the acolytes are the primary "doers" in the liturgy, and the Prayer Book, as we have said, is relatively silent about what to do. Why, then, would it not be silent about who does it?

In considering the acolytes, we mean a wide range of liturgical ministers who divide among themselves the essential practical tasks of making the liturgy unfold: the thurifer, crucifer, and torch bearers; the ones who hold the Altar Book open before the presider or who bear the Gospel Book at the proclamation; those who carry the vessels to the Lord's Table for the Great Thanksgiving, who wash the presider's hands, who bring the auxiliary vessels for the fractioning of the eucharistic Bread and Wine, who assist in clearing the altar after the Communion, and who see to it that any of the leftover elements are reverently consumed. The acolytes are like good waiters who tend to all the details that make the meal unfold gracefully, and draw as little attention to themselves as possible.

While the acolytes make the liturgy seem to unfold effortlessly, they actually must invest tremendous effort. They must learn to move in unison and discretely, to know when each liturgical object needs to be where it needs to be and to see that it is there at just the right time, to cultivate habits of reverent posture and comportment, and to master obscure actions and make them seem utterly natural. Being a good acolyte is hardly effortless.

In many congregations, children or young members of the assembly do some of these tasks, while others reserve the ministry of acolyte to adults. This is one ministry, however, where distinctions of age need not be drawn. The liturgy is an expression of what the church understands itself to be and what it aspires to do. In baptism, the members are initiated into an equality that transcends age. Often when we speak of the diversity of the church, we think of gender, socio-economic status, sexual orientation, and the various orders in the church. Just as important, however, is age. Most discussions of ageism in the church focus on the importance of fully including the elderly, but we must also include children—not only on special Youth Sundays or at children's services, but in the week-by-week common prayer of the congregation. If our prayer is to be truly common, it must fully integrate children. A baptized Christian does not have to be very old or very big to bear the Gospel Book, to carry a vessel to the Lord's Table, to assist at the lavabo, or to do any of a number of tasks in the liturgy.

At times an adult acolyte may gently need to shepherd a younger colleague. Far from being a misfortune, this is a further modeling of the Christian life at its best. Having adult helpers at hand for young acolytes does not excuse the youngsters from rehearsal and preparation. Children must practice as rigorously as the others, and they will likely not resent or resist it. They are used to practicing for sports activities and theatrical or musical events, and the level of practice required often conveys to them how important their participation is. By lovingly and patiently rehearsing children in their liturgical roles, the community impresses on them not only the seriousness of their ministry but also how seriously the community takes *them*. When a child can stand and minister with dignity, grace, and confidence next to an adult exercising the same role, important spiritual formation is taking place in the child. Even more important, perhaps, spiritual formation is taking place in the assembly that is witnessing this striking enactment of life in the Body of Christ.

The tasks given to acolytes are many and varied. For them to be done with as little fuss, as much dignity, and as "invisibly" as possible, more—rather than fewer—acolytes may be needed. This does not mean that acolytes should be used at a service for no good reason. Filling the church with people in albs or in cassocks and surplices for the sole purpose of creating a liturgical spectacle does not make sense and militates against the liturgy being the work of the entire assembly. At the same time, having one or two acolytes running back and forth, or having insufficient ministers to enact a full and rich liturgy comfortably, makes just as little sense. It also portrays a community that is lacking in gifts for ministry. The liturgy, on the contrary, should be an enactment of the church at its best: rich with spiritual gifts and skills for ministry.

THE COORDINATOR OF LITURGY

Even in small congregations whose liturgy is not complex, someone has to coordinate the various ministries, especially before and during the liturgy itself. This role has any number of names, such as the master of ceremonies (MC), verger, head acolyte. Often in smaller congregations, as noted below, the deacon performs or assists with this function, as "head servant" in the liturgy and as someone who has the continuity of serving in the liturgy every Sunday. The liturgy depends on a number of people acting in harmony so that, as we have said many times, the church's worldview and belief system can simultaneously be expressed by the assembly and impressed onto the assembly.

Before the liturgy, the coordinator (by whatever title the role is known) verifies that all of the assigned ministers are present, that they agree about who will do what, and that everyone knows how to do the assigned ministries. All of this has to be done before every liturgy, but especially before special events when the usual patterns will not be followed. The coordinator also verifies that all the ministers have ensured that the materials or objects they will use in the liturgy are in place and ready.

At every turn, the coordinator must remember that the assembly as a whole celebrates the liturgy, and that the ministers are first of all members of the assembly. They have been called forth for particular tasks, and from among them, the coordinator is chosen. In other words, this is a bottom-up, not a top-down arrangement. The coordinator is a servant chosen from among the servants of God's servants, not an overlord. As a minister's "power" and authority increases, so must the conscious commitment to model the servanthood of Jesus. "Power" in the church, and especially in the liturgy, is the opposite of what we usually understand power to be. The coordinator, who has a particularly powerful role, must take a particularly loving and humble stance.

This is not to suggest that the coordinator of the ministers should be weak, indirect, or sloppy. Strength, clarity, and order can be kind. Knowing that someone is overseeing the entire corps of ministers can put everyone at ease. The coordinator can reassure those who are nervous and instruct those who are uncertain. This is an important witness that life in the Body of Christ is not like life in the "world."

The church canons make the rector ultimately responsible for the liturgical life of the parish. Within the liturgy itself, however, if everyone, including the presider, has agreed that the coordinator is "in charge," then the coordinator is also in charge of the presider. The liturgy is a ritual act. No one, especially the presider, can act unilaterally. Especially the presider, in fact, must adhere to the ritual patterns and words that the assembly has agreed upon if the rite is to move smoothly. It cannot be emphasized enough that the liturgy is an act of the assembly, not a show that the presider "puts on" for the laity. The presider, like all the other ministers, is under submission to the rite. The job of the coordinator is to remind, instruct, and direct the ministers, and this includes the presider. If the presider is primarily responsible for coordinating the assembly as it enacts the liturgy, the task of the deacon, master of ceremonies, verger, or head acolyte is to coordinate the presider and the other ministers. It is a "backstage" sort of role.

For the liturgy to move smoothly, seemingly without effort and as if it were perfectly natural, the ministers must rehearse. There is no substitute for detailed rehearsal. Rehearsal is not to make the liturgy stuffy but just the opposite: to make it relaxed. If the leaders and servants of the assembly know intellectually and "in their bones" what to do, their actions will not be clumsy and uncertain, and they will not distract the assembly. Instead, they will convey a calm and ease that will transfer to the assembly, allowing everyone to celebrate the liturgy with confidence, attending fully to the Mystery revealed in the rite.

The coordinator, as well as being the "director" of the liturgy, is the leader of the rehearsal. This does not mean that the coordinator merely gathers the ministers and dictates what will happen. The best rehearsals involve the entire group of ministers in deciding what will work best: what will be most reverent, hospitable, transparent, gracious, and efficient. The best rehearsals also are not an intellectual exercise but a "hands-on" dry run. At an ideal rehearsal, the coordinator brings a strong sense of what must happen during the rite and then, as the ministers talk and walk through it, listens carefully to the insights of the entire team, seeks consensus, and then incorporates the new ideas into the choreography. This promises not only to create a better liturgy, but also genuinely to empower the ministers. In thinking about the rite and walking it through, the ministers will come to understand it more deeply and, over time, will be able to articulate a set of liturgical principles that they have thoroughly internalized.

In procession, the coordinator (unless it is the deacon) leads. Even the thurifer follows this person. Only if the coordinator thinks it best to pace the procession by "stepping off" each pair does the coordinator not come first. In that case, the coordinator enters the procession last, just before the presider.

In churches that already have a verger, this is the role the verger should have. If the verger does not serve a genuine and needed liturgical function, the role is antiquarian and, in many cases, precious, and should be reconsidered. The truth is, vergers often do no more than lead processions (carrying the processional staff or *virge*), and then move readers to and from the ambo. In fact, most readers do not need to be led around, and doing it seems pretentious. What the ministers do need, however, is someone to coordinate them. To have both a master of ceremonies and a verger is a duplication of roles, and they should be collapsed into one. A single liturgical coordinator, vested in an alb along with all the other liturgical ministers, or alternatively in a cassock with a full and long surplice, is usually a more appropriate role for a congregation.

SACRISTANS, ALTAR GUILD MEMBERS, AND ENVIRONMENTAL ARTISTS

The building in which the liturgy is celebrated and the objects used in it are formative. Their care, therefore, and how they are arranged are not incidental. There is probably not one Episcopal church that does not have an altar guild or a group of sacristans dedicated to the care of the concrete things that are required for the liturgy. These ministers launder and iron the linens, care for the vestments, polish the metalware, set the necessary items on the credence table before the liturgy begins, change the paraments, arrange the flowers, clean everything up after the celebration, and handle the work of ordering candles, bread, wine, and the other expendable material without which the liturgy could not be celebrated. Beyond these tasks that are commonly thought of as the purview of the sacristans and members of the altar guild, however, many others are increasingly becoming part of their work. For this reason, many congregations are expanding the scope of this ministry and sometimes changing its name. They speak not of the altar guild, for example, but of the art and environment committee.

In matters of environment, as in all other areas of the liturgy, the Prayer Book does not lay out many details, so decisions must be made. Long-established ways of doing things are not necessarily the best way of doing things. For example the "liturgical environment" has traditionally meant the decorations in the sanctuary (the space within the altar rail). If the liturgy happens only in that part of the room, then this pattern makes logical sense: the liturgical environment and the sanctuary are coextensive. If, however, the entire assembly celebrates the liturgy, and if it is enacted throughout the church, and if the focus shifts from place to place within the liturgy, then the ministry of the altar guild must expand far beyond the precincts of the altar.

Today it is commonly understood that the entire liturgical space—wherever the people are assembled—is the liturgical environment. In some places, for example, candles do not stand only alongside the altar but also near the lectern and even around the entire room through the use of sconces. Flowers adorn every place where key liturgical actions occur: the altar, the lectern, the font, and even the door of the church, as the marker between the lives of the individual members and the life of the Body. Banners, sculpture, monumental hangings that overshadow the entire assembly: these are all part of the liturgical environment.

In places where the members of the existing altar guild are not interested or gifted in devising schemes to enhance the entire liturgical space, new members can be added without faithful members being displaced. Knowing how to get wine stains out of a purificator so that it will be fitting for the Lord's Table is no less important or honorable than knowing how to weld iron into an Advent wreath that will hang above the assembled church or how to craft processional banners for a solemn occasion. The task of preparing the liturgical environment is broad and leaves room for people with many talents and interests.

USHERS AND MINISTERS OF HOSPITALITY

Church shoppers and religious seekers make their first visit to the Sunday Eucharist for many reasons. One of the regularly cited reasons they give for making their second visit is that they received a warm welcome the first time. Hospitality is not enough to convert a person, but it is a good way to start. Jesus distinguished himself by welcoming sinners and eating with them. It was so central to who he was that he put his life on the line for it. Just as this ministry was central to the life of the historical Jesus, it is a ministry the glorified Christ continues today. He welcomes sinners and eats with us. Many congregations are acutely aware that they are guests at Christ's Table, and through no merit of their own. And so, what they have received as a gift, they seek to give as a gift. Congregations like that, especially if they are invested in evangelical and social outreach, flourish and grow. Congregations that do not will almost certainly stagnate and die.

Hospitality is the work of the entire assembly. Still, like all the other ministries that are inherent in the Christian life, the church designates representatives to model hospitality. Ushers, increasingly called ministers of hospitality, embody the hospitality that the whole church is called to exercise. They are the "frontline" of a welcoming assembly. "Well begun is half-done," and if the congregation welcomes strangers, seekers, and even its own members as they arrive, a great beginning will have been made. The ministers of hospitality take the lead in this important service.

The ministry of hospitality transcends gender and age. Traditionally, ushers have been adult men. In fact, people of both sexes and of all ages can be gifted at this work. Children especially can offer an open and warm welcome to those who come for common prayer, and can put nervous visitors at ease. A Christian does not have to be very old to smile, offer a warm hand, and pass along an order of worship. Young people and even little children serving as ministers of hospitality bespeak the nature of the Body of Christ to those who come to our doors. They would see at first glance that this is a community where all are taken seriously, seen as equals, and valued.

In some churches, ministers of hospitality actually seat worshippers, as ushers do in a theater. When this is done, it must be approached very carefully: while visitors need to know that they are welcome and need to be given all they will require to participate at whatever level they choose, they also need to know that they are not captives. They will likely not feel comfortable if they are pushed into doing things that to a regular church-goer would seem effortless and natural but to them are odd. Being allowed to choose a place to sit in the assembly may be all it takes for newcomers to feel in control in an unfamiliar and uncomfortable situation.

Ministers of hospitality are often entrusted with taking the collection. Because of public scandals involving money and religion and the troubling stories people tell of being denied the sacraments and other ministries of the church because they could not pay for them, how money is handled in the assembly must be carefully considered and even more carefully done. In nearly every sphere of life, money is equated with power. In the church, however, money cannot be allowed to function as that kind of currency. The rich and the poor are equal before God and before one another in the assembly of the baptized. Anything that can be done, therefore, to rid the Offertory of its potential to embarrass the poor and aggrandize the wealthy will make the liturgy more hospitable. This is not to suggest that the church should be embarrassed to handle money. The Prayer Book directs the deacon or presider to place the monetary collection on the altar with the bread and wine, since it is a tangible token of the assembly's investment in the work of the gospel. Still, the amount of the gift does not equate with the level of investment and, above all, it cannot determine the level of rank or power one holds in the church. The plate should be passed quickly and simply. If a member of the assembly chooses not to put anything in it, the minister of hospitality should pay no attention—not delaying or looking quizzically at the person—but should move the action along. Money is a delicate matter in modern culture. The way it is dealt with in the liturgy should also be delicate.

The collection is often carried to the Lord's Table by the ushers or ministers of hospitality. By engaging the imagination, the ministers can experience the link between what they carry forward and the lives of all who have gathered. Those who present the offering at the Lord's Table are servants of the assembly's self-offering, not bankers.

Realizing that, in a sense, they are holding people's lives in their hands will transform their task from a transaction into a ministry.

At the receiving of Communion (and at other processions), the ministers of hospitality usually organize the people and tell them when and where to move. In this way, they are the coordinators of the assembly at large at this point in the liturgy. As we have said about the coordinators of the liturgical team of ministers, as a minister's "power" and authority increases, so must the conscious commitment to model the servanthood of Jesus. Through the gracious invitation of the minister of hospitality at the time of the Communion, Jesus invites the members of his Body to partake of his own Body. The invitation to move from the pew to the altar must be full of welcome and patience. The ministers must imagine that they are issuing a loving and coveted invitation, not giving marching orders.

Those who provide hospitality after the liturgy—food and drink—are usually not the same ministers who provide it during the liturgy. Holding joint meetings and formation sessions for these two groups, however, can ensure that Christ's hospitality extends from the time worshippers come in the door of the church until they go out the door of the hall.

Chapter 8

POSTURES AND GESTURES

If the building space and the liturgical year are the two "stages" on which the liturgy unfolds, the members of the assembly are the actors. As we have noted earlier, every member of the assembly is an essential actor. Still, the designated liturgical ministers have a unique role. By the ways they use their bodies, they demonstrate for the others a kind of prayer that is thoroughly incarnational. Part of their task as liturgical ministers is to embody the highest aspirations of the entire group with care and intention. In them, the assembly sees itself at its best.

Throughout the liturgy, the ministers should strive to be as mentally and physically centered as possible. While not being self-conscious, they should be self-aware. While not being stiff, they should be still. While not being rigid, they should be restrained. The bodily movements of the liturgical leaders both reflect their interior dispositions and foster those dispositions within them. The body, mind, and spirit are integrated, and what happens in one, influences the rest. Liturgical ministers, whether lay or ordained, often find themselves torn between praying and keeping track of what comes next. A step toward praying without becoming distracted from the demands of the ministry is to assume a posture of prayer. The body can lead the mind and the heart.

The bodily comportment of the ministers can also lead the minds and hearts of the entire assembly. Outside the liturgy, people know how much their environment can transform them. To feel invigorated, they go to an amusement park; to feel calm, they go to the wilderness. In the liturgy, the environment is no less influential. How the ministers carry themselves has a strong effect on the disposition of the rest of the assembly. As much as possible, the ministers should strive to be "transparent": to be part of the liturgical environment without drawing attention to themselves, especially to their idiosyncrasies. The impetus for becoming "transparent" is neither anti-incarnational nor self-abrogating. It is *kenotic*: it is self-emptying for the sake of a greater good, carrying on the self-emptying of Jesus for the sake of the world.

Because the liturgy is "dramatic," those with focal roles can, with every good intention, move with a flourish that draws attention to themselves and away from the Mystery they have chosen to serve. Clarity, strength, and directness are the qualities to which liturgical ministers aspire, and these are the kinds of traits that can easily trigger egocentric display. But they need not, and if the assembly is to experience the liturgy as what it is—an encounter with God in Christ present in the Spirit—the ministers will work to avoid any urge to draw attention to themselves.

PRAYING

The earliest depictions of Christians at prayer show them in the *orans* position: their arms spread and their hands open. In the liturgy, the *orans* is the appropriate gesture for all prayers, not only the texts prayed at the Lord's Table. For prayers prayed at other places in the room, an acolyte holds the book so the presider's hands are free. The acolyte stands perpendicular to the presider, rests the book against the forearm furthest from the presider, and extends the arm so the book is directly in front of the presider. The acolyte's other hand is used to steady the book by grasping the bottom corner. The acolyte steps forward to allow the presider space to extend the arms in prayer. The acolyte does not hold the book to the side, but holds it directly in front of the presider so the presider can maintain a forward gaze. The acolyte should adjust to the presider, not the other way around. The book should be brought to the presider a few seconds before it is needed so the text can be located on the page. At the Collect of the Day, for example, the acolyte brings the open book to the presider during the last phrases of the Hymn of Praise.

The presider opens the arms in the *orans* only during the actual prayer. The *orans* position is not used when the presider is addressing the assembly or proclaiming a text, but is strictly for prayer. At the Collect of the Day, for example, the presider greets the people with hands joined, says, "Let us pray," and only then assumes the *orans* position. The presider begins to bring the hands together again during the last phrase of the collect, so that they are joined as the prayer ends and the assembly adds its "Amen."

It should be noted that the *orans* is not used during the *Sanctus* or during the singing of metrical hymns, even though most of them are prayers. It is normally only used for congregational prayers that are not acclamations, said or sung. So, for example, the presider stands in the *orans* for the Lord's Prayer and the prayer after Communion, even though the entire assembly is singing or reciting the text. This is simply a matter of custom and cannot be defended on the basis of any clean logic or principle.

The *orans* is a stance of openness and vulnerability to God, as well as a gesture of reaching toward God. Keeping these and other personally relevant images in mind, the presider will integrate the internal disposition into the external gesture, making the *orans* more authentic in appearance and in fact. There are no "rules" for exactly how wide the arms should be spread, although there were specific guidelines in the Tridentine rubrics that became the norm among some Episcopalians. The gesture should reflect the interior attitude to which the presider aspires, and should be proportional to the room and the size of the assembly.

In some congregations, the entire assembly stands in the *orans* position as the presider prays in the name of all. Most congregations would resist such a practice, but it should not be rejected outright as "charismatic" or un-Anglican. The *orans* began as a gesture as common as folded hands are today.

SITTING

When we sit during the liturgy, it is not a time to be casual, but to be attentive. Both feet should be flat on the floor, and the hands should rest comfortably in the lap, palms down. Anything that suggests disinterest or draws attention, like throwing an arm over the back of a chair or pew, or crossing the legs, should be avoided. The way one sits in the liturgy, whether one is a liturgical minister or another member of the assembly, should mirror the way one sits in contemplative prayer. In the liturgy, because we trust that God is acting, we use posture to make the mind and the senses attentive.

WALKING

Walking in formal processions or from one liturgical focus to another requires intentionality. Liturgical walking is not just moving. It is moving *mindfully*, with attention to the self and, more important, to the object or the action to which one is moving. The eyes should be directed toward the thing, the person, or the activity, and the mind should be engaged with what the eyes see. Those walking in the entrance procession, for example, are not merely moving from the back of the church to the front. They are moving from a place outside the assembly of the saints into that assembly, and are drawing close to the Lord's Table. The engagement of the imagination and the practice of mindfulness bring the body into alignment with the mind and heart, which simultaneously brings the mind and heart into alignment with the body.

The pace should be purposeful but not rushed. Often, in the name of reverence, liturgical ministers move so slowly and with such gravity that the effect is lugubrious. Others move so quickly that they seem to lack attentiveness and awe. A balance between haste and sluggishness is the goal: moving with purpose toward something important, but not rushing to get there.

The hands should be joined as the minister walks. Throughout the liturgy, the hands are held to one another whenever they are not being used to hold something else. A comfortable folding of the hands, not a stiff pressing of palm against palm, conveys a sense of both centeredness and ease. The arms should never dangle or swing as the minister walks.

Ministers do not walk backward during the liturgy, even though it may sometimes seem like the quickest way to move. There is only one exception. Some congregations use two thurifers in the procession of the Sacrament to the place of reservation on Maundy Thursday. They walk in procession directly in front of the presider, who carries the Sacrament. One of the thurifers censes the Sacrament walking backward, then turns to walk forward, while the other turns toward the Sacrament and walks backward. This is the only possible exception to the general rule that ministers do not walk backward during the liturgy. Even if only a few steps are to be taken, the minister should turn in the direction of the movement.

STANDING

Standing is so natural and common that it might not seem to be a liturgical posture. Standing during the liturgy, however, is not the same as standing at a bus stop or on the street chatting with friends. Like every action in the liturgy, standing is an embodied prayer. In the liturgy, one stands consciously aware of being in the presence of God and God's people, and uses the body both to express and instill befitting attitudes. The feet are planted firmly on the floor, and the weight is distributed evenly to both. All ground is holy. The liturgy is a rehearsal for experiencing the holiness of all ground and for moving with reverence and gratitude upon it.

It is natural to shift from leg to leg after standing for a time, or to sway forward and backward. In the liturgy, the ministers should avoid the temptation. Moving nervously around, they distract the others in the assembly. Instead, they need to maintain a sense of groundedness, with the goal of inspiring a similar attitude in the others.

Standing, rather than kneeling, is the common posture of the entire assembly for prayer. As Marion Hatchett, one of the scholars most responsible for the liturgical books that emerged in the Episcopal Church in the 1970s and 1980s, summarizes in his *Commentary on the American Prayer Book:*

> Standing was the universal posture for [the eucharistic] prayer until late in the middle ages and continues to be the posture in the Eastern churches. The council of Nicea forbade kneeling for prayer on Sundays or during the Great Fifty Days of Easter, days when the Eucharist would be celebrated.... The 1549 Book assumed standing to be the posture for [the eucharistic] prayer; Prayer Books have traditionally embodied the principle that people stand for prayer unless expressly bidden to kneel, as at the prayers of confession and petition. Some older Anglican manuals direct the people, if they are kneeling, to stand when addressed by the priest, and specifically to assume a standing posture after the absolution when the priest says "Hear what comfortable words." Clearly, this meant that they stood for the eucharistic prayer which followed immediately.[8]

8. Marion J. Hatchett, *Commentary on the American Prayer Book* (New York: Seabury Press, 1981), 364.

GENUFLECTING

In places where it is customary to genuflect, the gesture is performed only in regard to the Sacrament, whether present on the altar or reserved for the sick. The body is  lowered onto the right knee, and the hands rest on the left. The body is kept perpendicular to the floor, and the right knee is brought all the way to the floor, not partway in the style of a curtsy. The hands that are resting on the left knee are used to push the body back into the standing position. There is no pause at the bottom of the genuflection. It is one continuous motion.

To genuflect at the Lord's Table, the minister places the hands shoulder-width apart with the fingers on the top surface (technically called the "mensa") and the thumbs pushed against the vertical surface. The right knee is  lowered to the floor while the back is kept perpendicular to the floor and the eyes are focused forward. As the minister stands, the hands hold the body steady.

Whether genuflecting in an open space or at the altar, it is important not to slouch forward. Genuflecting and bowing are two distinct gestures, and should not be combined.

BOWING

Although some customaries describe three degrees of bowing, simplicity suggests that only two are required: a bow of the head and a bow of the body. Both are gestures that acknowledge the sacredness of an object or person. As with every other gesture, authenticity and grace demand that the mind and heart be engaged so the gesture becomes more than empty ritual. Calling into mind the respect and love one has for the person, the person's role in the community, the object, or what the object signifies is the first step in making a liturgical bow more than "going through the motions."

Often, people bow during the liturgy in a way that looks more like bobbing. The bow should be deliberate and intentional, and not rushed. The eyes should follow the head downward and not stay focused on the person or object being honored. Throughout the scriptural record, when people realize that they are encountering God, they instinctively avert their gaze. The liturgical bow is a rehearsal for this kind of awe before the presence of God. To bow in the liturgy is both to express and to learn an attitude that is the opposite of being "stiff-necked."

In a bow of the head, the eyes and head move toward the floor while the body stays erect. After a momentary pause, the head is raised. In a bow of the body, also called a

solemn bow, both the head and the body are lowered toward the floor from the waist, along with the eyes. It may be helpful to think of this bow as "looking at your shoes." The hands can be run down the legs to the knees during a profound bow for stability and, when a number of ministers are bowing, for ensuring that they all bow to the same relative depth. The eyes must be lowered along with the body, not directed toward what is being reverenced, so that the pelvis does not jut backward and produce an irreverent, distracting, and even comic result.

During the Eucharist, one makes a profound bow only before the Sacrament and the altar, when receiving a blessing (as, for example, when the presider may invoke a blessing upon the deacon before proclaiming the Gospel), and when the assembly bows at the affirmation of the incarnation during the Nicene Creed. When it comes to bowing, there are no rules in the Book of Common Prayer. Therefore, it is important for an Episcopal congregation to arrive at a set of coherent principles.

This book has among its guiding principles that "less is more." In general, then, the number of bows—of the head or of the body—should not be exaggerated. Too much bowing draws attention away from the core action, distracting the assembly from the essential things and cluttering the ministers' imagination. One of the first questions liturgical planners and ministers must ask is whether what is being done supports the essential core or competes with it.

When a minister is carrying a ritual object other than a book or service leaflet, a reverent pause substitutes for a bow. For example, in a procession the thurifer, crucifer, and torch bearers do not bow but, instead, pause momentarily at the place where others bow.

KNEELING

Kneeling is the usual posture for acts of humility and penitence. Just as at a genuflection, the body is lowered onto the right knee when one kneels. The hands rest on the left knee, one atop the other, for stability. Then, the left leg is brought behind the body so that the feet are together. The body from the knees to the head is held perpendicular to the floor. The hips do not rest on the heels, nor does the body slouch forward. Just as genuflecting and bowing are two distinct postures, so are kneeling and bowing. To return to the standing position, the left leg is brought again to the front of the body, and the hands are used to push up from the knee.

Kneeling in vestments can be difficult. The feet can become caught on the alb so that when the person tries to stand, balance is lost and the person falls backward. This can be avoided by pulling the vestments to the side and away from the heels as the kneeling posture is assumed. Then, when it comes time to stand, the vestments will not be caught on the shoes.

When kneeling follows immediately upon sitting, the person first stands and then kneels.

TURNING

Purely as a matter of convention, the following rules govern how ministers turn around during the liturgy. This happens, for example, when ushers bring forward the monetary offering, give it to the deacon or presider, and then turn to move away from the altar.

- ◆ Those standing alone turn clockwise.

- ◆ Those standing in pairs turn inward toward one another. This rule holds even if another minister is between the pair. (The torch bearers flanking a crucifer, for example, turn inward toward one another.)

- ◆ A minister standing between a pair of ministers (such as a crucifer between two torch bearers) turns clockwise, as if standing alone.

Undeniably, this is a convention. It would be just as logical to do it another way. Still, if ministers, especially in groups, individually decide which way to turn, the effect is disorderly. Following the convention overcomes this problem.

CROSSING

The sign of the cross can be made over the self, a person or group, or a thing. In the Western style, the cross is traced from top to bottom, and then left to right.

When tracing the cross over oneself, the right hand is held flat with the palm facing the body. Beginning at the breast, the hand moves to the forehead, then to waist; to the left shoulder, then to the right. When the Trinitarian Name is pronounced during the gesture, the Persons are named in this pattern: "the Father" at the forehead; "the Son" at the waist; "the Holy" at the left shoulder; and "Spirit" at the right shoulder. The hand is then either touched to the breastbone or folded with the other hand. It is not allowed to simply drop to the side. The entire gesture is done deliberately but not dramatically. It is not exaggerated. The hand stays close to the body and does not extend beyond the head, shoulders, and waist.

At the proclamation of the Gospel, the minister traces a cross with the thumb of the right hand on the printed text, moving from top to bottom and then left to right, as the Gospel is announced. With the same thumb, the minister traces a small cross on the forehead, the lips, and the breast, as the other members of the assembly do the same. This custom began in the ninth century. At first, only the forehead was marked with a cross when the deacon greeted the people ("The Lord be with you") before the Gospel, or the forehead and breast at the announcement of the Gospel. Only in the eleventh century did the triple crossing become the norm, along with the marking of the cross on the page of the book. It was also common for the people to mark themselves with the cross *after* the Gospel. The custom of the final crossing did not endure.

The sentiments that accompany each of the three crossings before the Gospel are a matter of pious custom. Most people pray that the Gospel be imprinted in the mind, spoken with the lips, and loved with the heart. The Prayer Book does not mention, let alone require, the gesture, but most Episcopal lectionaries and Gospel Books have a cross printed at the beginning of each Gospel passage. In liturgical books, this is the typographical convention signaling that the sign of the cross is to be made.

When tracing the cross over a person or a group, the same pattern is followed as when tracing a single cross over one's own body, except that the hand is rotated ninety degrees clockwise so that the edge of the hand faces the people. The person tracing the cross does not touch his or her own body, but does confine the gesture to the size of the body, as if tracing the cross over the self. Only priests and bishops invoke a blessing upon others in the liturgy. When deacons or lay presiders (for example, at the Daily Office) invoke God's blessing, they alter the formula from the second to the first person (from "May Almighty God bless *you*," to "May Almighty God bless *us*") and touch their own bodies, as described above.

A cross is traced over an object exactly as it is traced over a person, except that the hand is brought close to the object. The size of the cross is proportional to the object. If the object is very small, however, the size of the sign must exceed the size of the object so that observers can recognize that it is a cross and not some indeterminate design that is being traced.

LOOKING

To help the assembly maintain focus, the presider and the other ministers should look toward the liturgical actions, even those in which they are not directly involved. For example, the other ministers should look at the lectors during the readings. The only exception is when looking at the liturgical action would require an awkward posture, such as looking over one's shoulder or straining forward. The head and eyes should always be kept basically forward, the feet flat on the floor, and the hands in the lap.

The presider should never close the eyes except when the entire assembly is engaged in silent meditation, such as after each of the first two readings. To close the eyes suggests distance from the assembly and a retreat into private prayer. The ministers responsible for directly assisting the assembly, especially the deacon and the acolytes, should never close their eyes but should be attentive to the assembly throughout the liturgy.

Ministers should look at the assembly when they are addressing it, and should continue looking at it if there is a congregational response. For example, during the greeting, "The Lord be with you," and the response, "And also with you," the presider should not look away from the assembly. Not only is this a matter of courtesy; it also makes the dialogue authentic. Liturgical dialogues are ritualized, but they are genuine dialogues.

By contrast, when the ministers, especially the presider, are addressing God, they should not look at the assembly. The eyes should be kept on the page where the prayer is printed, or, when asking God to hallow objects or persons, the eyes should be focused on them. For example, during the Great Thanksgiving, the presider looks at the book until the Institution Narrative, and then at the bread and wine as they are touched or elevated. Then, the eyes are turned back to the book.

We have emphasized that the assembly is a particular incarnation of the Body of Christ, and that in the Spirit, God is present in the entire liturgy and all its objects. This does not mean, though, that the presider should look around the room when addressing God, as if the presider were looking for God. While the presence of God is not concentrated in the book, keeping the eyes focused on the book helps in the following ways:

◆ It suggests that, while God is present in the assembly and the liturgical action, God also transcends all human realities. The presider looks at a symbolic non-place when addressing God.

◆ It cues the assembly that what is happening is a prayer rather than something else, like an announcement or an address, and triggers the appropriate mode of participation.

◆ It helps the presider to maintain a centered focus during prayer. "Custody of the eyes," as some spiritual teachers refer to it, is a classic aid to prayer.

Some writers suggest that the presider can attain the same effect as looking at the book by looking over the heads of the people at a point on the far wall. This, however, can make it seem like the presider has spotted something in the back of the room that no one else can see. It can also make it seem that God is "out there" somewhere: entirely beyond the assembly and its action—transcendent and not immanent—rather than both at once. It is best to look at the book.

CARRYING OBJECTS

As a general rule, ministers carry objects one at a time, and always with both hands. While it would be more expedient to carry two objects, one in each hand, the effect is irreverent and *laissez-faire*. This is not an arbitrary rule but a simple matter of observation. If many objects must be moved at once, as at the Offertory or the fraction, a tray can be used. Alternately, a number of ministers, each carrying one item, can move in unison. (If a purificator is laid over a chalice or rolled and placed in the bowl, the pair can be treated as one object. The pitcher of water and bowl for the lavabo, likewise, can be seen as a single ritual object.)

There are exceptions to the two-hands rule. A thurible, for example, is carried in only one hand. Whenever only one hand is used to hold an item, the palm of the other hand rests flat on the chest. The unused hand is never allowed to dangle or swing.

Because of the ancient suspicion and distaste for the left hand and left-handedness, only the right hand was used for formal or polite tasks. The convention is maintained in the liturgy in that the right hand is used to hold objects and to perform tasks (such as distributing Communion), though in most cases using the left hand would not be unsightly. For some gestures, however, it would seem very odd and draw attention to itself (when making the sign of the cross, for example).

EXCHANGING THE PEACE

Beyond the greeting between the presider and assembly, the Prayer Book does not give specific words or gestures for the assembly's exchange of the Peace. The Peace is more than a casual hello but it is not an act of personal affection. It is a gesture of mutual acceptance and forgiveness rooted in a shared humanity and the bonds forged by baptism. The Peace expresses and instills a confidence that equality in Christ (and the equality of all people before God) is rooted in something far more basic than whether people personally know one another. Members of the assembly greet who happens to be nearby, even if people across the room are more familiar or more dear to them. Clasping the others' hands with both hands and embracing others in a way that draws them close but does not cling to them are two ways to strike a balance between impersonal distance and personal intimacy.

The Prayer Book allows the Peace to be exchanged either before the Offertory or just before Communion. The latter is the current Roman custom but it is exceedingly rare in Episcopal congregations. Because the Confession and absolution usually come at the end of the Liturgy of the Word, keeping the Peace in the usual place makes it an act of gratitude for God's unearned and undeserved forgiveness, and a pledge to embody it. Also, this reflects the biblical injunction to make peace with one's neighbors before approaching the altar. Even if the presider is the only one in the assembly who physically approaches the altar at this point, it is in the name of all who have gathered and, in fact, the entire church. In most church buildings, the assembly as a whole does not physically approach the Lord's Table until receiving Communion, but in a more essential way, they draw near in the person of the presider at the Offertory, as the presider approaches the Table for the Great Thanksgiving.

KISSING

The custom of kissing the altar appeared as early as the seventh century. The custom of kissing the Gospel Book after the proclamation of the Gospel is attested to as early at the eighth century and echoes the Jewish custom of kissing the Torah before it is replaced in the ark. In both cases, the reverence is directed toward Christ, whose presence is symbolized by the book (or, more accurately, the proclamation that proceeds from it) and the Table (or, more accurately, the Food and Drink that proceed from it).

The presider, with the assisting priests, may kiss the altar as they enter and leave the liturgical space, or the presider may kiss it when approaching it at the Offertory. As with all liturgical gestures, it is important to engage the imagination and to allow the body to express what is in the mind and heart. At the same time, it is important to desire that the mind and heart will be formed by the physical gesture. While a liturgical kiss is not the equivalent of a romantic kiss, neither is it like a perfunctory peck on the cheek. The minister lays the hands upon the altar and kisses the top of it, mindful in both actions of greeting the Beloved Son who stands in the midst of the community as Table Servant, Food and Drink, and Lord of the Heavenly Banquet.

Until the rubrics of the Roman Rite were revised in 1969, the custom of kissing the Gospel Book after the proclamation was reserved to the presider (or the bishop, if present), even if a deacon proclaimed the Gospel. Currently, when a Roman deacon proclaims the Gospel, he, and not the presiding priest, kisses the book at the conclusion. This joins the gesture of reverence directly to the proclamation and recognizes the deacon's ministry as having its own integrity. While the Prayer Book does not mention kissing the Gospel Book, if the custom is observed, the person who proclaims the reading should kiss the book unless the bishop is presiding or is in official attendance. In that case, the book should be taken to her or him to be reverenced.

CENSING

Nearly every liturgical gesture is a common human gesture. Even the *orans* position is not really unusual, even though it might seem to be. Anyone who has stretched out the arms pleading for help, mercy, or forgiveness viscerally understands the *orans*. Anyone who has seen a child running toward a trusted adult with arms spread wide knows instinctively what the *orans* is and how it connects to the deepest levels of the psyche. Using a thurible, however, has no parallels in the repertoire of most people, and since not every Episcopal parish has a tradition of incorporating incense into their worship many Episcopalians are not familiar with or trained in its use. The use of incense is becoming increasingly common in Episcopal churches, however, so this guide goes into some detail for those who wish to introduce incense into a worship setting.

Incense, like the other elements of the liturgy, does not have a single meaning or even a limited number of meanings. It is evocative and primitive, and can inspire a wide range of insights, memories, and emotions in each member of the assembly. Within a Judeo-Christian context, the rising aromatic smoke also echoes innumerable scriptural references, and so draws deep from the well of the religious imagination. The first step in actually using a thurible is to engage the imagination and the senses. Without this, the swinging of a thurible can seem perfunctory at best and, at worst, distasteful and uncomfortable.

CHARGING A THURIBLE
The thurible may be charged (that is, the grains of incense may be added to the burning coals) in the view of the assembly, or it can be brought already charged to the person who will use it. If the thurible is to be charged publicly, it is brought to the minister, along with the boat (the vessel of incense). One person may carry each, or one person

may carry both: one in each hand. Having one person carry both vessels is preferable. In either case, the thurible is held at the top of the chains and is allowed to fall to its full length as it is carried. It is swung front to back as the thurifer walks, in rhythm with the thurifer's stride. As usual, the palm of the free hand is held against the chest if it is not holding the boat. The arm is not allowed to dangle.

The vessels are brought to the presider, who takes the boat. If a four-chain thurible is being used, or a single-chain thurible with a moveable lid, the thurifer raises the lid a few inches. Tightening the fist around the top of the chains will keep the lid open. The thurifer brings the clenched fist and the top of the chains to the chest and, with the other hand, grasps the chains as close as possible to the lid without being burned. (Thuribles become very hot. Touching the bowl, lid, or bottom-most portion of the chain can result in serious burns.) The thurifer

lifts the bowl so the presider can spoon grains of incense from the boat onto the burning coals without bending over. Then the thurifer allows the thurible to drop to the length of the chains, moving the clenched fist away from the chest, and loosens the grip so that the lid drops. The presider and the thurifer exchange items; that is, the presider takes the charged thurible and the thurifer takes the boat. The thurifer steps well out of the way and the presider begins the censing.

There is a formal way of carrying out the exchange of the thurible and the boat if there is a boat bearer. After the boat bearer has taken the boat and freed up the presider's hands, the thurifer places the top of the chain in the presider's left hand and the lower part of the chain in the presider's right hand. If this exchange is not done very precisely, it can appear fussy and often, because the thurifer has not handed the thurible to the presider so that the lower grip is in exactly the right place, the presider has to drop the thurible to its full length and start over. Unless the ministers are committed to extensive rehearsal, it is simpler for the presider to receive the thurible full-chained in the first place. In places where incense is seldom used, it is especially important not to complicate the matter.

Two factors must be kept in mind if the charging of the thurible is to look graceful and the essential element—the sight and the smell of the rising smoke—is to be the focus. First, the distance the lid is raised determines how close to the bowl the thurifer can grasp the chains. If the lid is raised only a few inches, the thurifer can grasp the thurible relatively close to the bowl. This allows the thurifer to keep the entire thurible—chain, lid, and bowl—in front of the chest while the presider charges it. If, however, the lid is raised high above the bowl (a foot or more, for example), the thurifer is forced to lift the lid overhead to bring the bowl to a comfortable height for the presider. The thurifer looks strained and the mechanics draws more attention than the rising smoke. The overall impression is ungainly.

A second point, related to the importance of raising the lid only slightly, is that the top of the chains must be held against the chest and not raised overhead. Most people's instinct is to raise the bowl to the presider by raising the *entire* thurible, including the full length of chain, straight up. Natural as this tendency may be, the result looks strained and is physically uncomfortable for the thurifer. Besides, unless the thurifer is exceptionally tall or has unusually long arms, this maneuver still does not get the bowl to the proper height for the presider. A standard thurible is about thirty inches long. To get the bowl to mid-chest using a grip at the top of the chains means stretching higher than most people can reach. If, however, the thurible is lifted not by grasping it thirty inches from the bottom but about twelve inches from the bottom (that is, just above the slightly raised lid) the bowl can be lifted to mid-chest by raising the hand only to the neck. The effect is compact and does not draw attention away from the smoke.

If a single-chain thurible with a fixed lid is used, the procedure is exactly the same, except there is no lid to raise. The thurifer simply brings the top of the chain to the chest, uses the other hand to grasp the chain near the bowl (taking care not to be burned), and raises the bowl to chest level.

USING A THURIBLE

Incense is customarily used at any of three times during the Eucharist:

1. In the entrance procession, leading to the censing of the Lord's Table.

2. At the proclamation of the Gospel, for censing the Gospel Book.

3. At the Offertory, for censing the offerings.

1. In the entrance procession

◆ A thurible is always carried with the chain fully extended. When a thurible is carried in procession, it is swung from front to back in pace with the thurifer's stride. When the thurifer is standing still, the thurible is swung in front of the body from side to side, just enough to keep the coals aerated and burning. In either case, the movement is created by the wrist, not the arm or the shoulder. The motion is very subtle. Once the thurible is set to swinging, it will continue to swing with only a slight movement of the wrist.

◆ The thurible is charged just before the procession begins. There is no need for the presider to bless the incense after it is added to the coals. Since the evocative potential of the incense is in both its smell and the movement of the smoke, enough incense should be used that the aroma and sight are clear and strong.

◆ In general, the thurifer always leads the procession. Only a master of ceremonies or a verger precedes the thurifer. Since the thurible is swung forward and backward during a procession, a significant space must be left between the thurifer and who precedes and follows.

◆ The thurible is swung in pace with the thurifer's stride throughout the procession. Although complex methods have been devised for negotiating turns while swinging a thurible, they tend to look stiff and even militaristic and are entirely unnecessary. They draw attention to the thurifer and away from the rising smoke.

◆ The thurifer arrives at the Lord's Table and waits on the side of the altar that will be to the presider's right (north for an altar facing the assembly, and south for an altar affixed to the east wall). When the presider arrives at the spot where he or she will stand during the Great Thanksgiving, the thurifer brings the thurible to the presider. (Or if the censing is to occur during the Hymn of Praise, as is the custom in some places, the thurifer waits until the beginning of the hymn to take the thurible to the presider.) There is no need for the deacon to act as an intermediary between the thurifer and the presider. The censing of the altar begins at the center. Therefore, the thurifer should bring the thurible to the center where the presider is already standing. The presider should not be forced to move away from the center to get the thurible. After the thurible has been passed to the presider, the thurifer moves well out of the way so that the action of the censing can become focal.

◆ There are two ways to swing a thurible:

❖ The Western custom is to grasp the thurible by the chains using one hand, palm down, close to the bowl. (Some find that holding it palm up allows more control. Each person should do whatever makes the censing look and feel natural.) The wrist is cocked to produce a swinging motion. The other hand holds the top of the chain to the chest.

❖ The Eastern custom is to grasp the thurible at the top of the chains, and to throw the full length of it outward from the body. As in the West, the free hand is held against the chest. The Eastern method is meant for an Eastern-style thurible, with chains much shorter than the standard thirty inches of a Western thurible.

It is very difficult to use a Western thurible in the Eastern way. Similarly, it is somewhat incongruous to use an Eastern thurible in a Western way. Nonetheless, Western thuribles are increasingly used in the Eastern way and Eastern thuribles are increasingly used in Western liturgies. The mixing and matching of vessels and methods must aim, above all, to allow the core element—the aromatic smoke—to dominate, and not the mechanics. The ministers must decide how best to negotiate the possibilities.

◆ The customs of throwing the thurible over the head in what is commonly called "a 360" and maneuvering it to produce "a figure 8" precisely draw attention to the mechanics and, worse, to the minister. These and other gesticulations involving incense are recent innovations. That alone is not a reason to advise against them; a recent development can be a genuine advance. Flamboyant uses of a thurible, however, are not an advance since they draw attention away from the essential to the incidental. Moreover, they draw attention to the peculiar skills of the minister. Never is self-promotion or self-aggrandizement appropriate in the liturgy. The liturgy is an expression of the Christ who "did not regard equality with God as something to be exploited, but emptied himself, taking on the form of a slave" (Phil. 2:6–7). Every member of the assembly, but especially the ministers, should aspire to the same attitudes as the Christ who is praying in and through them.

◆ If the altar is freestanding, the presider moves around it counterclockwise, censing it continuously. There is no predetermined number of swings, nor is there a complex pattern. Engaging the imagination and the eyes, the presider honors the altar, a symbol of Christ, by surrounding it and reverently "stroking" it with the perfumed smoke. The smoke envelops the altar and spreads from it through the entire room and into the midst of the people. The spreading of the smoke and the aroma is the crucial element of this action, not the number of swings or their performance according to some arcane set of rules. The best substitute for that kind of rigidity and precision is grace and reverence. Being able to use a thurible with grace and reverence, since it is a gesture without strong everyday parallels, requires a great deal of rehearsal outside the liturgy and practice within it.

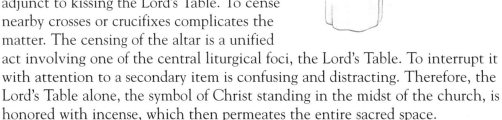

◆ If the altar is attached to the east wall, the presider moves from the center to the right, then reverses to the left, and then moves back to the middle, censing all the while. This is simply the long-standing convention and makes as much sense as anything else.

◆ The altar is being censed, not the cross or crucifix. The censing is a parallel or adjunct to kissing the Lord's Table. To cense nearby crosses or crucifixes complicates the matter. The censing of the altar is a unified act involving one of the central liturgical foci, the Lord's Table. To interrupt it with attention to a secondary item is confusing and distracting. Therefore, the Lord's Table alone, the symbol of Christ standing in the midst of the church, is honored with incense, which then permeates the entire sacred space.

◆ As the presider nears the end of the censing, the thurifer (and the boat bearer, if there is one) moves to the center of the Table where the action began, and receives the thurible from the presider. The thurible is then removed from the liturgical space as the presider moves to the chair for the Opening Acclamation.

At the proclamation of the Gospel

◆ The presider stands with the rest of the assembly as the pre-Gospel music begins.

◆ If the thurible is to be charged in the view of the assembly, the thurifer brings it, along with the boat, to the presider at the chair. The thurifer and presider charge the thurible according to the pattern outlined above.

◆ The thurifer moves into place before the altar, facing it and allowing space for the torches, the bearer of the Gospel Book, and the gospeller to approach the altar. (A diagram is provided in the ceremonial for the Liturgy of the Word, below.) The thurifer leads the procession to the place from which the Gospel will be proclaimed.

◆ After the gospeller has announced the reading, the thurifer passes the thurible to the gospeller. The gospeller censes the open book, making one swing to the center, one to the right, and one to the left.

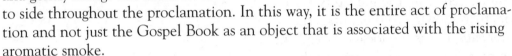

◆ The thurifer takes the thurible and moves to behind the gospeller, or to another convenient place near the book, and gently swings the thurible from side to side throughout the proclamation. In this way, it is the entire act of proclamation and not just the Gospel Book as an object that is associated with the rising aromatic smoke.

◆ At the conclusion of the Gospel, the thurifer leads the procession back to the place where the Gospel Book will be placed for the rest of the liturgy or, if the book is to be left on the ambo, back to the place where the torches will stand. As usual in procession, the thurifer swings the thurible from front to back, in pace with the stride.

3. At the Offertory

As Marion Hatchett points out in his commentary on the American Prayer Book, the Offertory is misnamed. The Great Thanksgiving is the liturgical offertory. The placing of the bread, wine, and monetary offerings on the Lord's Table is preparatory to the actual offering. While it is not helpful or even accurate to say exactly what the censing at the Offertory means (since it can evoke innumerable legitimate thoughts and feelings in the worshippers), it is primarily related to the gifts that have been set upon the altar and not the altar itself.

◆ As the presider completes the placing of the gifts on the Table, the thurifer (and the boat bearer) moves to the center where the presider is standing. The presider and the other ministers charge the thurible, as noted above.

◆ The thurifer (and the boat bearer) exchange vessels with the presider and move well aside so that the censing can be the focus. The presider first censes the offerings directly, and then moves around the entire altar as at the entrance. The offerings can be directly censed with one swing to the center, one to the right, and one to the left. Nothing more is required or even desirable. A complex pattern for censing the offerings was formalized in the Tridentine Missal and was adopted by many Anglicans. It involved a triple crossing, then a series of circles, first one way and then the other. This pattern is suggested by many Anglican customaries, including the famous and highly influential *Ritual Notes*. It seems, nonetheless, that the elaborate pattern draws more attention to itself than to the offerings. (It is, incidentally, not part of the current Roman Rite.)

◆ As the presider completes the censing of the offerings (and the Table), the thurifer comes to the center of the altar and receives the thurible from the presider. The thurifer then moves to the front of the altar, carrying the thurible with the chains fully extended. The thurifer censes all the ministers in the sanctuary, bowing to them first and afterward, if it is the local custom. The thurifer first casts smoke toward those in the center (including the presider), then those on the right, and finally those on the left.

◆ The thurifer then moves toward the assembly and censes it, just as the ministers have been censed. The assembly stands to be censed. The thurifer may have to signal this by raising in an upward motion the hand that is not grasping the thurible. It would break the unity of the entire censing for the thurifer to actually tell the assembly to stand, and a hand gesture usually suffices. If the thurifer bowed to the vested ministers before censing them, the rest of the assembly should be accorded the same sign of reverence. How the actual censing is done will depend upon the configuration of the room.

❖ In a longitudinal space without transepts, the thurifer censes the assembly either by making a number of swings to the left of the aisle and then to the right of the aisle, or by walking the length of the aisle, censing from side to side. The thurifer may bow to the assembly, and the members of the assembly may bow to the thurifer, before and after the censing.

❖ In a cruciform space, the thurifer censes each of the four arms of the cross, using one of the patterns for a longitudinal space, almost as if they were four distinct rooms.

❖ In a circular or other nonlinear space, the thurifer may move around the front of the circle, censing all the while, and may move down each of the aisles.

❖ In an antiphonally arranged space, where the seats face one another across a central aisle, the thurifer could walk the length of the room, censing one side continuously and then, returning toward the altar, censing the other side continuously.

◆ Because liturgical spaces can be arranged in so many different ways, there is no precisely correct way to cense the assembly. As in every other case, however, the question remains the same: What is this action meant to do? By engaging the imagination and bringing the mind and heart into harmony with the body, the thurifer will make it clear that, just as the bread and wine along with the monetary gifts have been prepared for the Great Thanksgiving, so too has the assembly been prepared as "a living sacrifice."

Chapter 9

THE GREATER
AND THE LESSER

In the Episcopal Church today, the Holy Eucharist is "the principal act of Christian worship on the Lord's Day and other major Feasts" (BCP 13), and, thanks to the Liturgical Movement, it is increasingly normative in other Christian traditions as well. As the ecumenical document *Baptism, Eucharist and Ministry* asserts, "As the eucharist celebrates the resurrection of Christ, it is appropriate that it should take place at least every Sunday."[9] A great many Christians, then, and nearly all Episcopalians, celebrate the Eucharist frequently enough that they know the rite by heart.

That is why those in training for liturgical ministries are often shocked at how lost they feel when their turn comes to "play church." How to navigate through the books, what to do with the hands, where to direct the eyes, when to move from place to place and what path to take, what to say and what *not* to say, how to set objects on the Lord's Table and how to maneuver them once they are in place: the details can be overwhelming, and neophytes can become so befuddled that they are paralyzed. They think they know the liturgy inside and out, and so they are confused by their own confusion. When they put on the vestments they discover that most of the details have completely escaped them.

The way forward through the details is not to commit them to memory and push through them as if they were a drill. To move gracefully through the tangle, liturgical ministers must go back to the basics, to what lies beneath all of the perplexing particu-

---

9. *Baptism, Eucharist and Ministry*, Eucharist III.31.

lars. Beneath them all is a simple, basic core that holds all the details together. Without it, the seemingly arbitrary and innumerable particulars are a confusing and essentially meaningless conglomeration. The core determines the details: which things belong and which do not belong, what should be said and what should not be said, what is to be done and what is not. Once the core is firmly grasped, it can function as a matrix into which all of the minutiae fit, and then a great deal of the confusion will evaporate.

Bells and whistles are important only if they are attached to a working bicycle, and a working bicycle is useful only if the person who wants to ride it knows how to make it go. Otherwise, the bells and whistles don't matter. They are fun and they are fancy, but they are useless. They are even a distraction from what really matters if the would-be rider is ever to get up and get moving. When a minister-in-training wants to learn how to serve at the Eucharist, the place to start is the liturgical equivalent of the bicycle frame and wheels, not the bells and whistles. What is this thing, what is it for, how does it work? After those questions are settled comes the time to think about the trim. There is time and reason to add trim, but the trim is secondary to the core.

An Order for Celebrating the Holy Eucharist (BCP 400–401) is the core of the eucharistic liturgy. When the boldface headings in the Prayer Book order are strung together, they form a sentence with "the people and the priest" as the subject: The people and the priest gather in the Lord's Name, proclaim and respond to the Word of God, pray for the world and the church, exchange the Peace, prepare the Table, make Eucharist, break the Bread, and share the gifts of God. That is the core of the eucharistic rite.

These actions are not arbitrary, nor are they strictly liturgical. They are the essential elements of the baptismal vocation: to gather together and recognize one another as the Body of Christ; to hear of the stirrings of the Spirit in the history of the church and to listen for the echoes of God's action in the world today; to serve as a "priestly people," making intercession for the world; to be reconciled to God and to one's neighbor; to give of oneself for the good of the church and the world; to be always thankful, especially for salvation in Christ; to recognize Christ present in the assembly, the Sacrament, and the world; and to unite oneself to him so that his mission can continue. This is the core, not of the eucharistic rite, but of the Christian life.

The liturgy, then, is not empty ritual or pompous ceremony. Rather, it is the distillation in ritual form of all that it means to be a disciple of Christ and a member of Christ's living Body. The core of the eucharistic liturgy is the core of the baptized life. It is a rehearsal for living in God's reign.

According to the Prayer Book rubrics, the Order for Celebrating the Holy Eucharist is "not intended for use at the principal Sunday or weekly celebration of the Holy Eucharist" (BCP 400). The complete rites of the Holy Eucharist, however, are essentially elaborations of this order. The questions a liturgical committee, as well as the liturgical ministers, must ask at every turn, then, are not about the "bells and whistles" except as they relate to the core of the rite highlighted in the order.

GATHERING

How can the opening rites be structured and celebrated so that the people and priest "gather in the Lord's Name"? What does it mean to be gathered in the Lord's Name and not merely gathered together? How is being "gathered" different from merely being in the same place at the same time? These are the sorts of questions that must be considered if the ceremonies of the Eucharist are to be more than pomp and formality.

If the opening rites aim to gather the people in the Lord's Name, should the planning team seize the Prayer Book's allowance that "a hymn, psalm, or anthem may be sung" (BCP 355) at this time? If so, which of the three? If the intention is to gather the church more than superficially, what kind of hymn would be best? It would seem that the primary considerations would be the familiarity, rhythm, drive, and energy of the hymn. And when imagery is considered, would not the principal concern be to select a hymn whose imagery taps into the essential truths and sentiments that make the assembly more than an accidental crowd, rather than images that reflect the "theme of the day"?

If the liturgical planning team were to decide not to use a piece of music at the beginning of the rite, what would they choose instead to facilitate the gathering of the church? How would the people be greeted, and by whom, as they arrived at the church? How would the ministers enter? Would silence or conversation be encouraged in the church? What actions could be used—whether by the entire assembly or by some of the ministers—to facilitate the group's transition from a conglomeration of individuals into an amalgamation of the members of Christ's Body?

Each of the following questions must be asked in light of the overarching purpose: for the people and the priest to gather in the Lord's Name.

◆ Does the liturgy begin with a procession? What is the order of the procession? What is the path of the procession?

◆ Will incense be used, and how?

◆ Where will the presider stand, and where will the ministers be stationed, for the Opening Acclamation? The Collect for Purity? The Hymn of Praise? The Collect of the Day? What gestures and what tone will the presider use for each of these?

◆ What elements will be part of the environment? How will they be arranged?

◆ What would militate against the intention of this part of the liturgy in the environment, the tone, the movements and gestures of all the members of the assembly?

◆ If the *Gloria* is appointed, how will it be performed? If it is not appointed, what other hymn might best support the gathering in the Lord's Name? (Note that the Hymn of Praise is mandated for every Sunday, while the opening hymn or processional is never required.)

PROCLAIMING AND RESPONDING

At every point in the liturgy, the search for the core must be prior to the consideration of the secondary details, and must be woven into the consideration of each of the particulars. In the next section of the Eucharist, the goal of the people and the priest is to proclaim and respond to the Word of God.

◆ Proclamations, by definition, are meant to be heard. What do people in our culture need to truly *hear* something—not just read it or have it read within earshot, but truly *hear* it? Is "proclaiming" different from "reading aloud"? How might readers be prepared to be proclaimers?

◆ What visual cues would suggest that the biblical proclamations are more than just ancient texts? What objects should be used, stances taken, tones projected, and attitudes fostered to suggest that these words are records of a people's experience of God *and* windows into what God continues to do in the world?

◆ What sorts of ritual might distract from the assembly's experience of the proclamation as an encounter with the Word of God, even if those rituals are commonly accepted? In a particular assembly, for example, would the use of incense heighten or reduce the people's experience of the proclaimed Word? A Gospel procession? An elevated pulpit? A worn lectionary? An ornamented Gospel Book?

◆ What would constitute a genuine response to the Word in a particular assembly? Clearly, the sermon is a response, but how can the entire congregation and not just the preacher be asked truly to respond, while still observing the canons and the rubrics?

◆ If a rite is to come after the proclamation (baptism, marriage, ordination, anointing, confirmation), how can it be presented homiletically and how can it be "choreographed" so that it is unmistakably a response to the Word that has been proclaimed?

PRAYING FOR THE WORLD AND THE CHURCH

The Prayers of the People are not prayers *about* the people and their individual needs. Just the opposite, they are the *people's prayer* for the entire created order. The baptized community is priestly insofar as it stands before God making intercession on behalf of the world, and stands in the midst of the world as a witness to the presence of God. The Prayers of the People are where the concrete realities of life enter most explicitly into the liturgy. The core of this part of the liturgy is intercession that is attentive to the most concrete needs of real life.

The forms of the prayers in the 1979 Book of Common Prayer are just that: forms. They are examples of how the Prayers of the People might be structured. They were generic even when they were written, and the world and the church of the 1970s is not the church and the world today. When these forms are used they need to be adapted and expanded; many churches write their own Prayers of the People. The following questions need to be asked when revising, expanding, or writing the prayers.

◆ What are the genuine needs of the world and the church *today*? What people and events cry out from the television, radio, newspapers, and the "word on the street"?

◆ What are the needs of those who differ in significant ways from the gathered assembly, or the person composing the biddings? What do children experience as truly needful in their lives? Young adults? New families? Retired people? People who sense death coming near? The span of age is only one of the variables that make people different. How can the church expand its consciousness so that it can "pray for the whole state of Christ's Church and the world" (BCP 328)?

◆ What mechanisms would help the people or groups who write the prayers to be aware of both global and local needs?

◆ How can the individual members of the assembly invite the people and priest to pray for the world and the church in ways that might not occur to the group, or for important needs of which the group might not have been aware?

◆ How can the prayers or the biddings be structured so that the individual intentions stand out, trigger a strong intellectual and emotional engagement from the members of the assembly, and elicit in them a desire, not only to pray, but also to do something about the need?

EXCHANGING THE PEACE

The Peace stands between the Liturgy of the Word and the Liturgy of the Eucharist. It is a ritual sign that the community is reconciled and can approach the Lord's Table in good conscience. It is the Body recognizing the Body and so, as St. Paul warns, not eating and drinking judgment against itself. The core of this rite is a simple human greeting that acknowledges the dignity of the others and accepts them, no matter who they happen to be.

The Peace is a *ritual* act of reconciliation just as the Eucharist is a *ritual* meal. It need not be protracted to be genuine, nor does every person have to greet every other person. The core of this rite is the embracing of any person who happens to come near. That does not require that every person in the room greet every other person. It especially means that members of the assembly should not move about in search of those they know or to whom they are related. The point is that in the Body of Christ, such distinctions are irrelevant.

◆ The Peace is an integral part of the liturgy, not a break in it. What sort of formation can help the entire assembly to recognize the Peace as a ritual action in which they all participate, not a recess in the ritual?

◆ The rubrics allow that "the Ministers and People may greet one another in the name of the Lord" (BCP 360). It suggests neither words nor gestures. How might the liturgical leaders model the Peace so that it both expresses and instills a spirit of reconciliation in Christ, and an openness to the unknown other?

◆ What gesture might the presider use when greeting the people before the Peace? What should the gesture convey? Is a gesture, in fact, even necessary or helpful?

PREPARING THE TABLE

To prepare the table for the Eucharist requires only that bread and wine be set upon it. These are the *only* things required. As the Catechism states, "The outward and visible sign in the Eucharist is bread and wine, given and received according to Christ's command" (BCP 859). Every object and every gesture that enters into this part of the rite should be oriented toward these essential elements. Nothing should distract from them.

Bread and wine are basic human artifacts. Like all primal things, they are rich with meaning. All the essential elements of the liturgy—bread and wine, water and oil, skin upon skin—are symbolically dense. That is, in and of themselves, they evoke thoughts, feelings, insights, and memories that go to the very heart of the human experience and, hence, to the human experience of God.

An old quip has it that most people can believe that Christ's presence is conveyed by bread, they just cannot believe that Communion wafers are bread. In other words, what is essential is commonly downplayed and minimized, and what is secondary rises to prominence. The core is allowed to become anemic and lost, while the "bells and whistles" are inflated and thrust to the fore. At the core of "preparing the Table" is setting bread and wine upon it in preparation for the Great Thanksgiving. Every decision about this part of the rite should be in service of that core.

The monetary offerings of the people, while not essential since they need not be collected at every Eucharist, are the sign that the assembly recognizes everything as God's gift. The 1928 Prayer Book included among the offertory sentences, "All things come of thee, O LORD, and of thine own have we given thee" (1 Chron. 29:14). The offering is also the assembly's concrete pledge to support the mission of Christ in the world, not only by contributing finances, but also by giving its life in service to the reign of God. The current Prayer Book includes this sentence from Romans: "I beseech you, brethren, by the mercies of God, to present yourselves as a living sacrifice, holy and acceptable to God, which is your spiritual worship" (BCP 343).

The Altar Book is not necessary, but it is important. The presider could attempt to pray the Eucharistic Prayer from memory, but this is risky, since even the most well-trained memory can fail. More important, however, the Altar Book is a visual cue that the prayer is not the *priest's* prayer, but is the *church's* prayer. The presider speaks aloud the prayer that Christ is praying in the gathered assembly and in assemblies like it across space and time. The Altar Book is not at the core, nor is it even as important as the monetary offerings. It is, nonetheless, an important sign of what the community is doing when it "makes Eucharist."

Beyond the primary things—bread and wine—and the secondary things—monetary offerings and Altar Book—everything else is tertiary. Often, however, the tertiary things are given such prominence that they would seem to be secondary or even primary. Even more commonly, the secondary things are treated as if they were the primary ones. (Think, for example, of the elaborate ceremony that often accompanies the procession and presentation of the alms. It smothers the essential action of setting the food and drink on the Table, and the huge alms basin sometimes dwarfs the food and drink themselves.) The primary and core things must be the focus of this part of the liturgy, just as the core things should be the focus of every other part of the liturgy.

- What kind of bread can be used so that all the evocative power of bread is available to the assembly?

- How can the wine be poured so the core action can be experienced (seen, heard, smelled) by the entire assembly?

- Where on the Table are the bread and wine placed so that they are experienced as the offering of "the people and the priest," and not only of the priest?

- Where do the presider and deacon stand in relation to the Table and the bread and wine so that, again, the elements and the action are experienced as communal and not private?

- How are the alms and Altar Book placed on the altar so that they do not achieve a greater importance than the bread and wine?

- What things and gestures can be trimmed away so that the core action of preparing the Table can come to the fore?

- What size, shape, and quality should other objects related to the Table have (candles, for example)? Where can they be placed so that they point toward and highlight, rather than distract from and bury, what is core?

- How can the unity symbolized by the one bread and one cup be conveyed even if there must be more than one vessel of bread or wine placed on the altar in a large assembly?

- The Prayer Book directs that it is the deacon who is "to make ready the Table for the celebration, preparing and placing upon it the bread and cup of wine...may be assisted by other ministers" (BCP 407). How can this all be done in a "decent and godly" fashion, so that the mechanics of handing things off from one person to the other, placing them on the altar, filling the cup, adding the water, and so on does not become so jumbled and complex that the core action—the setting of the bread and wine on the Lord's Table—is obscured?

MAKING EUCHARIST

The Order for Celebrating the Holy Eucharist directs that the priest pray the Great Thanksgiving "in the name of the gathering." Again, the emphasis is on the priest and the people entering into a common liturgical action. The name of the prayer is not The Prayer of Consecration, as the section of the Eucharistic Prayer after the *Sanctus* was called in previous editions. The current names—The Great Thanksgiving and The Eucharistic Prayer—mean exactly the same thing and reflect the content and intention of this prayer in all its classic forms. It is a Eucharist, that is, a thanksgiving, and by the community's act of giving thanks God transforms what is prepared on the Lord's Table. The bread and wine are consecrated not by any single act or phrase but by the church—not just the clergy—gathering around them and giving thanks for all God's mighty acts, especially for salvation in Christ.

The order provides two "forms" of the Eucharistic Prayer, which, like the entire order, are essentially outlines. Each of these outlines, however, has the same essential elements:

1. Introductory dialogue between the presider and the rest of the assembly;

2. Thanksgiving for God's work in creation and for the revelation of God in human history;

3. Praise of God for the world's salvation through Jesus;

4. Remembrance of the Lord's Last Supper;

5. Petition that God will send the Holy Sprit upon the bread and wine;

6. Petition that God will unite the assembly with Christ and accept each member's self-offering in communion with Christ's.

These are the same elements in each of the Eucharistic Prayers approved for use in the Episcopal Church, and are the core of the early, classic prayers.

In short, the Eucharistic Prayer is an act of thanksgiving for God's mighty acts, especially for the saving work wrought by Christ, with an invocation that the Holy Spirit will transform the bread and wine and, through them, unite the assembly with Christ in his life and mission. At the end of the prayer the entire assembly says, "Amen": an assent to the presider's words and a commitment to receive what God has been asked to give.

It should be noted that this prayer is not a reenactment of the Last Supper. Rather, it is a current enactment of what Jesus asked his disciples to do in memory of him. The remembrance of the Last Supper in the midst of the prayer—the Institution Narrative—expresses why the community is doing what it is doing. But what it is doing is not reenacting the Last Supper, but rather giving thanks, especially for the Lord Jesus, who commanded his disciples to eat and drink thankfully in memory of him. The Institution Narrative, then, is not a magic formula for transforming either the bread and wine, or the assembly. Rather, God transforms the bread and wine through the entire thankful action of the assembly and then, in turn, transforms the assembly through their communion in the Bread and Wine made holy.

◆ How can the ritual express that the entire assembly is praying, and that the priest is speaking aloud a prayer that is common to all?

◆ What tone is appropriate to this prayer, and how is the tone conveyed through ritual, gesture, inflection, pace, and music? This question applies not only to the presider, but also to the other liturgical ministers and the entire assembly.

◆ Since the prayer is one single prayer, from the introductory dialogue through the concluding "Amen," how can the unity of the prayer be expressed in music, gesture, posture, tone?

◆ A common misunderstanding of the Great Thanksgiving is that it is a reenactment of the Last Supper. How can the assembly pray the prayer so that its actual nature is conveyed? How can they intentionally counteract the misunderstanding of what the prayer is? What might be done, conversely, that would serve to reinforce the notion that the Eucharistic Prayer is a historical reenactment of the Last Supper?

◆ If the Great Thanksgiving is not a historical reenactment of the Last Supper, it follows that the presider is not "playing" Jesus. What, then, is the presider's identity during the Eucharistic Prayer? How does the presider express this accurately in tone, gesture, the use of the eyes, and so forth? What might the presider do that would only reinforce the misperception that the priest is an actor taking the role of Jesus? What might the presider do to express as clearly as possible the actual presidential role within the assembly's prayer?

BREAKING THE BREAD

The most ancient name for the Eucharist is the Breaking of the Bread. This single act lent its name to the entire event. The breaking of the Bread and the pouring of the Wine after they have been consecrated are actions that carry layer upon layer of meaning. From a strictly human perspective, the sharing of bread and wine is rich with significance. It conjures up images and ideas that go to the very heart of human existence and human community. When the particularly Christian significance of this act is added, the depth of the symbol—both the action of breaking and tearing, and the symbol of the one Bread being divided for the entire assembly—becomes fathomless. Silence is mandated in the two full rites of the Eucharist when the eucharistic Bread is first broken. This is the only mandatory silence in the entire eucharistic rite, suggesting that there is something in this action that is singularly worth contemplating.

The core of this moment in the liturgy is so basic that it seems too simple to stand alone as a key element of the rite. The core is, simply, making the consecrated Food and Drink ready for Communion by dividing them into sufficient pieces and sufficient vessels for the assembly. But because this rite is so dense with imagery and associations, it is a moment with the potential to trigger deep insight. It can be a hierophanic moment: an occasion when the Mystery is revealed in its complexity and richness. This entire rite is referred to as the fraction, and the music appointed is called the fraction anthem.

◆ What kind of bread has the greatest potential for triggering the rich potential insights and experiences of the Breaking of the Bread? Should it be leavened or not? Wafers or substantial bread?

◆ What kind of vessels allow the assembly to experience as fully as possible the Bread both before and after it has been broken, and the Wine both before and after it has been poured? If vessels must be used that do not meet these ideal standards, how can those who enact the rite compensate?

◆ How might the Bread be handled during the initial breaking? How high might it be held? How quickly or slowly should it be broken or torn? How long should the contemplative silence last?

◆ What can the presider do with the body, the face, the eyes to facilitate the assembly seeing this symbol in all its richness?

◆ The Prayer Book does not suggest any gesture to accompany the invitation to Communion, only the words, "The Gifts of God for the People of God" (BCP 364). Given the many layers of significance in the breaking and pouring, and in what has been broken and poured, what action would most effectively invite the community to feast in the broken Body and Blood of Christ, many and yet one? Should the presider alone be part of this gesture, or should other ministers join?

◆ How can the preparation of the elements and the invitation to Communion be followed as directly as possible by the movement of the assembly to Communion or the movement of the Sacrament to the assembly? How can the community's complex experience during the rich moments of the fraction rite be joined to their partaking in the gifts?

SHARING THE GIFTS OF GOD

The liturgy builds toward the sharing of Communion. In the full rites, there is a prayer of thanks to conclude the Communion, but then nothing more is prescribed but the dismissal. Nothing follows the Communion. It is both the pinnacle and the conclusion of the liturgy. The sharing of the gifts is the offering of Food and Drink, the acceptance of the offer, and the actual consumption. The core of this final part of the liturgy is the simple human act of eating and drinking together. Note the word "sharing." This is a communal, not a private, event. Everything that is done should refer to this core.

To eat and drink is basic to human existence and, as the dictum suggests, what is taken into the body is supremely consequential. "You are what you eat." To eat and drink something is to make it part of oneself. This is true in the spiritual as well as the physical sense, as the second postcommunion prayer makes clear:

> Almighty and everliving God,
> we thank you for feeding us with the spiritual food
> of the most precious Body and Blood
> of your Son our Savior Jesus Christ;
> and for assuring us in these holy mysteries
> that we are living members of the Body of your Son. (BCP 366; cf. 339)

Those who partake of the Body of Christ *are* the Body of Christ. The sharing of Communion, the prayer says, expresses what the church is and makes it what it is. In his first letter to the Corinthians, Paul makes the same claim: "Because there is one bread, we who are many are one body, for we all partake of the one bread" (1 Cor. 10:17). The

Sacrament and the church are mirror images of one another, and "make" one another. The Eucharist is the Body of Christ, brought forth by the prayer of the Body of Christ, in Communion with Christ, who makes the members of the church into his Body.

Because the Food and Drink, according to both the *lex orandi* and the *lex credendi*, are the Body and Blood of Christ, to eat and drink them is not casual snacking. The level of attention and care people give to eating and drinking varies according to the importance they attach to the food and the occasion when they are sharing it. To say that the core of this part of the rite is eating and drinking together is not to reduce the core to a purely biological function. Eating and drinking is a complex social phenomenon which, while biological, is more than that. How and what human beings eat both expresses and forms them at levels well beyond the purely physical.

- ◆ In the sharing of the gifts, the members of the church are joined both to one another and to Christ, through the Spirit. What does this suggest about the way the Food and Drink should be offered and accepted, administered and received?

- ◆ What is the proper balance between the distance and intimacy the minister and the communicant should enact to express what this offering, accepting, eating, and drinking does? Do they allow their eyes to meet or not? Do they allow their hands to touch or not? Is so, how and for how long?

- ◆ What kind of music should accompany the Communion? What should it convey in its tone and its text? When should it begin and when should it end?

- ◆ What posture should the members of the assembly be encouraged to take while others are receiving Communion? What bodily action would create the greatest congruence between what the assembly believes about the reception of Communion (the *lex credendi*) and their ritual behavior (the *lex orandi*)? To what should each member of the assembly attend as the other members offer, accept, eat, and drink?

- ◆ How are the vessels of Bread and Wine to be replenished? How can this be done to support most fully the core of this part of the liturgy?

All of these questions must be asked in the light of the core event that is happening: the Body of Christ is sharing the Body of Christ as Food and Drink.

PART II

THE SUNDAY EUCHARIST

Chapter 10

THE OPENING RITES

IN A NUTSHELL

Necessary Artifacts
- A "clean white cloth" on the Lord's Table (BCP 406)
- The vessels and small linens for the Lord's Supper, set on a credence table:
  - Corporal
  - Principal chalice and a purificator
  - Secondary chalices and purificators (if needed)
  - Secondary bowls, plates, or ciboria (if needed)
- The Altar Book
- A Bible and/or lectionary and/or Gospel Book

Optional Artifacts
- A pitcher of water for the admixture
- A bowl of water and a towel; or an empty bowl, pitcher of water, and towel for the lavabo
- Torches, altar candles, a thurible and boat

Necessary Ministers
- The assembly
- The presider
- One assisting minister

Optional Ministers
- A deacon
- A master of ceremonies
- A thurifer (and boat bearer)
- A crucifer, torch bearers, and sufficient acolytes to facilitate the liturgy
- A cantor or choir (One of these is necessary if the opening music or Hymn of Praise is responsorial or antiphonal.)
- An instrumentalist

Necessary Liturgical Elements
- A seasonal acclamation
- A Hymn of Praise
- The Collect of the Day

Optional Liturgical Elements
- A song before the acclamation
- The Collect for Purity

What does this part of the rite do?

The vitality of the liturgy depends on the entire assembly understanding and experiencing itself as the celebrant—precisely as an assembly and not as an aggregate of individuals. These initial moments of the service are key in fostering that common self-awareness. They mark the transition of the community into a keenly felt experience of what it is: the Body of the Risen One.

How is this goal accomplished?

How this awareness is instilled will not be the same in every community on every occasion. Planning teams and ministers must consider a number of factors, the most obvious being the shape of the room, the size of the assembly, the number of vested ministers, the musical possibilities, and the liturgical season.

GATHERING

MODEL 1: THE PROCESSION OF THE MINISTERS

Having the vested ministers move up the center aisle led by a cross and torches will not necessarily accomplish the transition, although it is the most common model. A procession is, essentially, a parade. On a great civic holiday, a powerful, energetic, well-arranged parade can sweep those lining the street into its energy so that they feel caught up not merely in the parade but also in the ideals it celebrates. A sickly parade, however, can have the opposite impact. Because it does not proceed with enough volume or vigor to draw the observers into its trajectory, they cannot "connect" to it or what it symbolizes. It leaves them feeling unconnected to the greater whole, or even disappointed in it. "Is this all there is?" they might ask, if only at an unconscious level. If the parade is poorly or gracelessly arranged it can trigger uneasiness, boredom, a lack of belief in the ideals being celebrated, and a breakdown of the people's faith in the organizers.

A "parade" at the beginning of the liturgy, therefore, should be strong enough and arranged carefully enough to draw the worshippers together into an awareness of their corporate identity and prepare them for the tasks that lie before them: listening with care, speaking with conviction, singing from the heart, watching with a contemplative eye, and touching, tasting, and smelling the action of God they are about to encounter. This is a tall order and calls for a vigorous, intentional procession.

The procession is an enacted symbol. Its allusions are many: the pilgrimage of the Christian life, movement from distraction to mindfulness, the journey to the kingdom, and other images that will naturally arise in the worshippers. A procession of just a priest

and one or two acolytes would hardly be capable of drawing the entire assembly into the sort of imaginative participation a procession is meant to elicit. Besides, the procession is not, as is sometimes said, for the purpose of "greeting the celebrant." Calling the entrance of just the presider and one minister "an entrance procession," then, hardly seems justified.

Since the Prayer Book does not prescribe a procession, neither does it address the order of the procession. The earliest and most enduring directives for arranging liturgical processions prescribe, essentially, that the ministers enter in order of ecclesiastical "rank." The ecclesiology of the 1979 Book of Common Prayer is baptismal; it begins with the equality of all the baptized and situates the ordained ministries within that context. The notion of rank does not find an easy home within our predominant notion of ourselves as a Body. At the same time, the Prayer Book understands the community to be ordered. It is not anarchy.

It is perhaps best, then, to order the procession in terms of how things and people *function* instead of what rank they hold. The procession is led by the community's sacred symbols (the cross or crucifix and, far more important, the Gospel Book). They can be flanked or led by torches, as a mark of honor. Banners would generally not be carried in procession on a typical Sunday. When they are carried, they should be few in number so as not to compete with the primary symbols, the Gospel Book and the people themselves. Banners can be interspersed in any way, such as after the choir and before the other ministers, but care must be taken that they not be carried so close to the Gospel Book that they overshadow it. As *The Church for Common Prayer* says concerning "Artwork, Flags, and Banners": "Things that are secondary ought never to eclipse or demean things that are primary." National flags are never carried in a liturgical procession. The Mystery celebrated in the liturgy transcends national boundaries.

If incense is used, it precedes the entire procession so that the smoke will encircle the symbols as well as the members of the procession. As the smoke diffuses, it also enwraps the rest of the congregation and helps to sweep it into the movement of the procession.

After the sacred symbols come the lay ministers, then the ordained who do not have specific ministerial roles in the liturgy, and finally the presider and the assistants. The deacon, as the custodian of the Gospel, bears the book near the head of the procession. The deacon enthrones it on the center of the altar and waits there for the presider to approach or, if the presider is not to approach the altar, meets the presider at the presider's seat. If there is no deacon, another minister, perhaps one of the lectors, can solemnly bear the Gospel Book into the assembly. If it is not borne in procession, the deacon walks to the right of the presider and remains to the presider's right throughout the liturgy.

Ordering the procession
While not every procession will include all of the following units, a standard order is:

Master of Ceremonies / Verger
Thurifer
Crucifer
Torch—Gospel—Torch
Choir
Acolytes
Vested Deacons
Vested Priests
Presider / Deacon

Directions for the use of incense as part of the entrance procession are given in chapter 8, "Postures and Gestures." Since the torches are associated with the Gospel Book, and usually will be carried with it at the proclamation of the Gospel, they should stand on either side of it where it is enthroned. If possible, these torches can also serve as the altar candles. Most Gospel Books will stand upright, and should be enthroned on the altar this way, in the view of the assembly.

If there must be a choice between bearing the Gospel Book and the cross in the procession, the book is chosen since it is an integral part of the liturgy. Like the altar, it is a symbol of Christ in the assembly. Again, as the document *The Church for Common Prayer* notes, "While the cross is a basic Christian symbol, it is not one of the primary liturgical focal points." When both a processional cross and the Gospel Book are borne in, the torches accompany the book. Since the torches are a kind of honor guard for the book, if the procession comes to a place where the three cannot walk abreast, the torches precede the Gospel Book.

1. If there is a processional hymn, the procession does not move until the hymn begins, and should be timed to finish before the hymn ends. If the Holy Table is to be censed, an interlude should be inserted into the hymn so the assembly can look up from the printed page to attend to this action and, by viewing it, participate in it as fully as possible. The censing of the altar is a visual and olfactory event, and the liturgy should be choreographed to allow the assembly to experience it as both.

2. As the procession reaches or passes by the altar, the ministers who are not carrying liturgical objects make a profound bow. Those who are carrying an object briefly pause instead.

3. A liturgical procession should have volume, strength, and trajectory. The people in it should move with enough space between them that as each pair pauses to reverence the altar, the procession does not stop, breaking the image of pilgrimage or journey. A

"stalled" procession is clumsy looking. It does not allow the assembly to be drawn in by its grace and beauty. Throughout the procession, the ministers should keep the eyes focused forward, toward the place they are moving. Sometimes at festive occasions when people gather who are not commonly together, the ministers, especially the priests, look around the room and even glad-hand as they move up the aisle. The basis of the liturgy is not personal intimacy, as the above section on exchanging the Peace discusses, and the procession should not be interrupted by personal and intimate greetings. Furthermore, given the latent clericalism in the church, having the liturgical ministers personally greet some of the people on the basis of personal knowledge but not all the people will feel like favoritism. It is completely contrary to the spirit and intention of the liturgy.

4. To ensure that the procession is spaced well, a liturgical minister can "step off" each person or pair in the procession, directing them to maintain the spacing for the duration of the procession. The master of ceremonies might do this, in which case the MC would fall into the procession just before the presider and deacon, rather than walking at the head of the procession.

5. Everyone in the procession, including the presider, is first and foremost a member of the assembly. Those who are not carrying a liturgical object should have hymnals or orders of worship, and should sing the hymn with the other members of the assembly. This both models active participation and witnesses to the equality of the baptized. As the procession approaches the altar:

◆ The ministers set the objects they are carrying in the designated places and take their stations.

◆ The deacon (or, in the absence of a deacon, an acolyte) takes the hymnal or order of worship from the presider so the presider will not have to set it on the Lord's Table in order to kiss and/or cense the altar. *Extraneous items should never be set on the altar.* All that should ever rest on it during the course of a normal Sunday liturgy are the offerings, the Gospel Book, the Altar Book, the secondary vessels into which the Bread and Wine may have to be divided, and, if they do not stand on the floor, the candlesticks. (It is interesting to note that *The Church for Common Prayer*, in listing the items that the altar should be large enough to accommodate, says "sometimes" candlesticks. This is not to suggest that candles should not be used. Rather, they are meant to honor not only what is *on* the Table, but also the Table itself, and to flank it rather than stand on it.)

◆ The presider may kiss the altar (see chapter 8, "Postures and Gestures").

◆ The presider may cense the altar (see chapter 8, "Postures and Gestures").

◆ The presider, deacon, and bearer of the Altar Book move to the place from which rest of the opening rites will be led (see "Positioning the Ministers," below).

MODEL 2: AN INFORMAL GATHERING WITH CONVERSATION

Another option would be for the entire assembly, including the vested ministers, to gather informally and circulate freely for conversation. The ministers' role in this model is to embody the spirit of hospitality and equality that is essential to the church's health and the authenticity of its liturgy. Those who seem to be most ill at ease or isolated, especially newcomers, would call for the most attention from the clergy, the parish lay leadership, and the other vested ministers.

This model might serve well, for example, in a parish with a strong influx of new members or where injuries within the Body need to be healed, or where the community has not yet grasped that the liturgy is a communal, rather than an individual, action. Perhaps the greatest pitfall of this model, however, is how easily it can draw the assembly away from the sacred purpose for which it has gathered. Unscripted conversation among the members of the church can certainly be sacred in itself. At the same time, conversation can distract people from mindfulness of the Divine Presence and even be a way to avoid it.

When this mode of gathering is used, then, a further transitional activity will be necessary: a gradual movement of the members of the assembly to their places, a signal that a time of recollection is about to begin, and, most important, a time for the entire community to sit silently and, perhaps, to listen to a prelude. If a hymn is to be sung, the sound of the instruments would be the assembly's signal to stand.

MODEL 3: AN INFORMAL GATHERING IN SILENCE

At times, especially during Advent and Lent, the community, including the vested ministers, can enter informally and individually, in silence. This is also a good model for a congregation that is striving to deepen its contemplative focus. Liturgical silence can be explained homiletically as an activity of great fullness and beauty, not only emptiness and deprivation. A group gathered in silence, intentionally focused on the Divine Presence within, among, and beyond the assembly, can reach a state of intense attentiveness. Something greater than the group and yet not detached from it can begin to be sensed: the God who is both transcendent and immanent. In this way, both reverence and hospitality—awe before God and awe before the neighbor, openness to God and openness to the neighbor—can be experienced as a single reality.

If there is an entrance hymn, the sound of the instruments would be the signal for the assembly to stand. If not, the presider's standing is the cue for the rest of the assembly to stand. "Stage directions" are unnecessary here and elsewhere in the rite if it is well designed, the ministers are well rehearsed, and the order of worship contains clear rubrics. As long as the ministers know that they are to stand when the presider stands, the rest of the assembly will follow their lead. A clear and simple rubric in the order of worship can also be useful, such as, "As the presider stands, the entire assembly stands."

If the presider has to tell everyone else what to do at each turn, the presider comes to be in control of the liturgy and the other members of the assembly become passive followers, waiting to be told what to do. Everything that can be done to make the entire assembly and every member of it into competent liturgical actors advances the cause not only of the liturgy, but of the Christian life it encapsulates.

MODEL 4: A COMBINATION OF MODELS

Models 1, 2, and 3 can also be combined in various ways to good effect. The presider, the other ministers, and parish leaders might greet the members of the assembly as they arrive, on the sidewalk or at the door, in the style of Model 2. When the liturgy is to begin, the ministers can then enter in solemn procession, in the style of Model 1. Or, after greeting people on the sidewalk or in the narthex and chatting with them, the ministers might enter the worship space individually and informally, quietly taking their places. The rest of the assembly would already be seated there in silence.

Not every combination, however, is felicitous. An ineffective combination of the models, for example, would be for the ministers to circulate and have conversations with the assembly in the actual worship space, leave momentarily, and then process into the room as if they had never been there. The liturgy is ritual, but it is not pretend. To enter, leave, and enter again as if you had never been there does not foster a spirit of authenticity.

THE ELEMENTS OF THE OPENING RITES

POSITIONING THE MINISTERS

In the chapter on liturgical space, various models were outlined for where the presider, an acolyte holding the Altar Book, and the deacon might be stationed during the liturgy. If the ministers are behind the altar or to the side of it, they lead all the opening rites from there. If, however, they choose to stand in the center of the chancel in front of the Holy Table, they should orient themselves in the same direction as the rest of the assembly, that is, toward the altar except during the acclamation and the dialogue before the Collect of the Day. At those two points, the presider, but not the other ministers, faces the assembly since the presider is addressing it. During prayers, however, the presider is not addressing the assembly but is speaking to God along with and in the name of the assembly and so, with the others, stands facing the symbolic place of God: east, the altar, or the reserved Sacrament. This is not in any way to suggest that God is more in any of those places than God is in the midst of the assembly. It is only to say that, since the liturgy is a *symbolic* action, the body must be used intentionally to symbolize different kinds of speech. A prayer is not a sermon or an announcement, and the way the person stands in the building while praying is an important signal of the distinctions.

THE OPENING ACCLAMATION

The 1979 Book of Common Prayer provides three acclamations: for the Easter season, penitential occasions (especially Lent), and the "green" seasons. *Enriching Our Worship 1* provides variations, and includes a proper acclamation for Advent. In one of the most ancient existing customaries, the first of the early eighth-century *Ordines Romani* (Roman Orders), when the bishop crossed himself in silence at the start of the liturgy, the assembly seemingly was to join him. Many, if not most, Episcopalians have adopted this custom. The sign may be made during any of these acclamations, but is especially fitting for the first acclamation in the Prayer Book because of its Trinitarian language.

If the acolyte is to hold the Altar Book before the presider for the acclamation, it should be brought into place a few seconds in advance so the presider can find the text. Generally, the acclamations are so familiar that the Altar Book may not be needed.

The presider's part of the acclamation is neither a prayer nor a ritual dialogue, but an invitation. It invites the people to a statement acknowledging and praising God. The presider should look at the assembly during the acclamation and not assume the *orans* position. (See "Looking" and "Praying" in chapter 8, "Postures and Gestures.")

THE COLLECT FOR PURITY

In the Sarum usage, the priest recited this prayer in the sacristy before the liturgy, along with other preparatory acts. Archbishop Cranmer moved the prayer into the public part of the rite in the 1552 Prayer Book. In the Collect for Purity the assembly acknowledges that the very ability to celebrate the liturgy is predicated upon God's grace. This text began as a preparatory prayer for the priest but is now a preparatory prayer for the entire community. It is, in any case, optional.

The presider will almost surely know this text by heart and, therefore, may not need the Altar Book. If the book is not used, however, the presider must be careful neither to glance around the room nor to close the eyes during the collect. The advantage of having the Altar Book held before the presider is that it gives the presider a place to focus the eyes, and conveys clearly that this is the church's prayer, not the presider's personal devotion or original composition.

The ancient Christian posture for prayer is standing, with the arms open in the *orans* position. (See "Praying" in chapter 8, "Postures and Gestures.") Symbols work best when they are used consistently, and so the *orans* position should be assumed whenever the presider prays aloud. The acolyte moves away with the book as soon as the people have said the "Amen."

THE HYMN OF PRAISE

Although the *Gloria* and the alternate texts given in the Prayer Book are prayers, it is not customary for the presider to assume the *orans* position during acclamations sung by the assembly. The one-sentence rubric before the *Gloria* includes the words "hymn," "song," and "sung," making it clear that this text is to be rendered musically. The rubric does allow that it may be recited, but that is clearly not the Prayer Book's intention, and for good reason. The overall goal of the opening rites (to unify and prepare the assembly) would not be advanced by people blandly reciting a text. The goal would be more likely achieved with a well-sung metrical hymn than by a recited *Gloria*, *Kyrie*, or *Trisagion*. The rubric allows that "some other song of praise" can be used during most of the year in place of the given texts, and this option should certainly be taken if the alternative is to recite the texts.

The Hymn of Praise is acclamatory in nature. Even the *Kyrie*, which to modern ears might seem like a plea rather than an acclamation, was originally a sort of cheer accorded the emperor as he passed, lauding his lordship and power. The *Kyrie* is an acclamation of God's saving power in Jesus, not a bewailing of our sins.

THE COLLECT OF THE DAY

Near the end of the Hymn of Praise, the acolyte brings the open Altar Book before the presider. With hands joined, the presider looks at the assembly and says the greeting, is greeted in return, and says the invitation to prayer. All of this is a dialogue, and so the presider does not look into the book until after saying, "Let us pray." After a brief pause, the presider assumes the *orans* position and prays in the name of all. When the assembly has prayed the "Amen," the presider waits for the acolyte to close the Altar Book and then returns to the assigned seat. Since all liturgical ministers, including the presider, wait for one another (see "Sitting" in chapter 8, "Postures and Gestures"), the ministers then sit in unison for the Liturgy of the Word.

Chapter 11

THE LITURGY OF THE WORD

IN A NUTSHELL

Necessary Artifacts
- ◆ A Bible or lectionary
- ◆ A binder containing the Prayers of the People

Optional Artifacts
- ◆ A Gospel Book

Necessary Ministers
- ◆ The assembly
- ◆ The presider
- ◆ One lector to proclaim both readings, lead the Psalm, and lead the Prayers of the People
- ◆ A minister ordained to proclaim the Gospel (deacon or priest)
- ◆ An ordained or licensed preacher

Optional Ministers
- ◆ A second lector
- ◆ A Psalmist or a choir/group to lead the Psalm
- ◆ A deacon or other member of the assembly to lead the Prayers of the People
- ◆ Two torch bearers

- A bearer of the Gospel Book
- A thurifer (and boat bearer)
- An instrumentalist

Necessary Liturgical Elements
- Two readings before the Gospel
- A Gospel reading
- A sermon
- The Nicene Creed
- The Prayers of the People
- Confession of Sin (unless it has been said earlier, or a decision has been made to omit it "on occasion")
- A bidding of Peace by the presider

Optional Liturgical Elements
- The exchange of a sign of Peace

What does this part of the rite do?

The Judeo-Christian tradition is based on a conviction that God acts in and through human history and that, in a particular way, God has revealed the Divine Self through the history of the Jewish people. Christians see this divine self-revelation reaching its fullness in Jesus and especially in his Paschal Mystery: the pattern of life triumphing over death, and salvation over sin. In the Liturgy of the Word, the assembly:

- recalls the narrative;
- recognizes itself as part of the narrative;
- acclaims the God who has acted and continues to act;
- asks God to act in specific ways today;
- acknowledges its failure to be the agent of God's saving actions in accordance with the Baptismal Covenant and asks God's forgiveness;
- signifies that, as it has been forgiven, it pledges to be forgiving.

How is this goal accomplished?

This goal is accomplished by the assembly hearing the Judeo-Christian story as its own and asserting its willingness to embody the saving action of God today.

THE FIRST READINGS

PROCLAIMING

1. The assembly having just been seated, the first reading does not begin until they are completely still and focused on the place from which the reading will be proclaimed. This not only allows the rite to do what it is meant to do, but is also a courtesy to the assembly. Whether the readers' seats are with the other liturgical ministers or in the midst of the assembly, the movement to the ambo is paced and deliberate, creating both a pause and a visual focus for the assembly. The reader stands at the ambo in silence until the assembly is still and ready truly to listen.

2. The readers should be rehearsed in how to move to the ambo. They should also be familiar with the lectionary. The liturgical coordinator meets with the readers before the service to point out any anomalies in the day's texts (that one of them is printed in the lectionary under a different liturgical day, for example). At a normal parish Sunday Eucharist, the reader, if well informed and rehearsed, will know when to move to the ambo. To have someone lead the readers to the ambo and then lead them back to their seats suggests that the liturgical ministers are incompetent and encourages them to be incompetent. At some special services, a person from outside the Episcopal Church or even a visiting Episcopalian who does not know the congregation's patterns may be asked to read. In that case, it may be helpful to have a minister (usually the master of ceremonies or verger) escort the reader to the ambo at the appropriate time.

3. The reader announces the reading. The Prayer Book allows the reader to say either, "A Reading from," or "A Lesson from," and then to name the book. The word "lesson" in this case is an Anglicization of the word "lection" (reading). The two options, then, mean exactly the same thing. To modern ears, however, the word "lesson" does not mean "reading," but most often implies a hard-earned and often painful learning: "That will teach you a lesson." Thus the simple English word "reading" conveys the more accurate sense.

4. The Prayer Book allows the citing of chapter and verse. Unless the assembly is following along in Bibles, this is extraneous and distracting.

5. The reader should not glance around the room during the proclamation, as if what is being said were the reader's own words. The eyes should be kept on the book.

6. The reader pauses slightly after the announcement, proclaims the text, pauses slightly again, and says the concluding statement, such as "Hear what the Spirit is saying to God's People" (*Enriching Our Worship 1*, 53). A number of concluding statements are given in the Prayer Book and in *Enriching Our Worship 1*. All but one—"Here ends the Reading (Epistle)"—require the response, "Thanks be to God." The statements that elicit a response are preferable since they allow the people to acclaim and assent to what they have heard, supporting the overall intention of this part of the liturgy. Since this statement is addressed to the assembly, the reader looks at the assembly while speaking and continues looking at them during the response. The reader moves from the ambo only after the assembly has responded.

RESPONDING

1. "Silence may follow" each of the readings (BCP 357). Since the Liturgy of the Word is not only meant to convey historical or theological information, but also to allow the assembly to find its place within the Judeo-Christian narrative, this silence is crucial. It allows those who have heard the text to listen for echoes in their own lives and experience of what they have heard. In a sense, the silence allows the members of the assembly mentally to compose their own sermons—their own personal applications of the text—and it creates a context in which they can listen for the voice and search for the movement of God. Such a silence must be far more protracted than a momentary pause. Catechesis about sacred silence will help the assembly to understand the potential of this often neglected and omitted liturgical action. It is pastorally wise to increase the length of the silence only gradually. Since silence is uncommon in this culture and even in church, inserting too much silence too quickly can cause the assembly to become uncomfortable, or to wonder if someone has forgotten what to do next. Even a year may be needed gradually to extend the periods of silence after each reading to a full minute. Anything less than a minute, however, does not allow for the depth of contemplation upon which the success of the Liturgy of the Word depends.

2. After each reading, "A Psalm, hymn, or anthem" may follow. This triad suggests music. Even though the Psalms are sometimes recited in worship, they are, in fact, intended to be sung. The introduction to the Psalter in the Prayer Book allows for the recitation, rather than the singing, of psalmody, but the genre itself suggests that this is not ideal (BCP 582). As the introduction to the Psalter in *Evangelical Lutheran Worship*, which is based on the Prayer Book Psalter, says, "Their meaning can certainly be communicated when spoken or read silently, yet this ancient poetry is inherently musical." Moreover, nowhere in any Episcopal lectionary, whether for the Eucharist on Sundays, festivals, or weekdays, or for the Daily Office, are psalms given as readings.

Whatever comes between the readings, then, is to be sung. While the Prayer Book allows for anthems (apparently pieces rendered by the choir) between the readings, the assembly as a whole should be given opportunities to respond to the proclamations. Care must be taken not to miss this important goal of the Liturgy of the Word. If, for example, a choir anthem intervenes between the first two readings, congregational song should come between the second reading and the Gospel.

The Prayer Book directions Concerning the Psalter describe four methods by which psalmody can be rendered (BCP 582). Musical settings are readily available for all of the lectionary Psalms in each of these styles. Church canons authorize the use of many versions of the Bible for liturgical *readings*, but are not clear whether this extends to the Psalms. In his authoritative *Commentary on the American Prayer Book*, Marion Hatchett suggests that it does when he notes that the versification of the Prayer Book Psalter must guide the use of other versions, which may versify or even number the Psalms differently.[10] Moreover, in the Additional Directions for the Daily Office, permission is given for using even metrical versions of the Invitatory Psalm and the canticles after the readings (BCP 141). This suggests that the Prayer Book is open to various translations and forms of the Psalms. The many musical settings of the Psalms in all the authorized versions provide a rich resource for enriching Episcopal worship.

Responsorial psalmody has a great deal to recommend it. These settings are especially plentiful, and the recurring antiphon allows even preliterate children and visually impaired worshippers to participate by hearing and repeating. A strong cantor or schola is key to successful responsorial psalmody. In the Roman Church especially, cantors often gesture to the assembly when the antiphon is to be sung. This is entirely unnecessary if the music is well crafted, making the place for the antiphon obvious. To tell the assembly what to do except when it is absolutely necessary, even by a nonverbal cue, promises to render them passive and liturgically incompetent. Visitors and seekers, of course, will need direction, but this can be given in a well-designed and rubricated order of worship. Besides, visitors who find themselves in a competent and hospitable assembly can easily follow the rite by following those around them.

Many contemporary liturgies, including *Evangelical Lutheran Worship* and the Roman Rite, explicitly suggest a sung Alleluia before the proclamation of the Gospel, except during Lent. *Common Worship: Services and Prayers for the Church of England* suggests it also when it says, "An acclamation may herald the Gospel reading" (252). *Enriching Our Music 1*, published for the Episcopal Church by the Standing Commission on Liturgy and Music in 2003, contains musical settings for a pre-Gospel acclamatory Alleluia, along with "Alleluia verses" for every Sunday in the three-year lectionary cycle (144ff). More musical settings are provided in *Enriching Our Music 2* (2004). As with responsorial psalmody, an extensive body of ecumenical music is readily available for the acclamatory Alleluia. The same setting can be repeated, perhaps for an entire season, once again making it possible for those who cannot read words or music to participate fully,

10. Hatchett, *Commentary on the American Prayer Book*, 35.

confidently, and competently. Also, as with responsorial psalmody, a skilled cantor or choir is essential to a successful performance. When neither is available, a strong metrical hymn will have more of an acclamatory impact than a weak or recited Alleluia with a verse.

The assembly remains seated for both readings and the responses, unless the responses are metrical hymns or acclamatory Alleluias. For those genres of responses, the assembly stands.

THE PROCLAMATION OF THE GOSPEL

1. The Prayer Book directs the assembly to stand for the proclamation of the Gospel. If an acclamatory Alleluia or a metrical hymn precedes the Gospel, the sound of the instruments is the cue for the entire assembly—both the ministers and the others—to stand together. If there is no acclamatory music, the presider stands as the cue for the others to stand.

2. If incense is to be used, and the thurible is to be charged in the view of the assembly, the thurible and boat are brought to the presider during the music. A service that does not merit music does not merit incense.

3. If there is to be a procession with the Gospel Book, it takes place during the music. In some places, the procession forms during a hymn or anthem, and then moves during an acclamatory Alleluia. In most congregations, simplicity is best. One piece of music suffices.

The Gospel Book is the visual focus of the Gospel procession and a primary symbol of Christ present in the midst of the people. It is the only symbol that is carried. A processional cross is only a distraction in this case and is not carried in the Gospel procession.

4. A deacon assisting at the liturgy proclaims the Gospel. The Roman Rite directs the deacon to ask a blessing from the presider before taking the book. This custom is observed in some Episcopal congregations, though because deacons are given the "authority to proclaim God's Word" (BCP 545) by the bishop at ordination, and minister "directly under [the] bishop" (BCP 543), this gesture can be misleading, suggesting that the deacon ministers at the behest of the presiding presbyter. If, however, the parish understands the ecclesiology of the Episcopal Church and understands that

the blessing is not a sort of quasi-ordination or commissioning, the Roman form is a logical one to use.

◆ After the thurible has been charged, and as the members of the processional party move into place, the deacon stands before the presider. Looking directly at the presider, the deacon requests, "N., give me your blessing." (In the Roman Missal, the request is, "Father, give me your blessing." In the Book of Common Prayer rite, this is adjusted according to the gender and preference of the presider: Father, Mother, Brother, Sister, or the Christian name of the presider.)

◆ The deacon then makes a profound bow to receive the blessing, as the presider says, "The Lord be in your heart and on your lips that you may worthily proclaim his gospel." Then, making the sign of the cross over the deacon, the presider adds, "In the name of the Father, and of the Son, and of the Holy Spirit."

◆ The deacon responds, "Amen," and moves immediately to take up the Gospel Book.

5. A common way for the procession to be arrayed, whether the presider, another presbyter, or a deacon is the gospeller, is:

ALTAR

Torch—Gospeller—Torch
Thurifer

If the Gospel is to be proclaimed in the midst of the people, a person other than the one who will proclaim it may walk in front of the gospeller and then, while the Gospel is being proclaimed, hold the book open. This must be done if incense is to be used so the gospeller's hands will be free to take the thurible. A common way for the procession to be arrayed is:

ALTAR

Torch—Gospeller with Gospel Book—Torch
Book Bearer
Thurifer

6. When all are in place facing the Lord's Table, the ministers watch for the gospeller to take up the book and turn away from the altar (toward liturgical west). They turn in unison with the gospeller, and the procession begins.

The gospeller holds the book overhead, just as one would hold a cross, until the procession reaches the place of the proclamation. Various places are possible. While it has become customary in most congregations for the Gospel to be proclaimed from the midst of the people, the Additional Directions for the Eucharist do not list this as the preferred option: "It is desirable that the Lessons be read from a lectern or pulpit, and that the Gospel be read from the same lectern, or from the pulpit, or from the midst of the congregation" (BCP 406). This preference for all the readings to be proclaimed from a single lectern is repeated in *The Church for Common Prayer*: "A single prominent piece of furniture for reading and proclaiming the word should be located so that the congregation can hear and maintain eye contact with the speaker. Space around the pulpit should be open enough to allow for a procession with the gospel book." Clearly, the expectation is that the procession will move to the lectern, not into the midst of the people, and that the Gospel will be proclaimed from there. Still, this is not the only allowable option and so a pastoral choice must be made among three options.

◆ The use of a single lectern emphasizes that the Word proclaimed in all the texts is the same, and that the narrative is unified. In most spaces, the lectern is elevated and equipped with a microphone. This makes the proclamation visually and aurally accessible.

◆ The use of a pulpit apart from the lectern emphasizes that the Gospel is not like the other readings. Since the pulpit is usually elevated and larger than the lectern, it creates the impression that the Gospel is not only different but also superior, that is, above. It also heightens visibility and audibility, as the lectern does.

◆ The proclamation of the Gospel from the midst of the people creates the sense that Christ is living in the midst of the assembly. It brings the members of the assembly face to face, with the proclaimed Word at their center: the unifying force. In a large room, however, this arrangement can make it difficult and even impossible for some members of the assembly, including children, to see the person proclaiming the Gospel. If it also makes it impossible or difficult for some to *hear* the proclamation, this arrangement will have done a major disservice to the assembly and undercut one of the primary aims of the Liturgy of the Word.

7. The processional path and the way the ministers will array themselves for the reading will depend upon many factors, including the width of the space and the various levels on which the ministers will stand. For example, if the Gospel is to be read from the aisle, the width of the aisle will determine how the processional party can be arranged. If it is to be read from an elevated pulpit, it may be necessary for the torches to stand below the pulpit. In any case, the general arrangement when the procession ends is:

Thurifer—Gospeller
Torch—Gospel Book/Book Bearer—Torch

In most worship spaces, this will put the thurifer and gospeller facing liturgical west, book bearer facing liturgical east (or the book on the reading desk), and the torch bearers turned inward, facing the book.

The hymn must be long enough to cover the entire Gospel procession, including the preparation of the incense and the blessing of the deacon. If it is not, interludes are inserted. If an acclamatory Alleluia is added, the procession moves as it is sung.

If the proclamation is being made from the aisle and a person other than the gospeller is holding the book, the gospeller may need to adjust the height and angle of the Gospel Book.

8. Just after the processional music ends, the gospeller announces the reading, using the formula either in the Prayer Book or in *Enriching Our Worship 1*, and makes the triple sign of the cross, if it is the custom. (See chapter 8, "Postures and Gestures.") After the assembly responds, the thurifer, if incense is to be used, passes the thurible to the gospeller, who censes the Gospel Book. (See chapter 8, "Postures and Gestures.") The thurifer then takes the thurible, and moves behind the gospeller. Throughout the reading, the thurifer swings the thurible slightly from side to side.

9. With hands joined if the proclamation is in the midst of the people, or with hands resting on the reading desk if it is from the lectern or pulpit, the gospeller proclaims the text, keeping the eyes in the book. The reader does not open the arms into the *orans*, since this is a proclamation and not a prayer.

10. At the end of the reading, the gospeller pauses slightly, looks at the assembly, and says, "The Gospel of the Lord." After the assembly has acclaimed the Christ they have encountered in the proclamation, the gospeller kisses the page of the book, if it is the custom. This can be done while the book bearer is holding the book, or the gospeller may take the book, kiss it, and then pass it back to the book bearer. This is the better solution if a child is holding the book and the gospeller could not easily or gracefully bow low enough to kiss it.

When saying, "The Gospel of the Lord," the reader does *not* elevate the book. The assembly is being invited to acclaim the Lord Christ present in the event that is taking place, not in the book. In other words, "The Gospel of the Lord" suggests that "You have just encountered the Gospel of the Lord, living and active," not, "This book is the Gospel of the Lord." The Gospel proclaimed in the assembly is an event—the revelation and action of Christ—not an object. Raising the Gospel Book during the concluding acclamation makes no more sense than raising the lectionary during the phrase, "The Word of the Lord."

11. The procession then essentially reverses, with the Gospel Book again held on high. At the end of the procession:

◆ The preacher will have moved to the place from which the sermon will be delivered. (The preacher may not be the same person who proclaimed the Gospel.)

◆ The gospeller, if not also the preacher, will have returned to the assigned seat.

◆ The torches and the thurible will be returned to their places, and the torch bearers and the thurifer will be at their seats.

◆ The Gospel Book will have been left on the reading desk from which the sermon will be delivered, or will have been set in another place of honor, but not on the altar.

How all of this will proceed will depend on any number of factors that must be worked out in each particular case. Always, however:

◆ The thurifer leads the movement.

◆ The ordained minister walks at the end of the procession.

◆ The torches accompany the Gospel Book or, if the book is to be left on the reading desk from which the Gospel was proclaimed, the torches walk side by side.

For example, if the Gospel is proclaimed from the midst of the assembly and the gospeller is also the preacher, the procession after the proclamation proceeds in this way.

◆ The gospeller steps to the side.

◆ The thurifer turns around and moves in the direction from which the procession came, usually liturgical east.

◆ The torches and the bearer of the Gospel Book follow the thurifer, moving past the gospeller.

◆ The gospeller takes up the rear.

◆ The torch bearers accompany the Gospel Book to the place where it will be placed, or they stand the torches on either side of the altar while the Gospel Book is being set in a place of honor.

◆ The gospeller goes to the lectern or pulpit and, only after the other ministers have returned to their seats, begins the sermon.

THE SERMON

The sermon holds a middle ground between proclamation and response. It is a prophetic, contemplative grappling with how God is acting in the assembly's particular time and place in the light of God's action in the biblical record. The sermon explores how, by virtue of baptism, the assembly had been called to participate in God's ongoing saving work. Liturgical preaching is not about texts or the past but about people and the present. Paul Marshall, now the Bishop of Bethlehem and formerly professor of homiletics at Yale, writes that the church does not need sermons about biblical archeology: "The sunset [in Jerusalem] or ancient domestic arrangements may help illustrate a useful sermon, but the focus needs to be our growth into the full stature of Christ and what that concept means in the world today."[11] How is God in Christ, present in the church through the Spirit, continuing the saving work exemplified in the biblical texts? The task of the preacher is not to answer this question definitively. Rather, it is to invite the assembly to hold in tension the ancient record of God's action, the current situation of the world, and the hope celebrated in the Eucharist. In the sermon, Bible, liturgy, and life are entwined.

Because of the role of the Bible in this triad, the sermon is generally preached from the same place where the Scripture has been proclaimed. A visual link should be made between the proclamation and the preaching. Some preachers prefer to deliver the sermon from the chancel step or from the midst of the people. In some pastoral situations, this may have value. It can, however, impede visibility and audibility, and can easily convey the impression that the sermon is not integrally linked to the rest of the liturgy and the proclaimed Scripture.

1. The sermon should follow directly upon the proclamation of the Gospel since it is a direct response to it. If there is a sequence hymn, it should not be broken, with half coming before the Gospel and half coming after it. Instrumental processional music accompanies the movement of the ministers as they travel from the place where the Gospel was proclaimed to their next stations.

2. The custom of beginning the sermon with the sign of the cross, a prayer, or a verse began at a time when sermons were not delivered during the Eucharist. They were preached after it or entirely apart from it. Something had to mark the beginning, and these three devices came to be used. Since the Reformation churches, and now the

---

11. Paul Marshall, *Preaching for the Church Today* (New York: Church Publishing, 1990), 41f.

Roman Church, restored the sermon to its proper place in the liturgy, these devices have become the poetic equivalent of asking the assembly to sit down. They are certainly better than the clumsy, "Please be seated." In order to place as little distraction as possible between the Gospel and the sermon, however, the briefer and more formulaic the cue, the better. Long quotes, and especially protracted and self-referential prayers, create a space between the rest of the liturgy and the sermon, and draw attention to the preacher rather than the preaching.

3. After the sermon, the preacher returns to the assigned seat. If the sermon has successfully brought to light the action of God in the world, and invited the assembly to both an interior and an exterior response, a period of silence paralleling the silence after the readings is important, and for the same reason. Deep realities and significant challenges do not settle into the heart and mind quickly or easily. Whether the members of the assembly find themselves more comforted or convicted, they deserve a time for listening to the Mystery reverberating among them after the sermon. Other liturgical traditions recognize this, even though the Prayer Book—always spare on rubrics—does not. Both the Presbyterian *Book of Common Worship* and *Evangelical Lutheran Worship* include a rubric suggesting silence at this point in the rite. *The United Methodist Book of Worship* in "An Order of Sunday Worship" lists silence as one of the appropriate responses to the sermon. Similarly, the *General Instruction of the Roman Missal* directs that "After the homily a brief period of silence is appropriately observed." So that the members of the assembly, including the preacher, can rest and reflect on the experience of the Word present in their midst, nothing less than a full minute of silence will suffice.

The preacher is seated with the rest of the assembly for the period of silence, and models a relaxed contemplative posture. Unlike during prayers, the preacher may close the eyes in meditation.

4. If the Creed is to be recited, not sung, the presider stands when sufficient silence has passed. This cues the assembly to stand. It is important that the assisting ministers do not close their eyes during the silence so they can remain attentive to the presider and poised to stand. If the Creed is to be sung, however, the sounding of the instruments is the cue for the entire assembly, including the presider, to stand. This means that the director of the instrumentalists and the presider must agree in advance how long the silence should last, or must agree to trust one another's judgment.

THE NICENE CREED

The Nicene Creed was composed at the Council of Nicea (325) to denounce heresy, and was redacted by the Council of Chalcedon (451) further to clarify the orthodox faith. It was not intended to be a liturgical formula, and made its way only gradually into the Eucharist, becoming nearly universal only seven hundred years after it was written. Some Protestants have historically rejected it as being non-scriptural and thus not appropriate for worship, although in the ecumenical spirit of the Liturgical Movement, it has been widely reintroduced. Among Anglicans, with fleeting exceptions, it was never suppressed.

Pastorally, the Nicene Creed can present significant challenges. Its precise and arcane language can alienate some seekers and even some baptized Christians, who see it as a test of orthodoxy that counts them in or out. A number opt out, feeling that they cannot in conscience publicly and formally declare what they do not believe. Others pick and choose among the articles of the Creed, saying some, not saying others, and even altering some according to their personal belief. This crisis of conscience is born at least in part of a modern mindset that does not recognize that all religious language is metaphorical or analogical. The Creed seems to many people to be a scientific or mathematical formula that is true or not according to laboratory-like standards. A troubled member of my own parish, to give a vivid example, came to me suffering a genuine crisis of conscience because in a universe where the notions of up and down are meaningless he thought it was absurd to say, as the Creed does, that Jesus "ascended into heaven." He also did not believe that "heaven" is a physical place to which one can go, whether by ascending or descending. This created a genuine crisis for him. He believed that because he could not assent to the *literal* sense of the Creed, he could not recite it and, therefore, he could not remain a member of the liturgical assembly. This thoughtful, deeply principled man is not unique. Believing that "the church" inserted the Creed in the liturgy precisely to alienate and exclude people like him, he had concluded that he did not belong.

Without contradicting even one word of the Creed, parish clergy and other religious educators can ease the consciences of many faithful Christians by exploring in religious formation programs and sermons the nature of all religious speech: that it is an attempt to express in language what is ultimately beyond the scope of human understanding. Within the liturgy, the most fertile solution is to treat the Creed like an acclamation, not a manifesto. I credit my own bishop, Paul Marshall, with the insight that by singing, rather than reciting, the Creed, the assembly experiences it as an acclamation of what it has experienced in the proclamation of the Word. *The Hymnal 1982* provides three musical arrangements of the Creed; especially the setting by Calvin Hampton (S-105) creates a sense of festivity and acclamation, and undercuts any notion that the Creed, at least in its liturgical use, is a series of loyalty tests.

1. Two gestures—neither mentioned in the Prayer Book—are sometimes performed during the Creed.

◆ During the words "by the power of the Holy Spirit he became incarnate from the Virgin Mary, and was made man," a genuflection or, more commonly, a profound bow, is made. (In the current Roman rubrics, the genuflection is only made on Christmas and the Feast of the Annunciation, although it was previously made whenever the Creed was recited. Now, the bow suffices.) This phrase in the Creed celebrates what is commonly called "the divine condescension," that is, the willingness of God to humble Godself for the sake of humanity. In awe before such divine humility, the assembly humbles itself and makes a symbolic gesture of gratitude. In communities where this sort of piety is common and acceptable, the entire assembly should be invited to participate in it, and catechesis should be provided. If only the presider or the ministers would perform the gesture, it is better omitted. Since the entire assembly celebrates the liturgy, every attempt should be made to avoid gestures that isolate or singularize some members. (This general principle does not apply, of course, to gestures that must be performed by a minister in the exercise of the ministry.)

◆ At the end of the Creed, during the phrase "and the life of the world to come," some Episcopalians cross themselves. This gesture has ancient precedent and was included in the rubrics of the Tridentine Mass, but it is not part of the current Roman Rite. *Ritual Notes*, the widely circulated Catholic Revival rubrical guide to the Prayer Book, also has this directive. It came into the modern Anglican tradition during the nineteenth century. The meaning is obscure: Is it an attempt to ward off death? A fearful reaction to the mention of the dead? A reminder that one is sealed with the cross against "the great and dreadful day"? The custom is becoming less and less common, and is certainly not part of the ecumenical Western pattern.

THE PRAYERS OF THE PEOPLE

The Prayers of the People are intercessions made, in the language of the Prayer Book, "for the whole state of Christ's Church and the world" (BCP 328). They are not prayers *about* the assembled people or their personal concerns, but, instead, are prayers *by* the assembled people for the entire created order. They are an exercise of the baptismal priesthood.

1. One of the four places when announcements can be made is just before the Prayers of the People; they can also be made before the liturgy, before the Offertory, or at the end of the service (BCP 407). Making announcements before the prayers allows people to explain material in the prayers that may not be readily understood. This is especially appropriate if something, such as a death, will be mentioned that may confuse or shock the assembly and distract it from prayer. Practical announcements, however, should be made at another time in the service.

2. The pulpit and lectern are for the proclamation and preaching of the Word, and may be used for the Prayers of the People. They are not for reading announcements. These pieces of furniture are treated as sacred because they are used for a sacred purpose. Because they are treated as sacred, the reverence for what happens at them is heightened.

3. The Prayer Book explicitly requires that six categories of need be included in the Prayers of the People (BCP 359):
   - The church
   - The nation
   - The world
   - The local community
   - The suffering and troubled
   - The dead, with an optional commemoration of a saint, presumably the local patron or the saint of the day.

4. Since deacons are ordained "to interpret to the Church the needs, concerns, and hopes of the world" (BCP 543) and have traditionally been the leader of liturgical intercessions, the deacon is the appropriate leader of the Prayers of the People.

5. The forms appended to the liturgy illustrate the various ways the Prayers of the People can be constructed. Since the Prayers of the People should be timely and concrete, the

given forms are best understood as models to be followed, not actual liturgical texts to be read. The forms are:

◆ Form I: biddings, that is, invitations, addressed to the assembly in the style of a litany, with a repeating response, followed by silence and a collect.

◆ Form II: biddings addressed to the assembly, with a time of silence after each when the members of the assembly may pray silently or aloud.

◆ Form III: a responsive reading, alternating between the leader and the assembly, concluding with free prayer and a collect.

◆ Form IV: a series of prayers, each followed by silence and a repeating versicle and response, concluding with a collect.

◆ Form V: a litany addressed to God with a repeating response, followed by silence and a collect.

◆ Form VI: a responsive reading, alternating between the leader and the assembly, ending with free prayer, leading directly to an optional prayer for forgiveness (that substitutes for the Confession), with the absolution or a collect.

6. It is common for the leader of the Prayers of the People to stand in the midst of the assembly, suggesting that these are truly the prayers of the *people*, lay and ordained. Especially in longitudinally arranged and chancelled churches, focusing the liturgical action in various parts of the room has the advantage of conveying that the liturgy is celebrated by all who are present, not just those in the sanctuary. It is important, however, that the leader be audible.

7. After time has been allowed for prayer intentions to be explained, the deacon or presider signals that the actual prayers are about to begin by saying, "Let us pray," "Let us pray for the church and the world," or a similar brief phrase.

◆ The assembly stands and the leader moves quickly into place. When the assembly is still, the leader begins.

◆ When a silence is called for, it must be long enough for the people to actually do what they are being asked to do: to call to mind and mention specific needs in each of the categories. If the leader works to bring concrete needs to mind during each pause even as the assembly is doing it, the leader will have a good sense of when to move on to the next unit. The presider and the liturgical planning group may decide, however, that it is best to predetermine the duration of the periods of silence. If so, this must be communicated to the leader and, ideally, should be indicated in the printed text from which the leader reads.

◆ When the leader invites the assembly to mention needs, these should be spoken distinctly so that all present can make intercession for what is being proposed. Often, the members of the assembly mutter personal prayers during these pauses. While this is not a destructive pattern, neither does it encourage the entire assembly to exercise its priesthood by praying for the needs of the church and the world of which all the members may not be aware. In religious formation and preaching, the leaders of the community can explore how the Prayers of the People are an opportunity to solicit the prayers of the entire community for wide-ranging needs.

◆ When the prayers include biddings—such as Forms I through V—as the biddings end, the presider, remaining at the chair, opens the arms in the *orans*, says the concluding collect, and joins the hands just before the assembly's "Amen." If Form VI is used, however, members of the assembly may kneel when they are invited to pray for the forgiveness of their sins. The ministers also kneel, or, as noted in the next section, they may profoundly bow. A period of silence long enough for the people to actually call to mind their sins and sinfulness—at least a full minute—is allowed. The leader then reads the first line of the prayer, and the assembly continues. Near the end of the prayer, the presider stands, faces the assembly, and, after the "Amen," pronounces the absolution. (The manual gestures for this are described in the next section on Confession.) After the absolution, the people stand.

◆ The leader stays in place, standing or kneeling with the rest of the assembly, until after the collect or the absolution.

THE CONFESSION OF SIN

The Confession of Sin is normally celebrated after the Prayers of the People, unless the liturgy has begun with the Penitential Order (BCP 351). The use of the Penitential Order at the beginning of the service establishes a penitential tone for the entire liturgy, and is especially appropriate for Lent. In general, however, it is better for the Confession to follow the Prayers of the People. That placement ties the words of reconciliation to the gesture of reconciliation, the Peace, which follows immediately.

The Confession may be omitted "on occasion" (BCP 359). The Council of Nicea (325) forbade kneeling during the entire Fifty Days of Easter, and so the Easter season could well be considered an appropriate time for omitting the Confession. Other great feasts are similarly appropriate.

1. After the Prayers of the People, the presider may read one of the Scripture sentences from the Penitential Order. If so, an acolyte holds the Altar Book before the presider, open to the appropriate page. In general, however, it is best to omit nonessential texts, especially in a word-laden section of the rite. Since three readings, a sermon, the Creed if not sung, the announcements, and the Prayers have just been read, more words would only be burdensome.

2. The deacon or the presider, looking at the assembly, invites them to confess their sins.

3. The entire assembly, including the ministers, kneel. If it is not possible for the ministers to kneel because of their vestments or a lack of kneeling cushions, they make a profound bow in unison and remain bowed as long as the rest of the assembly is kneeling.

4. The Prayer Book then notes that "silence may be kept." In order for the assembly to engage its heart and mind in a genuine act of penitence, this silence is crucial. It must be lengthy enough that the prayer of confession that follows will emerge from a genuine and concrete awareness of failure to live the baptized life. Like all periods of silence in the liturgy, the silence for considering the sinfulness of one's life cannot be imposed all at once. Pastoral discretion and a plan gradually to build to a suitable silence will be necessary. Catechesis will help the assembly to know how to engage this silence, since to many it will seem unusual and potentially uncomfortable.

5. The deacon or presider reads the first line of the prayer of confession, and the entire assembly takes up the rest. In addition to the form given in the Prayer Book, *Enriching Our Worship 1* provides a text that is more focused on social sin.

6. Near the end of the prayer of confession, the presider stands and faces the assembly. If the presider is stationed anywhere but on the central axis of the room, the presider moves to the center as the prayer is nearing its close.

7. If the presider does not know the formula of absolution by heart, an acolyte stands at the same time and holds the Altar Book before the presider, open to the absolution. Looking at the people, the presider addresses them in the words of the absolution. Since this is a blessing, it is customary to trace the sign of the cross over the assembly as the text is read (see chapter 8, "Postures and Gestures"). The tracing of the sign should be paced to coincide with the length of the absolution. At the end, the presider brings the right hand back to the left, which has been resting on the chest.

THE PEACE

The people then stand for the exchange of the Peace.

1. The presider, looking at the people, opens the arms expansively, and wishes them the peace of the Lord. This gesture is not like the *orans*. In this gesture, the presider reaches outward, as one does toward approaching friends. The presider continues looking at the assembly until they have responded to the greeting.

2. Although the rite does not mandate, but only allows, the people to greet one another, the option is almost universally taken. The Peace is a gesture of equality and mutual respect based in a common baptism. While the presider and other ministers must take care not to isolate themselves from the rest of the assembly during the Peace, neither should they circulate widely about the room as if their greeting of Peace was "special." This delays the liturgy and is contrary to the baptismal ecclesiology of the Prayer Book. It is important that the clergy and the other vested ministers model at this time that they are members of the baptized community, not its upper caste whose greeting counts for more than anyone else's. The Peace is a symbolic gesture that need not be personal and should not be protracted. (See chapter 8, "Postures and Gestures.")

◆ It may be necessary for a signal to be established to end the Peace, such as a bell, if the community has a tendency to make it protracted. If the group responsible for preparing and leading the liturgy determines that the Peace has grown disproportionate to the rest of the rite or has become a social event rather than a ritual gesture, careful and sensitive catechesis should come before any heavy-handed attempts to rein it in.

3. The people are seated after the Peace. If no signal has been given that the Peace is completed, the assembly will need a cue to sit. In general, while straightforward directions are efficient, they are not graceful and put the presider in an unnecessarily controlling role. "Please be seated" is not the best option. An offertory sentence is a better one, or the beginning of the offertory music, unless a brief announcement (see below) is to be made at this point, in which case some directive will be needed. The important thing is that there be a demarcation when the community moves from standing precisely as a community to when it is seated as a community. The Peace, like the rest of the liturgy, is a common action, not a private one, and so people should not take their seats when

they decide individually that they have had enough. They should take their seats as a body.

ANNOUNCEMENTS

The Additional Directions for the Eucharist allow announcements to be made at this point. Pastoral comments related to Holy Communion, especially explaining that all people are welcome to approach the Lord's Table for a blessing or to receive the Sacrament, and to give instructions as to how that may be done, are especially appropriate here. In general, however, protracted announcements, especially concerning mundane topics (such as a parish fundraiser or parking policies), do not belong here. They are an intrusion into the liturgy and, paired with the Peace, can make both seem like a "time out" or an intermission rather than integral ritual moments.

Chapter 12

THE LITURGY
OF THE EUCHARIST

IN A NUTSHELL

Necessary Artifacts
- ◆ A vessel containing bread
- ◆ A chalice containing wine, with a purificator
- ◆ The Altar Book

Optional Artifacts
- ◆ A flagon of wine
- ◆ A vessel of water for the admixture
- ◆ The vessels for the lavabo: a bowl of water or an empty bowl and a pitcher of water, and a towel for drying the presider's hands
- ◆ A thurible and boat

Necessary Ministers
- ◆ The assembly
- ◆ The presider
- ◆ An acolyte or a deacon to move the vessels to the Lord's Table at the Offertory and fraction and to place the Altar Book on it, to assist with the lavabo, and to perform numerous other tasks
- ◆ Ministers to gather the assembly's offerings and bring them to the Holy Table

Optional Ministers
- ◆ A team of acolytes to divide the tasks among them
- ◆ Eucharistic ministers

Necessary Liturgical Elements
- ◆ The placing of the bread and wine on the altar
- ◆ The Great Thanksgiving, during which the presider must touch the bread and wine
- ◆ The breaking of the Bread and the pouring of the Wine into chalices, if more than one is needed
- ◆ A fraction anthem
- ◆ The invitation to Communion
- ◆ The administration and reception of Communion
- ◆ The postcommunion prayer

Optional Liturgical Elements
- ◆ The censing of the bread, wine, monetary offerings, the Holy Table, the ministers, and the rest of the assembly
- ◆ The lavabo

What does this part of the rite do?

In the Liturgy of the Eucharist, Christ welcomes the church into communion with himself even as he unites the members in a profoundly intimate way with one another. As they are shaped more perfectly into the image of Christ, they are sent as his Body to serve the world and proclaim the Good News.

How is this goal accomplished?

As the assembly offers its sacrifice—its thanks and praise for the saving acts of God in history, and especially what God accomplished in Jesus—Jesus joins their sacrifice to his one, sufficient sacrifice. By the outpouring of the Holy Spirit, bread and wine become the means by which Jesus becomes tangibly present to the assembly, and by partaking of these gifts, the community gives itself to Christ that they corporately might be his Body in the world today.

PREPARING THE TABLE

1. The presider may signal the beginning of the Offertory by proclaiming one of the offertory sentences given in the Prayer Book, or some other sentence of Scripture, or the invitation, "Let us with gladness" (BCP 376–377). These sentences all mark the transition between the Liturgy of the Word and the Liturgy of the Table, and cue the assembly to be seated. None of this is necessary if there is offertory music. As the assembly is seated, the presider and the ministers not directly involved in the preparation of the Table are seated also. Only the deacon or liturgical minister who will prepare the Holy Table, the acolytes who will assist in the preparation, and the ministers who will collect the monetary offerings remain standing.

2. The collection is begun. In some congregations the oblationers bring the bread and wine to the deacon or acolyte prior to the collection so the minister can begin preparing the bread and wine at the altar while the collection is taking place. However, at this point in the Offertory all that is needed is for the Table to be set, and the Prayer Book rubric would seem rather to envision a single offering of bread, wine, and money presented as one.

3. During the collection, if a corporal was not spread on the Lord's Table before the liturgy, the deacon or acolytes spread it now. The purpose of the corporal is to catch crumbs that fall from the eucharistic Bread and splatters of the Wine. Corporals are often reused a number of times between launderings, and crumbs can accumulate. To ensure that crumbs are not scattered, the folded corporal is placed in the very center of the table and unfolded flap by flap. It is not shaken open above the altar.

4. The acolytes bring a chalice with a purificator and the Altar Book to the Lord's Table. The purificator is set on the corporal, aligned with the lower right corner. The Altar Book and the chalice (and the bread and wine that will soon be carried to the altar) can be arranged in a number of ways. Each arrangement functions differently. What is optimal in each pastoral situation will depend upon a number of personal and architectural factors. Experimentation, especially during rehearsal, will make the best solution clear.

   ◆ The most common arrangement is to place the Altar Book on a stand to the left of the corporal, and to set the chalice, flagon, and bread on the corporal.

This arrangement elevates the book and makes it easier for some presiders to read the text. It also makes the Altar Book evident and signals that the presider is reciting the church's prayer, not one of his or her own devising. It forces the presider to look away from the central axis, however, which weakens the visual focus on the bread and wine. In many cases, the book-stand is so large or ornate that it visually competes with the vessels containing the elements—the essential objects.

◆ The Altar Book can be placed flat at the center of the altar edge nearest the presider, with the chalice, bread, and flagon beyond it. Because the presider looks straight ahead when the book is in the center of the altar, this arrangement

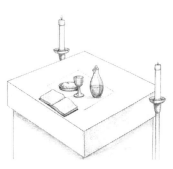

creates a strong, focused visual impact. The presider's eyes and body, as well as the eucharistic elements, align on the central axis. In addition, this arrangement, because it puts the elements further from the presider, relates them more to the assembly as a whole. They stand between the presider and the rest of the assembly and, because they are the largest and most elevated items on the Table, they become the visual focus. Unless the Altar Book is placed with some deliberation, however, this arrangement can make it seem that the presider is praying an extemporaneous prayer rather than the church's liturgical text. Furthermore, reading from a flat book can be difficult for some people and might cause the presider's head to be bowed over the book for most of the Eucharistic Prayer, unless the presider stands some steps back from the altar.

◆ The Altar Book can be placed flat on the altar, on the far edge of the corporal, with the chalice and the other items between it and the presider. This allows a central visual focus, and allows the presider to raise the head and eyes more than if the book is on the near edge of the altar. The vessels can block the presider's view of the book, however, and turning the pages with the altar arranged this

way threatens to topple the chalice. This arrangement also relates the elements more to the presider alone than to the assembly as a whole.

5. In some places, the unfortunate practice has arisen of filling the chalice from a cruet or flagon brought from the credence while the collection is being taken. This is apparently to "get it out of the way" before the gifts are brought forward. The Prayer Book clearly directs, however, that one flagon is to be carried to the altar and from it the chalice is to be filled. To do otherwise undermines the eucharistic sign of unity: one vessel of wine (from which a chalice is poured) and one vessel (ideally, one loaf) of bread.

Nonetheless, for an unusually large assembly, numerous flagons of wine or vessels of bread may have to be consecrated. In the spirit of the Prayer Book, they are all carried to the Lord's Table and placed upon it at the same time, in one unified action. No matter how many flagons are presented, however, only one chalice is poured, and it is poured from one of the flagons that is presented. (See chapter 5, "Vesture and Vessels," regarding the use of numerous flagons of wine and vessels of bread.)

6. When the Altar Book and the chalice have been placed, representatives of the assembly carry the bread, wine, and monetary offerings to the Lord's Table. Often, those who have collected the monetary offerings present them, although others may perform this ministry. (See chapter 7, "Liturgical Ministries.")

◆ The people stand as the offerings are brought forward (BCP 361). This is a multivalent sign that suggests, for example, that the assembly is joining itself with the gifts on the altar and expressing its desire to be "a living sacrifice." That, however, is but one of the meanings this action can stir in the hearts and minds of the people. It should not be said to have only one static meaning.

◆ Many congregations sing what is commonly called the Doxology, which is a verse from the hymn "Praise God from whom all blessings flow" by Thomas Ken, as the offerings are brought forward. This custom probably took root during the days when Morning Prayer was the primary service on Sunday, but in the midst of the Eucharist it obscures the fact that the Eucharistic Prayer *is* the doxology—the prayer of thanks and praise. It does not need to be supplemented or, worse, overshadowed. The Offertory is merely the preparation of the food, drink, and monetary offerings for the Great Thanksgiving. It should neither preempt it nor compete with it. Often, the accompaniment of the Doxology arises out of a dramatic modulation of the anthem, leading to a great crescendo, and then the people with gusto sing the verse. Compare the performance of the Doxology in most churches to the assembly's "Amen" at the conclusion of the Eucharistic Prayer. Which expresses and instills a sense that a ritual pinnacle has been reached?

7. As the collection is completed and the procession of the offerings is ready to begin, the minister who will receive the offerings moves to the station where the offerings will be received. The deacon is the preferred minister, though the presider or a priest other than the presider may also perform this ministry.

◆   The offerings may be received at a number of places: the chancel step, in front of the altar, or across it. Receiving them across the altar is the simplest, since they can then be placed upon it directly. This also brings the representatives of the assembly all the way to the altar and most directly involves them in the preparation. If the presider will receive the offerings across the altar, the presider may kiss it upon approaching it.

◆   The gifts are merely set upon the altar. They are not lifted up in a gesture suggesting that they are being offered. As Marion Hatchett notes in his commentary on the 1979 Prayer Book, the current edition, unlike its predecessor, does not give a sentence for the presentation of the offerings "since the oblation is spoken of in the eucharistic prayer which immediately follows. Making use of such a sentence in a proleptic fashion diminishes the force of the oblation in the prayer itself."[12] In other words, the offering occurs not during the so-called Offertory, but during the Eucharistic Prayer. The Church of England's *Common Worship* omits the word "offertory" altogether. It calls this part of the liturgy "Preparation of the Table, Taking of the Bread and Wine." In this, it is similar to the Roman Missal, which uses the title "Preparation of the Gifts." Since the oblation occurs during the Eucharistic Prayer, then, no gestures suggesting offering are made as the bread, wine, and money are placed on the altar. Above all, the monetary gifts are not dramatically elevated and treated with more seriousness than the bread and wine—the essential things.

◆   The monetary offerings, along with the bread and wine, are placed on the Lord's Table. They are symbols of the assembly, and the Prayer Book rubric is entirely reasonable. Many parishes do not follow this rubric, however, perhaps in imitation of the Roman Rite, which specifically forbids the placing of money on the altar (see *General Instruction of the Roman Missal*, II.73). The rubrics of the Prayer Book should be followed, not only because they are binding, but because they put the most realistic token of the assembly's self-offering on the altar where it belongs.

◆   It should also be noted that the Prayer Book does not suggest that if the deacon or a minister other than the presider receives the offerings, the minister should set them beside the corporal so the presider can formally move them onto it. This is suggestive of the presider as a sacrificial priest, who is making a priestly

12. Hatchett, *Commentary on the American Prayer Book*, 348.

offering. The deacon or other minister simply receives the gifts, sets them in place on the Lord's Table, and fills the chalice.

8. As the offerings are being placed on the altar, an acolyte brings a vessel of water to the deacon or priest who is preparing the Table. The acolyte moves all the way to the center of the Table so that the minister can simply reach out and take the vessel. The minister adds water to the wine in the chalice. The water is a symbolic addition. It is not a necessary ingredient in a magical potion or a catalyst in a chemical formula. The water is added only to the chalice, not to each and every vessel, as if it were needed so that the consecration of the wine in that vessel will "work."

◆ Whenever liquid is poured into a vessel on the Holy Table, a purificator is held at the lip of the vessel and drawn across it as the pouring is completed. This catches any drops that cling to the lip and prevents them from falling onto the altar coverings.

◆ If the deacon or an assisting priest has prepared the Lord's Table, this minister steps back, and the presider approaches the center of the Table and may kiss it. The gifts, the ministers, and the other members of the assembly may be censed. (See chapter 8, "Postures and Gestures.")

9. The presider's hands may be washed. The Roman Rite directs the presider to recite Psalm 51:2 privately as the hands are being washed: "Wash me through and through from my wickedness and cleanse me from my sin." In the Episcopal Church, both the verse and the entire action are at the discretion of the presider.

◆ If one acolyte is to assist the presider with the lavabo, a towel is draped over the acolyte's left arm. The acolyte holds either a bowl of water in both hands, or an empty bowl in the left and a vessel of water in the right. The acolyte moves to the presider. The presider either dips the hands in the bowl of water or holds the hands over the empty bowl as the acolyte pours water over them. The acolyte then brings the left arm in front of the body so the towel is near the presider. The presider dries the hands, folds the towel without ceremony, and drapes it again over the acolyte's arm. The acolyte then returns the items to the credence table. (The folding of the towel is incidental and, while it should not be careless, it should not be exaggerated and given more attention than the folding of a handtowel merits.)

◆ If two acolytes are to assist the presider, the one nearest the altar holds either a bowl of water in both hands, or an empty bowl in the left and a vessel of water in the right. The other one holds a towel stretched between the hands at the level of the bowl. The acolytes move to the presider. The presider either dips the hands in the bowl of water or holds the hands over the empty bowl, and the acolyte with the vessel pours water over them. The presider then takes the towel from the other acolyte and dries the hands. Stretching it out as before, the presider returns it to the acolyte. The two acolytes then return the items to the credence table.

MAKING EUCHARIST

The Prayer Book directs the assembly to stand for the beginning of the Eucharistic Prayer. This will have already happened, in fact, as the offerings were brought to the Lord's Table. In most church buildings, the congregation now simply turns its attention toward the altar. In rooms where the altar is surrounded with a large space, however, the assembly can also gather about the Table. They could also move to the Table earlier, as offerings are carried to it.

The presider faces the assembly, as the Prayer Book directs. If the Holy Table is against the east wall, the presider turns away from it toward the other members of the assembly. If the presider is facing the assembly over the altar, however, or the assembly is gathered around it, the presider simply begins the Great Thanksgiving.

The deacon generally stands to the presider's right, although if the Altar Book is to the left and the deacon will turn the pages, the arrangement is reversed. An acolyte or eucharistic minister may also stand to the presider's left and turn the pages. The deacon should stand close enough to assist the presider and to be able to reach objects on the altar at the appropriate moments. At the same time, the deacon should allow ample space for the presider to assume the *orans* position and should not seem to be co-presiding.

THE SURSUM CORDA

1. The assembly and the presider exchange the responses in the Preface Dialogue, sometimes called the *Sursum corda*. Since this is a genuine dialogue, the presider looks at the assembly during all of it.

2. The gestures most presiders make during the dialogue are not recommended:

   ◆ "The Lord be with you." The presider opens the hands and arms in a modest gesture toward the assembly.

   ◆ "Lift up your hearts." The presider raises the hands straight up, as if literally to illustrate the command.

   ◆ "Let us give thanks to the Lord our God." The presider moves the hands outward and upward, in a circular motion, bringing them down across the forehead and face, and joining them at the chest.

Despite their pedigree, these gestures seem, on the one hand, contrived (the circular motion at the end), and, on the other hand, simplistic (the literal raising of the hands during the command for the assembly metaphorically to lift their hearts). A more natural way to use the body, and one that unifies these three exchanges into a single dialogue, is for the presider to maintain one posture throughout. The hands are joined loosely at the chest, and the eyes are kept on the assembly until the final response, "It is right to give him [our] thanks and praise." Far more is accomplished by the presider actually looking at the assembly while speaking with them, than by making a series of complicated hand gestures.

3. The presider then turns toward the Holy Table if it is against the east wall, opens the arms in the *orans* position, and continues with the Great Thanksgiving.

THE PREFACE

The first section, called the Preface, is an integral part of the Great Thanksgiving. It is not a prelude to it. The title of each Eucharistic Prayer in the current edition of the Prayer Book comes before the introductory dialogue and no other title appears before the final "Amen." The 1928 Book of Common Prayer followed a different convention, inserting a new title, "The Prayer of Consecration," after the *Sanctus*. The 1979 Prayer Book directs the entire assembly to stand during the Preface. To make the unity of the Great Thanksgiving clear, the assembly should remain standing even after the Preface, throughout the rest of the Eucharistic Prayer. While the Prayer Book does allow kneeling as an option for the second part of the prayer, standing is the preferred posture. (See the discussion on standing in chapter 8, "Postures and Gestures," especially the comment by Marion Hatchett.)

It should be noted that the rubric here, paralleling other rubrics in the Prayer Book, says what "the people" might do. This does not mean individual members, although it is often read that way. It means the people as a group. Common posture is an element of common prayer. "The people stand or kneel" does not mean that some of the people may do one thing and some may do another. "The people" is a collective subject and implies a collective action. In congregations where some stand and some kneel, homiletics and religious formation should explore how this is contrary to the spirit of common prayer, while not being dictatorial or offensive to anyone's piety.

1. The Eucharistic Prayer is addressed to God, not to the assembly. The presider, therefore, looks into the Altar Book throughout the prayer, except when directly referring to the bread or wine. Then the eyes are turned to them.

2. Near the end of the Preface, just before the *Sanctus*, the presider begins to close the arms so that, just as the *Sanctus* begins, the hands meet at the chest. Near the end of the *Sanctus*, the presider again opens the arms in the *orans*. Two gestures are common during the *Sanctus:*

◆ From the beginning "Holy, holy, holy" to the end of the first "Hosanna in the highest," the assembly may make a profound bow. If the gesture is made, it should be by the entire assembly. It is not a presidential or ministerial gesture and should not be reserved to the vested ministers. Catechesis may be required to explain the gesture to the assembly and to encourage them to perform it along with the ministers, if the liturgical planners adopt it and the parish culture would support it.

◆ At the word "blessed" some Episcopalians make the sign of the cross over their bodies. This custom is based upon a misunderstanding. When a blessing is being invoked, some people cross themselves as the presider says the word "bless." For example, when the presider says, "May Almighty God *bless* you," many Episcopalians begin to cross themselves. When the word "blessed" occurs in the *Sanctus,* they also cross themselves, by association. In the *Sanctus,* however, the word is not related to the invocation of a blessing. Therefore, while the custom cannot be forbidden, for the designated ministers, especially the presider, to do it in the sight of the assembly would perpetuate this misreading.

THE INSTITUTION NARRATIVE

A few general notes are in order concerning the function of the Institution Narrative in the Eucharistic Prayer, given the variety of conceptions (and misconceptions) about the meaning and purpose of this part of the Great Thanksgiving. The Prayer Book directs the presider to lift or to lay a hand upon the bread and the cup as each is mentioned during the Institution Narrative. This gesture is commonly, if not almost universally, misunderstood. It is not in fact an opportunity for the priest to impersonate Jesus, although priests often treat it that way. They lift the bread and gaze at the assembly, saying, "Take, eat," as if the Eucharist were a tableau of the Last Supper and the priest were playing the role of Jesus. Often, they pivot with the bread and then the cup, holding them out to the people as if Jesus (played by the priest) were reenacting the Last Supper.

All of the Eucharistic Prayer is precisely a prayer, and so it is addressed to God. *The memorial of the Last Supper embedded in the Eucharistic Prayer is also addressed to God, not to the assembly.* A number of key moments in Jesus' life for which the assembly gives thanks *to God* are enumerated. The Last Supper is among them because it is the mandate for what the assembly is doing.

In fact, the Last Supper does not have to be mentioned for a Eucharistic Prayer to be authentic and orthodox. In at least one ancient Eucharistic Prayer, commonly called the Prayer of Addai and Mari, the words of institution are entirely absent. Liturgists and sacramental theologians, nonetheless, recognize it is a complete, valid, and orthodox Eucharistic Prayer. In 2003, even the Roman Pope acknowledged that the churches that have used this prayer since the patristic era celebrate a Eucharist that is not in the least defective.

The celebration of the anointing of the sick, to suggest a parallel example, does not depend on the church explicitly recalling the mandate for what it is doing. The letter of James is the mandate: "Are any among you sick? They should call for the elders of the church and have them pray over them, anointing them with oil in the name of the Lord" (5:14). The Prayer Book includes this reading as an option but does not require it; clearly, not reading the text from James does not make the rite ineffective.

This is not to suggest that the Western church should abandon the custom of reciting the Institution Narrative during the Eucharistic Prayer. The church should, however, be clear about what it is doing. It is recalling *before God* the institution of the Lord's Supper, not reenacting the last meal Jesus shared with his disciples. Whether the presider raises the bread and wine or lays a hand upon them, the presider is not imitating Jesus. The presider is designating *which* bread and *which* wine is being consecrated. (It would seem, since the church clearly means to consecrate what has been placed on the altar, that the gesture is not strictly necessary. Still, the Prayer Book mandates the gesture and so the presider may not omit it.)

To clarify another misconception: The gesture of touching the elements is not required because the priest has "magic" hands. Similarly, none of the words are magic words. There are no specific words that effect the eucharistic transformation or are required to effect it. The Great Thanksgiving—the entire action, not any particular words or gestures within it—leaves the bread and wine transformed. Therefore, the ringing of bells along with bows and genuflections after the Institution Narrative, while common in the West for many, many centuries, is ill-conceived and cannot be defended.

As the consideration of the *epiclesis* (the calling of the Holy Spirit upon the elements) will show, the very structure of the Eucharistic Prayers in the Episcopal Church make it clear that the words of institution and the accompanying gestures are not consecratory.

1. The presider remains in the *orans* from the end of the *Sanctus* until the end of the Great Thanksgiving except at the Institution Narrative and the *epiclesis*. At the Institution Narrative, the presider brings the hands together and turns the eyes toward the food and drink.

◆   If the bread and wine are to be lifted: Only one vessel of bread and one of wine are lifted, even if numerous vessels have been placed on the Lord's Table. The presider lays a hand on the other vessels before lifting the principal one. For example, if a flagon of wine is being consecrated in addition to the chalice, the presider lays a hand upon the flagon at the beginning of the text concerning the wine, but then lifts only the chalice. The elements are raised only inches above the Table, not even to chest level, in order not to suggest that this is a consecratory gesture. The bread is held throughout the part of the Institution Narrative referring to it, and then replaced on the altar. The wine is held in the same way. In elevating the chalice, the presider grasps the node (the knob-like ring on the stem) in one hand and pinches the base with the other.

◆   If the bread and the wine are to be touched but not lifted: The presider may use one or both hands, in proportion to the size of the vessels. The gesture should be strong, and deliberate. If one hand is used, the other remains on the chest. If there are numerous vessels, the presider purposefully touches each one. The presider should attend reverently to each vessel and not merely tap them, one after the other.

THE *EPICLESIS*

The *epiclesis* is an essential element of classic Eucharistic Prayers. It expresses the church's understanding that the Holy Spirit is the active force in the transformation of both the elements and the assembly. Besides the *epiclesis*, no further blessing needs to be invoked upon the food and drink, and the authorized Eucharistic Prayers of the

Episcopal Church contain none. Additional gestures of blessing, like numerous signs of the cross over the elements, are not only unnecessary but also detract from the single invocation of the Spirit and bespeak theological confusion.

During the Middle Ages, it is true, signs of the cross multiplied during the Eucharistic Prayer. The priest traced it again and again over the elements, usually in sets of three. This sort of multiplication is theologically baseless, however, and it muddles the assembly's view of what it is doing. Modern theologians, in agreement with their ancient predecessors and the great minds of the Reformation, teach that the Holy Spirit is the active force in the Eucharist. The ritual (the *lex orandi*) should reflect this consensus (the *lex credendi*), and not imply that the bestowal of the Spirit is insufficient to enact the Eucharist.

The authorized Episcopal texts follow the pattern of the most ancient Eucharistic Prayers, which is the pattern still used in the Eastern churches. This pattern places the invocation of the Holy Spirit *after* the Institution Narrative. If the Institution Narrative is the consecratory formula, to invoke the Holy Spirit upon the elements afterward is absurd. Clearly, according to the logic of our authorized prayers, the Institution Narrative is not a consecratory formula and the gestures of the presider during it are not consecratory gestures. The entire Great Thanksgiving must be thought of as the consecratory act, and no words or gestures in it should be singled out, nor any moment demarcated, as *the* point of consecration.

1. At the *epiclesis* of the elements: The presider brings the hands together from the *orans* and joins them at the chest. They are then outstretched over the elements and held there throughout the invocation of the Spirit. This is the same gesture as laying hands upon people and invoking the Holy Spirit upon them. Forming the hands into a rigid pose with the thumbs interlocked in a particular way is not necessary and can even be distracting. The *epicletic* gesture is essentially the laying on of hands, something every priest instinctively knows how to do prayerfully and thoughtfully. The presider then moves the hands back to the chest.

2. At the *epiclesis* of the assembly: The Holy Spirit is invoked upon the *entire* assembly, including the presider, during the Eucharistic Prayer. Commonly, Episcopalians, including the presider, cross themselves during this *epiclesis*. If making the sign of the cross is not the local custom, a profound bow would be appropriate instead. In all but one of the authorized Eucharistic Prayers, the *epiclesis* over the people follows directly upon the *epiclesis* over the food and drink. The right hand is used to trace the sign of the cross over the body as the Spirit is invoked upon the assembly, and then the right hand is brought back to the chest. The presider then resumes the *orans* position.

3. That is the usual pattern. Eucharistic Prayer 3 from *Enriching Our Worship 1*, however, reverses the two *epicleses*, so that the Spirit is first invoked upon the assembly and then upon the bread and wine. When praying this prayer:

◆ The presider joins the hands at the beginning of the Memorial Acclamation ("Dying you destroyed our death") and brings them to the chest. The presider then asks God to "Send the Holy Spirit upon us," and simultaneously traces the cross over the body with the right hand while not moving the left. The right hand is brought back to the chest and then both hands are extended over the gifts. Finally, the hands are brought again to the chest, and then opened into the *orans*.

THE DOXOLOGY AT THE EUCHARISTIC PRAYER

The eucharistic Presence arises out of the community's entire prayer of thankful remembrance as it gathers around the Bread and Wine. The "Amen" that concludes the Great Thanksgiving, therefore, is the culmination and the seal of the very heart of the eucharistic liturgy. This is the proper place for the energy and drama that is often diverted to the Doxology at the Offertory.

1. The Roman Rite instructs the presider to elevate the Bread and Wine during the entire doxology, beginning at "By him...." This gesture is fitting, not because it is Roman, but because it brings into harmony theology, liturgical text, and bodily action. The doxology of the Eucharistic Prayer is a crescendo, and by the combination of a strong gesture, strong music, and a strong text, the significance of this moment becomes vivid. Such a clear and strong performance not only expresses a liturgical and theological understanding, but also instills it in the assembly. Like the entire liturgy, this is a formative moment.

2. The gesture can be done in a number of ways. The most common is for the presider to take a Host in one hand, and then to hold it above the chalice grasped in the other hand, and then to elevate them together. While this makes the Bread visible, it involves only one piece of it. Another possibility is to elevate an entire vessel of Bread next to the chalice of Wine. This is a stronger gesture, especially if it is done with vigor and the vessels are held high.

3. The deacon assisting at the Lord's Table elevates the cup. The presider does not hand the cup to the deacon. Rather, during the last sentence of the Great Thanksgiving, just before the doxology, the deacon moves close to the Table so that, as the presider takes the vessel of Bread, the deacon can take the vessel of Wine. In this way, the doxological text with its accompanying gesture flows directly out of the Eucharistic Prayer without a gap or fumbling. The two ministers elevate the vessels side by side, so that the vessels almost touch and are kept at the same level. The eucharistic Presence is one Presence under two forms, so the vessels should be related to one another. The presider remains in the central, presidential place during the elevation. The deacon stands at the right hand of the presider. The vessels are held steady until the assembly has completed the "Amen," even if it is sung numerous times to an elaborate and extended melody. The ministers then replace the Bread and Wine on the Holy Table.

4. If the custom is to make a profound bow or to genuflect before the eucharistic Bread and Wine, it is done now, the entire Great Thanksgiving having been prayed.

BREAKING THE BREAD

1. If the assembly is kneeling, they now stand. The "Amen" of the Great Thanksgiving is their cue.

2. Looking at the assembly, the presider invites them to pray the Lord's Prayer. The text of the invitation signals which version of the prayer is to be prayed. This should be explained to the parish homiletically or in Christian formation. The presider assumes the *orans* position and joins the rest of the assembly in the Lord's Prayer. As the prayer is nearing its end, the presider begins to lower the arms so that the hands are joined just at the "Amen."

3. The presider steps far enough back from the Table, either here or before the invitation to the Lord's Prayer, so that the deacon and acolytes can prepare the altar for the

Breaking of the Bread. The presider does not step to the side, off the central axis. As much as the configuration of the room will allow, the presider should always be in a place that denotes presidency but not dominance.

4. Two acolytes approach the altar. One removes the alms. Since the only text left for the presider to say is the invitation to Communion ("The gifts of God . . ."), the other acolyte removes the Altar Book. Every priest has this text in memory, or should. The removal of the alms and book should be simultaneous for the sake of simplicity and to minimize visual clutter.

5. Acolytes bring to the Lord's Table the auxiliary vessels into which the Bread and Wine will be fractioned. (See "Carrying Objects" in chapter 8, "Postures and Gestures.") They set them to the side of the corporal—not on it—so the presider will have easy access to the eucharistic Food and Drink. Purificators are also brought.

6. If Communion will be taken to the sick from the celebration, the vessels in which it will be carried—vials for the Wine and pyxes for the Bread—are also placed on the Lord's Table now. As the Eucharist is fractioned for the members present in the room, it is also fractioned for those who are necessarily absent. This expresses the unity of absent members with the rest of the church, and it instills that awareness in the assembly.

7. As the acolytes move away, the presider moves back to the altar, takes the Bread, and holds it high. In a paced, deliberate way, the presider breaks the Bread. This is the only time in the entire eucharistic rite when the Prayer Book demands a time of silence. This silence is not an option. As at the Emmaus table, this breaking of the Bread at the Lord's Table is a hierophanic moment. It is full of expectation that the Holy One who is surely present will become evident, even if only for a moment, before vanishing again. "Their eyes were opened," the Scripture marvels, and that is the expectation of the liturgy: that the assembly's eyes will be opened. The breaking of the Bread is not a functional gesture but a heavily freighted one. "Be known to us, Lord Jesus," the anthem sings, "in the breaking of the bread." And so the church gazes and, full of expectation, waits.

◆   During the Breaking of the Bread, as the presider holds the fractured Bread before the assembly, it is fitting for the presider to look downward if the two pieces are held far apart, or, if they are held close together, to look upon them even as the assembly is looking upon them. Every visual cue must point toward the Bread. Nothing should draw attention away from it.

◆   The silence that ensues is not perfunctory. It must be protracted. It is full of promise.

8. After a marked silence, the fraction anthem begins. The presider lowers the Bread and begins to break it into enough pieces for the entire assembly. The presider holds the Bread high above the Table so that the rest of the assembly can see what is being done, and tears it piece by piece, placing the pieces as they are broken off into the vessel or vessels from which Communion will be administered. All of this should be done in such a way that the assembly can witness the fractioning.

◆   As the presider begins the fractioning of the Bread, the deacon or an assisting priest begins to pour the auxiliary chalices from the flagons. If there is no assisting ordained minister, the presider pours the Wine after all the Bread has been divided. As each flagon is emptied, an acolyte approaches the altar and removes it to a credence table.

◆   The fraction anthem should accompany the entire action. *The Book of Occasional Services* gives multiple refrains and suggests psalm verses so that the fraction anthem can be performed responsorially and extended as long as necessary (BOS 20f). Some musicians have composed "troped" versions of the *Agnus Dei* in which various titles for the Christ (Bread of Life, Prince of Peace, Saving Lord) are sung in place of "Lamb of God" until all the eucharistic Food and Drink is prepared. Whatever method is chosen, the liturgical preparation team, especially the musicians, must devise ways to lengthen the fraction anthem so that it accompanies the entire fraction.

◆   The presider and the deacon arrange the vessels on the corporal or, if there are a great many, across the altar. When all is ready for Communion, the fraction anthem ends.

SHARING THE GIFTS OF GOD

1. The presider invites the assembly to Communion, facing the people. If the altar is affixed to the east wall, the presider takes a vessel of Bread in one hand and a chalice in the other, turns toward the assembly, and extends the vessels toward the people. The presider says the invitation. If the presider is facing the assembly across the altar or they are gathered around it, the presider lifts the vessels and says the invitation. If a deacon is ministering at the Table, the deacon may hold the chalice.

Alternatively, if the presider is facing the assembly across the altar or the assembly is gathered around it, the presider may leave the vessels on the Table. Standing back from them and gesturing strongly toward them, the presider says, "The Gifts of God." Then, expanding the arms as if to envelop the assembly, the presider continues, "for the People of God." This gesture is especially fitting if there are more vessels on the Holy Table than the presider and deacon can elevate at once (for example, one vessel of Bread, two chalices, a flagon, and vessels containing Communion for the sick).

2. All the ministers of Communion—ordained and lay—move to the altar immediately after the invitation, standing beside and just behind it. They wait there to receive Communion and to be given their vessels.

3. The Prayer Book directs the clergy to receive Communion first and, without delay, to administer it to the rest of the assembly. The Communion of the assembly should follow the invitation as closely as possible and not be delayed by the Communion of the clergy. If there is a deacon or an assisting priest:

◆ The presider consumes the eucharistic Bread and Wine, proceeding with reverence yet without delay. The presider then wipes the lip of the chalice with a purificator.

◆ Meanwhile, the deacon or assisting priest moves up to the altar and stands just next to the presider, facing the presider. The presider administers the eucharistic Bread and Wine to the deacon or assisting priest, who retains both the chalice and the purificator.

◆ If other members of the assembly will assist in administering Communion, the presider then administers the Bread to them, and the deacon administers the Wine. Ministers of the Wine keep the chalice and the purificator after the deacon has administered it to them. The deacon or assisting priest takes another chalice from the altar for each lay minister.

◆ Lay ministers who will administer the Bread return the chalice and the purificator to the deacon or assisting priest. The presider then gives those ministers vessels of Bread.

◆ When each group of ministers has received their vessels, they move immediately to their station and begin administering the Sacrament.

If there is no deacon or assisting priest:

◆ The presider administers the eucharistic Bread to all of the ministers, then the Wine. As they receive the cup, the ministers each retain it, along with the purificator.

◆ If one of the lay ministers is to distribute the eucharistic Bread, that minister does not retain the chalice but returns it to the presider. After all the ministers have received the Wine, the presider gives a vessel of Bread to that minister.

◆ The groups of ministers move to their stations as soon as they all have their vessels in hand.

4. The procession of the assembly begins immediately after the invitation. In many churches, the ushers or ministers of hospitality coordinate the procession. (See chapter 7, "Liturgical Ministries.") The configuration of the liturgical space will determine the best way to organize the procession.

◆ Unfortunately, it is common for the assembly to be seated immediately after the invitation and to stand, row by row, only when it is their turn to receive Communion. After receiving Communion, they sit again or kneel according to taste. These are extremely privatizing postural shifts suggesting that during Communion the members of the assembly, as individuals, are one by one engaging in private devotional acts: praying privately or receiving Communion privately. In fact, while Communion certainly has a strong personal aspect, the reception of Communion is, as the word suggests, a communal action. It is the

Body as a whole partaking of the Body that binds it together. Ideally, then, the entire assembly stands in solidarity throughout the Communion procession. Standing, furthermore, expresses and fosters reverence for the eucharistic Presence. Kneeling has a similar impact, but kneeling during Communion is not as strong a mark of unity since, at any time, some will be kneeling and some will be on their feet moving to Communion.

◆   If Communion is distributed at stations rather than at the rail, the stations should be placed in the room so that all the members of the assembly move toward the altar, not away from it. The ministers of the eucharistic Wine must stand at some distance from the minister of the Bread to allow room for the people to queue. Otherwise, the Communion procession will bottleneck.

5. None of the administration formulae in the Prayer Book includes the communicant's name, and ministers do not normally address communicants by name. The ministers will know the names of some but likely not all, and certainly not strangers. To name some and not others is alienating and exclusive, even as it aspires to be hospitable and inclusive. The ministers may interact with the communicants according to either of two principles.

◆   In order not to intrude into this singularly personal encounter between the communicant and the Christ, the minister does not make eye contact with the communicant. Human contact is minimized so that as little as possible will interrupt the communicant's prayer and experience of the Presence. Maintaining this sort of distance and impersonality stresses that the Sacrament does not depend on the minister. The hands barely touch and the minister does not linger. If this approach is taken, the minister must guard against being cold or mechanistic, or rushing from one communicant to the next.

◆   Because the Christ is present in and through human relationships, and because Communion binds a person to Christ's Body, the church, as well as to Christ in glory, human contact conveys a central and essential aspect of the eucharistic Mystery. The minister looks the communicant in the eye during the formula, and deliberately touches the communicant's hand in administering the Sacrament. If this approach is taken, the minister must guard against being "chummy" or personal.

6. The Prayer Book, as an option, directs the communicant to say, "Amen," in response to each of the formulae for the Bread and the Wine. The custom is very ancient: Augustine attests to it in the fourth century. By responding "Amen," the communicant assents to what the minister has said, and takes a more active role in the sacramental exchange. The communicant receives the Sacrament, including under the form of Wine, only after the "Amen."

◆   While all the members of the assembly ideally assume the same postures at the same time when Communion is distributed at the altar rail, in most congregations some stand and some kneel. It would be pastorally insensitive to suggest, even subtly, to any of the communicants that their piety violates some "rule." Homiletically and in Christian formation classes, however, exploring posture as prayer and, therefore, common posture as an element of common prayer, would give people an opportunity to consider how they use their bodies in the liturgy.

◆   Previous editions of the Prayer Book were clear that the eucharistic Bread was to be given into the hands of the communicant; the current edition does not. Some Episcopalians prefer to receive directly on the tongue, presumably in imitation of the Roman and Eastern churches, and as a witness to the Real Presence. Yet since the custom is relatively uncommon, without adequate preparation the minister of the Sacrament may become confused and unwittingly convey to the communicant displeasure or discomfort. Everything should be done to avoid such signals. When placing the Bread in the mouth of the communicant, the minister must take care not to touch the tongue and transfer saliva onto the fingers. Only the Bread, and not the minister's hands, should touch any part of the communicant's body.

◆   The Prayer Book is clear that the normative practice is to receive the eucharistic Bread and Wine separately, but the two may be received simultaneously, usually by intinction—that is, the dipping of the Bread into the Wine before it is consumed. This can be done in a number of ways. One minister can take a piece of Bread, dip it into the Wine held by another minister, and place it on the communicant's tongue. Or the communicant can receive the Bread into the hands and then dip it into the Wine. The communicant can also receive the Bread and wait for the minister of the cup to take it, dip it into the Wine, and deliver it into the communicant's mouth. The Additional Directions suggest that it is up to the bishop to establish diocesan policy regarding the manner in which Communion is received (BCP 409).

◆ Members of the assembly who cannot physically approach the Lord's Table for Communion should alert a designated minister—usually one of the ushers or the coordinator. A minister of the eucharistic Bread and one of the Wine move together to the person to administer the Sacrament, usually at the end of Communion. Ideally, the weakest members of the assembly should receive first, but that would mean delaying the Communion procession, which should begin as soon as the invitation is made. While any ministers may take the Sacrament to those who are infirm, there is pastoral value in having the presider (the official representative of the entire community) administer the eucharistic Bread.

◆ Traditionally, people are instructed to cross the arms over the chest to signal that they desire a blessing rather than the Sacrament. Only bishops and priests may officially impart a blessing, not lay eucharistic ministers and deacons. Neither the words nor the gesture for such a blessing is given in the liturgical books. Often, the minister traces a cross upon the person's head or lays a hand upon it and says the Trinitarian blessing, but this is entirely at the discretion of the minister. Whatever is done, however, should not be so protracted or personal that it disrupts the flow of the Communion rite, or obscures that it is essentially a common, rather than a private, encounter.

◆ In the Eastern churches, Communion is given to infants exactly as to adults, using a liturgical spoon, though infants receive only the eucharistic Wine, not the Bread. Since the Western churches do not distribute Communion using a spoon, the eucharistic minister may communicate infants by dipping a finger in the Wine and touching it to the infant's lips. The finger is dried with the purificator. Often, infants suckle when Communion is administered to them this way.

◆ If the communicant is standing, the minister raises the chalice to the level of the communicant's mouth. The minister does not force the communicant to bend to the level of the cup in an undignified and uncomfortable way. The minister allows the communicant to grasp the chalice and guide it to the mouth to prevent the cup from hitting the communicant's teeth.

◆ Ministers of the chalice wipe the rim of the cup after each communicant has received from it, and rotate the chalice. If consecrated Wine remains in the flagon, a minister is assigned to distribute it into the chalices as Communion progresses. As chalices empty, the ministers of the Wine signal the one bearing the flagon by an agreed upon sign, perhaps turning toward the altar. The minister who carries the flagon also carries a purificator and draws it across the lip of the flagon after pouring.

◆ While Communion under the forms of both Bread and Wine is an important part of our Reformation heritage, both are not necessary. In other words, the sacramental encounter with Christ is not thwarted when only one form is received. Those who are not able to consume gluten, sulfites, or alcohol may not be able to receive both forms of the Eucharist, but this in no way lessens the Real Presence of Christ in their Communion. It is also possible to develop ways of honoring the Sacrament without consuming it; those who cannot drink alcohol, for example, sometimes kiss the chalice as it is presented to them, or touch it to the forehead.

Some congregations consecrate some gluten-free bread for members known to have a gluten allergy. If hosts are used, then having some of them be gluten-free does not lessen the symbolic strength of the Sacrament since every communicant is receiving a separate, "personal" piece of bread anyway. When a loaf of bread is broken and distributed to all but one or two communicants, having gluten-free wafers for those few may slightly weaken the impact of the symbol of unity for those distributing Communion, but none of this is observable as the congregation looks at the Table during the Great Thanksgiving. When a chalice of grape juice is consecrated alongside the chalice of wine, however, the visual impact is unavoidable; the symbol of the one bread and the one cup is lost. Pastoral sensitivity must come into play here as congregations with communicants who are not able to share in the eucharistic Wine discern how to address this concern without diminishing the symbol of the one cup. Remembering that when people receive in only one kind their Communion remains the full and Real Presence of Christ, it would seem best to preserve the common symbol of one bread, one cup. The pastoral care these issues demand cannot be stressed strongly enough.

8. If consecrated Bread and Wine remain after Communion, ministers may consume them immediately at the Holy Table or at a credence table. They may also veil them on a credence table and consume them afterward. Not all the ministers need to perform this task. The others place their Communion vessels (and purificators) on the altar or credence table and, without ceremony, return to their seats. If the leftover elements are consumed at the altar, acolytes carry the vessels, as they are emptied, to the credence. Nothing is to remain on the altar after Communion except containers for carrying the Sacrament to the sick.

The corporal may be folded and moved to the credence table as the last vessels are removed, or after the liturgy. The final cleansing of the vessels is not done until after the liturgy. The leftover Elements are not carried from the church (for example, to the sacristy), either during or after the liturgy. For those who are not well-formed in the Episcopal understanding of the eucharistic Presence, taking the Sacrament away can create the impression that the leftover Bread and Wine will be discarded or stored for reconsecration. How the leftover Elements are treated can shape the community's eucharistic theology and piety.

9. If Communion is to be taken to the sick from the celebration:

◆ During Communion or immediately after it, acolytes bring to the altar containers into which the pyxes and vials of Wine will be placed to be carried to the sick. The acolytes may place the vessels into the containers then, or the presider may do it immediately after Communion, while the other ministers are consuming the leftover Bread and Wine.

◆ If the eucharistic visitors—those formerly called lay eucharistic ministers (see Canon III.4.7)—will be sent out even before the liturgy ends, the presider presents the containers to them after Communion but before the postcommunion prayer. The containers should be delivered to them directly from the Lord's Table. The liturgical preparation team, the pastoral care group, and others associated with the parish ministry to the sick may compose a text to be read as the Elements are handed over to the ministers. It should include the names of those to whom the Sacrament will be taken. The eucharistic visitors proceed immediately to the sick. They do not carry the Sacrament back to their seats. Taking the Sacrament to the sick immediately after Communion is ideal, since it links the Communion of the sick most directly to the Communion of the assembly.

◆ If, however, the eucharistic visitors will go later that same day (perhaps after the coffee hour), the containers are left on the altar and the altar candles are kept burning until the Sacrament has been carried away. In this case, the names of those to whom Communion will be carried are mentioned in the Prayers of the People.

◆ If the ministers will go to the sick later in the week, the presider or another minister moves the containers to the aumbry while the other ministers are consuming the leftover Bread and Wine. Again, those to whom the Sacrament will be taken should be mentioned in the Prayers of the People.

AFTER COMMUNION

1. The presider, assisting clergy, acolytes, and other ministers who have assisted in consuming the leftover eucharistic elements and clearing the altar then return to their places. The acolyte assigned to hold the Altar Book for the presider carries it from the credence, where it was moved before the fraction, to the chair.

2. The assembly may be seated for a period of silent prayer. Just as after the readings and the sermon a time of quiet allows the assembly to reflect upon its experience and to listen for echoes of God's voice, the time after Communion calls for a similar time of silence. The Book of Common Prayer does not mention this silence, although other rites do, including *The Book of Alternative Services of the Anglican Church of Canada*, Order One in the Church of England's *Common Worship*, and the Roman Missal.

3. "A hymn may be sung before or after the postcommunion prayer" (BCP 409). If before, then the sounding of the instruments cues the assembly to stand. An acolyte brings a hymnal or order of worship to the presider so the presider can join in the hymn. If a hymn is not sung before the postcommunion prayer, the presider, when sufficient silence has passed, says, "Let us pray," and the assembly stands.

4. Assuming the *orans* position, the presider leads the postcommunion prayer. The arms are lowered during the final words of the prayer and are joined just at the "Amen." An acolyte may hold the Altar Book open before the presider for the prayer.

5. If a hymn has not preceded the postcommunion prayer, one may be sung now. An acolyte brings a hymnal or an order of worship to the presider so that the presider can join the rest of the assembly in singing the hymn.

Chapter 13

THE CONCLUDING RITES

IN A NUTSHELL

Necessary Artifacts
- The Altar Book

Optional Artifacts
- A binder containing the weekly announcements

Necessary Ministers
- The assembly
- The presider
- An acolyte to hold the book of texts

Optional Ministers
- A deacon
- Parish leaders and coordinators of parish events
- A team of acolytes

Necessary Liturgical Elements
- The dismissal

Optional Liturgical Elements
- ◆ A hymn after the postcommunion prayer
- ◆ Announcements
- ◆ Music for the retiring procession

What does this part of the rite do?
The concluding rites draw the liturgy to a close and send the assembly into mission in the world.

How is this goal accomplished?
Without pause, the liturgy turns its focus from what is happening in the worship space to what is happening beyond it. The rite does this either by immediately and explicitly sending the people out of the room, or by allowing announcements to be made about the larger life of the parish, the church, and the world. Then, the rite sends the assembly on its way. Little intervenes between the Communion and the time when the assembly is dismissed.

GENERAL OVERVIEW

The concluding rites required by the Prayer Book are the dismissal and nothing else. Three additions are optional: a hymn after the postcommunion prayer, a presidential blessing, and announcements (BCP 407). A hymn between the blessing and dismissal, or after the dismissal, has become ubiquitous in the Episcopal Church. The Prayer Book, however, does not envision one.

The rite's structure, especially its brevity, suggests that the sending of the church into the world in mission is linked directly to Communion. The people receive the Sacrament, pray the prayer of thanks—still part of the Communion action—and go forth to embody what they have received and express what they are.

THE BLESSING

1. While it is customary in most places for the presider to invoke a blessing upon the assembly, it is in fact optional. The Prayer Book does not give a formula in Rite II, but does provide two in Rite I (BCP 339), which can be adapted to contemporary language. An acolyte holds the Altar Book before the presider if the text is not committed to memory.

◆ The presider may trace the cross over the assembly at the naming of the Trinity in either formula. At the same time, the members of the assembly cross themselves or bow profoundly. (See the descriptions of crossing and bowing in chapter 8, "Postures and Gestures.")

◆ Since the presider is speaking to the assembly, the presider looks at the assembly throughout the blessing.

2. *The Book of Occasional Services* provides Seasonal Blessings for Advent, Christmas, Epiphany, Easter, Pentecost, Trinity Sunday, and All Saints. If one of these is used, the acolyte must have that book at hand, or the appropriate texts must be copied and inserted into the Altar Book.

◆ Some of the seasonal blessings are threefold and require the assembly to respond "Amen" to each of the three lines. Since there is nothing in the language of these texts, however, to cue the assembly when to respond, music that provides such cues is provided in the musical appendix of the Altar Book. A Trinitarian blessing is appended to each triplet and, again, the people respond, "Amen." These texts are all addressed to the people, not to God, and so the presider looks at the people throughout.

◆ The texts for Lent are, in fact, not blessings but Prayers over the People, an ancient liturgical form.

❖ The deacon (or the presider, if there is no deacon) bids the people to bow. Oddly, a rubric in *The Book of Occasional Services* then says that they should kneel. This is bound to cause confusion. If the minister says, "Bow down before the Lord," following the text in *The Book of Occasional Services*, then the people should be expected to bow. If the liturgy planning team decides that the assembly will kneel, the formula should be altered to "Kneel before the Lord."

❖   The presider may extend the hands over the entire assembly—not in the *orans* but in an *epicletic*, palms-flat gesture—during the prayer. It is the gesture historically associated with this kind of text. Each prayer ends "through Christ our Lord" or "for ever and ever," so the people naturally respond, "Amen."

❖   These are prayers, so the presider keeps the eyes focused on the book during them.

❖   A Trinitarian blessing is not added.

ANNOUNCEMENTS

Since the rite moves so quickly from Communion to life beyond the confines of the liturgy, this is the logical time to make practical announcements, though they may also be inserted before the blessing. These announcements are the assembly's first step in engaging the world.

1. The wardens and other parish leaders, especially the coordinators of projects and committees, can make the announcements. To have leaders of the parish other than the presider make announcements displays the ministerial gifts spread throughout the community. It also allows parishioners visually to identify the leaders coordinating the various aspects of common life.

2. The link between the Communion and the sending will be lost if these announcements are protracted. They should be quick pointers beyond the liturgy, not complex explanations. Details are better provided in print, usually in the back of the Sunday leaflet. If the announcements are so long that the assembly must be seated, they are too long.

DISMISSAL

When all is completed, the deacon (or, in the absence of a deacon, the presider) dismisses the people.

1. If there is a procession of the ministers out of the room, the beginning of the procession is the beginning of them actually leaving. They should not begin to leave until the deacon or presider dismisses them. The deacon or presider, therefore, should give the dismissal before anyone makes a move to leave. The dismissal should not wait until the end of the (ubiquitous but not envisioned) hymn at the retiring procession, unless the ministers stay in place throughout the hymn. If they move during the hymn, the dismissal should be given before the hymn begins.

2. The Prayer Book provides four forms. The last, "Let us bless the Lord," has historical associations with penitential occasions. Clearly, that is not the intention of the Prayer Book since is allows festive Alleluias to be added to it during Easter. The other dismissals plainly tell the people to go, suggesting that they are, indeed, to leave immediately. On the face of it, the dismissal "Let us bless the Lord" does not assume that the people will leave immediately. This form would seem most appropriate, then, when the people are in fact not leaving. When a rite is appended to the Eucharist or the parish is holding a plenary meeting, for example, "Let us bless the Lord" would be a suitable way to conclude the liturgy.

3. When festive Alleluias are appended to any of the dismissals, they are likewise appended to the people's response.

THE DISBANDING OF THE ASSEMBLY

Just as the Prayer Book gives no directives for how the assembly is to gather, it gives none for how it is to disband. Each community must arrive at the best solution, taking into consideration how the rite began, what will follow it, and where. Symmetry would seem appropriate so that, for example, a liturgy that began with an informal gathering generally should not end with a grand procession. If the liturgy will end with a formal recession of the ministers, the order is as follows.

1. After the dismissal, those who will lead the procession gather and array themselves in front of the Lord's Table, with the one who will lead the procession taking the place farthest from the altar and the presider and deacon, the one nearest. The presider may reverence the altar with a kiss before moving into place in the procession.

◆ The ministers, with the exception of the thurifer, gather in the same order in which they entered in procession, although in reverse, so that those who would have reached the altar first are now farthest from it, and the presider, who would have reached the altar last, is now closest to it. The thurifer, without the thurible, may walk directly behind the processional cross.

◆ After the presider moves into place, the group may profoundly bow before the altar in unison. Since the presider will be standing in the view of everyone else in the processional group, they watch for the presider to make the reverence. The entire group joins so that the action is done in unison. Ministers carrying objects other than books or booklets do not bow or genuflect. (See chapter 8, "Postures and Gestures," concerning the profound bow.)

◆ If the Sacrament is reserved on the central axis of the church, and if it is the custom in the parish to genuflect before the Sacrament, this may replace the reverencing of the altar. If the Sacrament is not reserved, however, it is not appropriate to genuflect. The altar is accorded a bow, not a genuflection.

◆ As the presider turns away from the altar, the rest of the ministers turn in unison. (See the discussion of turning in chapter 8, "Postures and Gestures.")

2. As the procession advances, those who were not arrayed in front of the altar, such as a vested choir or the baptismal party on the occasion of a baptism, fall into the proces-

sion in the place indicated in the chapter on the Opening Rites or the chapter on Baptism during the Sunday Eucharist. The ministers who were arrayed before the altar pause to allow these others to join the procession.

◆ The procession generally moves out of the worship space by the same route it entered. The clergy and other parish leaders may leave the procession and move to the door of the church to greet worshippers and to meet visitors. The other ministers continue in procession to the sacristy or choir room with the same decorum they used in church.

◆ The liturgical objects—cross, torches, and so on—must be handled with the same reverence after the liturgy as they were during it. The ability of these objects to evoke and express the piety of the church depends upon them being treated as sacred objects, not as theatrical props. Unlike props, they remain what they are even after the public event is ended.

Chapter 14

 # CELEBRATING BAPTISM DURING THE SUNDAY EUCHARIST

IN A NUTSHELL

Necessary Artifacts
- A font and a ewer of water or several pitchers of water, or an immersion pool
- The Altar Book (if the Thanksgiving over the Water is sung)

Optional Artifacts
- A vessel of chrism
- A bowl of soapy water and a substantial towel for removing the chrism from the presider's hands
- A towel to dry each neophyte
- A blanket to enwrap each neophyte
- The paschal candle standing near the font
- A baptismal garment for each neophyte
- A baptismal candle for each neophyte

Necessary Ministers
- The assembly
- The presider
- A leader of the prayers
- Two assistants: deacons and/or acolytes
- Two sponsors for each baptismal candidate

Optional Ministers
- A deacon
- A large team of acolytes
- Catechists and other parish leaders to assist the baptismal party

Necessary Liturgical Elements
- The presentation of the candidates
- The examination of the candidates and sponsors
- The pledge of the assembly's support
- The Baptismal Covenant
- The filling of the font, unless it is permanently full
- The Thanksgiving over the Water
- The pouring of water as the Trinity is named
- The signing of the forehead with the cross
- The collect "Heavenly Father, we thank you" (BCP 308)
- The assembly's statement of welcome

Optional Liturgical Elements
- Congregational song or instrumental music during the procession to the font and during the drying and vesting of the neophytes
- Chrismation
- The vesting of the neophytes in a baptismal garment
- The presentation of light from the paschal candle

What does this rite do?
This rite initiates members into the church, the Body of Christ, and forges an indissoluble bond between the neophyte and God. It invites the rest of the church to participate vicariously in the experience of the initiates. It puts the assembly in mind of its own conversion and initiation, and challenges it to live the grace it received at baptism.

How is this goal accomplished?
The rite accomplishes its purpose by the baptismal candidate or the sponsors freely requesting initiation, explicitly professing the faith of the church, and undergoing water baptism in a rite carried out by the entire local assembly during its weekly Eucharist.

BAPTISM IN TODAY'S CHURCH

For centuries, and nearly millennia, to be a citizen of many nations was to be at least nominally Christian. Increasingly, however, in a world that has become "post-Christian," membership in the church is a choice, not an accident of birth. Most people are not pressured to be baptized even by their families, either as children or, certainly, as adults. Baptism, therefore, marks for many if not most people a conscious and counter-cultural choice for Christ and the church. The church must treat every baptism as a moment of true conversion, when a person, against the odds, chooses the Christian way.

While the majority of those who are baptized are children, the normative candidate—that is, the fullest embodiment of what this rite intends—is an adult who, through a process of discernment and conversion, has freely chosen the Christian life. The church in the twenty-first century dares not take even one baptism for granted, treating it as a pious family event: the christening of a cute baby followed by a domestic celebration. Rather, the modern church must see every baptism as a revolutionary choice—not only in the life of the person being baptized or in the life of the church, but in the life of the world. The liturgy of Holy Baptism must reflect the importance of what it effects.

The Prayer Book, in all its rites, assumes that every member of the church shares in the priesthood of Christ by baptism. Famously, the Catechism lists the baptized as first among the ministers of the church. In other words, contrary to long-standing patterns and assumptions, the church is not an outgrowth of ordination but of baptism. It was always so, but now this is the operative theology. The life of the Episcopal Church, including the liturgy, is increasingly ordered around a baptismal center.

The Prayer Book strongly prefers four feasts for the celebration of Holy Baptism: the Great Vigil of Easter, the Day of Pentecost, All Saints' Day or the following Sunday (if the feast is transferred to that day), and the Feast of the Baptism of Our Lord, though other Sundays and feasts are not excluded (BCP 312, 298). Whenever the bishop is present is also appropriate, but this book does not consider episcopal liturgies. Because Lent is by nature a period of baptismal preparation, the Sundays of Lent, while not excluded by the Prayer Book, are not appropriate days to celebrate the sacrament. (See chapter 6, "The Liturgical Year.") Since "Holy Baptism is full initiation by water and the Holy Spirit into Christ's Body the Church" (BCP 298), it should always be celebrated as part of a major assembly, with as many representatives of the Body present as possible.

Like similar pastoral and episcopal offices that are celebrated during the Eucharist, most of the rite occurs after the sermon and before the Offertory. It is here that the normal pattern of the Sunday Eucharist is most disrupted. The celebration of Baptism also alters the opening of the liturgy by inserting versicles and responses after the Opening Acclamation; the Liturgy of the Word by proposing that the baptismal sponsors proclaim the readings; and the Offertory by suggesting that the sponsors present the offerings. Also, although the Prayer Book does not mention it, the celebration of Baptism also affects the distribution of Communion, since the newly baptized should logically be the first to receive at the Lord's Table.

WATER: THE PRIMARY SYMBOL IN THE CELEBRATION OF BAPTISM

The primary and essential sign in baptism is the flowing of water over a human being as the Trinitarian name is spoken. Nothing should overshadow it, and everything possible should be done to highlight it.

Water is a primal element that echoes deeply in the human mind, and resonates with specifically Christian associations. The two primary images in the Christian tradition that have been associated with baptismal water are amniotic fluid (highlighting that baptism is a rebirth) and the primordial chaos (highlighting that baptism is a burial of the old self in a watery grave). The readings at the Great Vigil of Easter, the occasion par excellence for baptism, are replete with references to water, and all of them open a window into what it means to be a baptized person in a baptized community. Yet, even they are not exhaustive.

A multiplicity of images, thoughts, and feelings not specific to the Judeo-Christian tradition can be stirred by the pouring of water. Water refreshes the parched tongue and the tired body. It cleans away stains, brings forth plant life, signals the coming of spring, and cascades off mountains with a deafening roar. People swim and play in water. The water of the ocean seems to go off into eternity. All of these images and others that fascinate the mind and stir the heart reveal something of what baptism does.

In each culture and for each person, water can evoke innumerable insights—often inchoate—about what baptism does to a person, a community, and the world. For the water of baptism to have this full impact, however, it must be experienced fully *as water*. A few drops of water dripping off a shell are plenty to make a baptism valid, but they are hardly enough to strike the conscious and unconscious with the complex changes that baptism creates. The baptismal liturgy demands a great volume of water.

THE ARCHITECTURAL SETTING FOR BAPTISM

All of the major Western liturgical traditions agree that a pool in which an adult can be immersed is the ideal. *The Church for Common Prayer*, for example, suggests that "water in abundance should be provided for. Ideally, the font will be able to accommodate the immersion of an adult. It should at least be large enough to immerse an infant and/or pour water over an adult." (That does not mean over only the head of an adult.) Likewise, the Anglican Church of Canada's *Book of Alternative Services* (1985) is very direct in saying, "In the celebration of baptism, the symbolic aspects of water should be emphasized. There should be water in quantity, enough for members of the congregation to see and hear when it is poured.

An act of immersion would vividly express the Christian's participation in baptism, in the death, burial, and resurrection of Christ" (BAS 148).

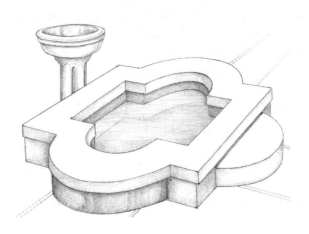

Other Christian traditions are also encouraging the model of immersion for baptism. *Evangelical Lutheran Worship*, for example, lists immersion first among the options for how the water bath is to be administered. The illustration that appears on the first page of the baptismal rite in that book shows an assembly gathered around a cruciform font sunk in the floor. A person stands in the font, seemingly a man, with water reaching above the waist. He is naked, at least from the waist up. One member of the assembly waits at the end of the font with a full-sized bath towel, a sign of just how wet the newly baptized person is. The choice of this image by the Evangelical Lutheran Church in America cannot have been made without the clear intention to illustrate a new and yet ancient model.

The Companion to the Book of Common Worship of the Presbyterian Church USA, an official church publication, agrees: "The power of the symbolism of water is particularly dramatic where a baptismal pool or font is kept full of flowing water." As early as 1978, the American Roman Catholic Bishops' Committee on the Liturgy advised in their publication *Environment and Art in Catholic Worship*, "New baptismal fonts...should be constructed to allow for the immersion of infants, at least, and to allow for the pouring of water over the entire body of a child or adult." The more recent and more authoritative United States Roman Catholic document, *Built of Living Stones* (2000), repeats this principle.

Finally, the United Church of Christ walks a middle line in its *Book of Worship*, noting that water's "presence and use should be boldly dramatized in the service," but adds that "the candidates, or their parents and sponsors, in consultation with the pastor, may elect sprinkling, immersion, or pouring" (BW 130). This witnesses an evolving reappropriation of the ancient way of using water in the baptismal rite.

If the presider and the assisting ministers—deacon and acolytes—will stand in a baptismal pool, their albs must be weighted at the hem. Some manufacturers produce these vestments. Rust-proof drapery weights can also be sewn into the hem of a regular alb.

How the baptismal candidate will dress for immersion is an important consideration, and will be determined by the sensibilities and age of the person and the culture of the congregation. The most ancient custom, of course, was for the person—no matter how old—to strip off everything, including jewelry and pins holding the hair in place. Modesty was maintained by the sexes being segregated at the font and only a few people being present for the actual water bath. There is evidence that women—deacons, perhaps—accompanied the women into the font while the bishop or priest—a man—stood on the other side of a curtain and put his arm through an opening to scoop the water.

Although the actual baptism took place in a semiprivate place, it was not a private event by any means. The liturgy began with the baptismal candidates in the midst of the assembly. For the actual water baptism, the person, the sponsors, and the ministers went into a separate room (a baptistery) for the bath. Meanwhile, the assembly carried on with singing or prayers. The newly baptized were then formally brought back into the assembly and, in some places, anointed by the bishop, even if they had been anointed at the font.

This ancient solution, however, will not work in the contemporary church. Hardly an adult today would elect to be baptized naked, no matter how few people were present or how segregated by sex. Besides, having the baptism in a room apart would lessen the assembly's participation in the essential moment of the rite. Perhaps, then, as an alternative to nudity, a swimming costume or a gym outfit in black or another neutral color—to provide a contrast to the white post-baptismal garment—would be suitable. None of this, however, can be decided by fiat. The entire group, including the liturgical preparation committee, the vestry, the ministers, the people being baptized and their sponsors, and the presider, must work it out, taking into account the dignity of the rite and the sensibilities of everyone concerned.

For most mainline Christian traditions, this is new territory. (Actually, immersion or "dipping" has been listed as the first option for performing baptism in the Book of Common Prayer from the very beginning. The size of fonts in Anglican churches up until now, however, shows that the reality failed to match the rubric.) To consider nudity, bathing suits, and how to contend with a person dripping on the terrazzo seems peculiar, if not inappropriate, in a book about the liturgy. Nonetheless, the liturgy is precisely about God's use of created matter, including human bodies, as a means of grace. It is not always tidy, and sometimes it should not be.

There is nothing to prevent a baby being naked for baptism. It remains the norm in all of the Eastern churches to this day. Some anxious parents in Western churches imagine all sorts of things that might happen while the child is naked, especially when it is lowered into the water. The Orthodox churches are proof that nothing usually happens and, when it does, it can be dealt with. Even with a naked and unpredictable child, the rite can unfold with dignity. The parents may bring the child to the church diapered and swaddled. After the water has been blessed, the parents remove the blanket and the diaper, and give the child into the arms of the presider for immersion.

Even in churches where a font, rather than a pool, will hold the water for baptism, a significant volume of water must be used. If the font is so small that it cannot contain enough water to have a strong sensual impact, a larger bowl should be set in it. The concern is not validity. Baptism can be celebrated in a neonatal ICU by one minister—not necessarily an *ordained* minister—and a baby, and nothing more than water from an eyedropper. Because the sacraments are "sure and certain means" of grace, God acts in them, no matter how minimal the symbols (BCP 857). Rather than validity, the issue is how the celebration can express as fully as possible what the church believes this sacrament does, and impress that belief upon the church as firmly as possible. The issue is the building up of the Body of Christ.

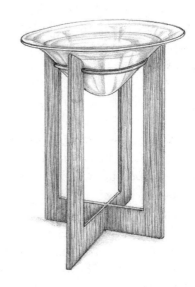

When temporary or auxiliary vessels are set up, they must be, as all liturgical objects must be, of high quality. A plastic punch bowl, for example, is not a suitable vessel for baptisms, even if it is very large and is placed where the entire assembly can see it. Finding suitable objects and vessels is worth the effort. Baptism effects a transformation that changes a person and changes the Body of Christ forever. Nothing shoddy or disposable has any place in so profound and timeless an event.

If the font is stationary in a part of the church that is not accessible to the assembly, it should be abandoned and another one should be set up in a more accessible place. Since baptism marks entrance into the church, it is fitting that the assembly should pass by the font as they enter the worship space. It should be near the door.

OPTIONAL BAPTISMAL SYMBOLS

THE WHITE GARMENT

From the earliest centuries of the church, Christians have been vested in white after being baptized. Being stripped of their old clothing and baptized with water, they were anointed and clothed in a white garment, the prede-cessor of our alb. The old was stripped way, and some-thing new and pure replaced it, enveloping the neophyte completely. The ancient custom has endured in those places where it is customary for infants to be carried to the font dressed in white gowns. Now, however, the putting on of the white garment has become misplaced in the ritual sequence.

Ideally, the person should be vested in white only *after* baptism, and this is entirely within the scope of what the Prayer Book allows. To be immersed as the Prayer Book proposes, a person must be stripped naked, or nearly naked. Therefore, while the Prayer Book does not explicitly mention vesting as part of the post-baptismal rites, immersion demands it. It could be argued, then, that the Prayer Book does not merely allow but even envisions the vesting of the neophyte after baptism. (See the discussion on the alb in chapter 5, "Vesture and Vessels.")

THE CHRISMATION

After undergoing water baptism, the neophyte is sealed with the cross upon the forehead and may be anointed with chrism. Only the bishop can consecrate chrism, so this anointing suggests the link between this person, this parish, and the life of the wider church. While the chrismation at baptism is not the same as Confirmation in the Episcopal Church, which values the personal contact between the bishop and the confirmand at the time of a mature profession of faith, it does call to mind that baptism is initiation into the wider church, not the congregation.

The minister of the sacrament marks a cross on the forehead of the neophyte and declares the person "sealed with the Holy Spirit" and "marked as Christ's own forever." Baptismal chrismation is a kind of branding that signifies that the person now belongs to Christ. Fourth-century records describe the neophytes being anointed from head to foot, and glistening as they walked into the assembly. This was an anointing that went far beyond a small cross on the forehead: it was an unrestrained response to an unrestrained grace. The Scriptures speak of similar uses of oil at the anointing of priests, prophets, and kings, when the oil flowed over them like the "fine oil" that flowed from Aaron's head, over his beard, and onto his robes (Psalm 133:2–3). Baptism initiates a person into a community that is priestly, prophetic, and royal, because it is the Body of Christ, who is the prophet, priest, and king. As the prayer for the consecration of chrism says, "We pray you to consecrate this oil, that those who are sealed with it may share in the royal priesthood of Jesus Christ" (BCP 307). The use of chrism, then, like the use of water, is highly evocative, but only if it is used liberally and strongly.

It should be noted that chrism, in addition to being oil, is perfume. Perfume, too, is rich with evocative potential, but it will be squandered if the minister uses so little chrism that no one, and especially not the assembly as a whole, can smell it. Dioceses must supply parishes with ample amounts of chrism, or at least make it available, if this rich sign is to accomplish all it can.

THE PASCHAL LIGHT

A candle, optionally lit from the paschal candle, may be given to the neophyte after the baptism (BCP 313). Since it would be very unwieldy for a person holding a candle to be lavishly anointed or ritually clothed in white, the giving of the light should come at the end of the post-baptismal sequence.

Lighting the neophyte's candle from anything but the paschal candle weakens the web of symbolic links within the Prayer Book liturgical system. The water, the white garment, and the paschal candle are a linked triad. They are used for Christian initiation, ministry, and burial. As a symbolic group, they associate these moments in the life of the church and the individual Christian with Christ's birth, servanthood, and resurrection. For the light taken from the paschal candle to have meaning, however, the Great Vigil of Easter must first have a powerful impact upon the assembly, so that the event is burned into the hearts and minds of the church and informs the rest of the year.

THE BAPTISMAL LITURGY

PREPARING THE MEMBERS OF THE BAPTISMAL PARTY

The celebration of Holy Baptism requires the active and confident participation of a number of people who may not be liturgical ministers: the candidate, the parents, and the sponsors. A rehearsal close to the day of the baptism is essential. The rehearsal must involve both an explanation of the service and a walk-through. The liturgical ministers and the baptismal party should rehearse together. The rehearsal will allow the rite to unfold smoothly. This will benefit the assembly as a whole but especially the candidates, parents, and sponsors. They will be able to participate in the liturgy with confidence and calm. Like all other liturgical rehearsals, a baptismal rehearsal should encourage all the participants to explore how to make the rite flow as naturally and powerfully as possible.

Because the chosen sponsors may not be Episcopalians and may not even be regular churchgoers, the director of the rehearsal must be particularly patient and warm. This is an opportunity to welcome people into the church and a time for the church to show itself at its most accepting and embracing. Baptismal sponsors should be practicing Christians, but the realities of pastoral life often mean that "practicing" must be given a very broad definition.

Texts that members of the baptismal party recite in unison must be carefully rehearsed. A number of repetitions may be necessary, since the candidates and their sponsors must learn to speak in unison and to project their voices in order to be heard by the entire assembly, and to convey conviction.

The sponsors should be asked to take the lead in the actual liturgy so the candidates and parents will not have to trouble themselves with practical details. If the sponsors seem unable to provide leadership, ministers of hospitality or suitable representatives of the parish—such as catechists or the wardens—should patiently but purposefully assist the baptismal party during the liturgy.

Just before the liturgy, the liturgical coordinator gives the members of the baptismal party copies of the texts they will need to participate in the rite. These should be in the same format as the copies they used at the rehearsal.

THE OPENING RITES

1. The assembling of the church and the seating of the ministers can proceed according to any of the models described in the chapter on the Opening Rites of the Eucharist, or another pattern created by the community. For example, those to be baptized and their

sponsors could greet the arriving assembly, along with the ministers and the parish leadership. It may be necessary to reserve seats for the baptismal parties, but they may also be seated informally throughout the assembly.

2. The Opening Acclamation, as usual, is the first required element in the rite. The Prayer Book includes both the Trinitarian acclamation, intended for most of the liturgical year, and the Lenten acclamation. (This implies that baptisms might be celebrated during Lent, but only for serious pastoral need.)

3. After the usual Opening Acclamation, two versicles and responses are added (BCP 299). The presider then greets the assembly as usual and prays the Collect of the Day.

   ◆ Alternatively, the *Gloria* may be sung before the Collect of the Day (BCP 312). If the assembly did not sing an opening hymn, a sung *Gloria* could help to unite the assembly. If the assembly did sing a hymn or psalm, a sung *Gloria* would tend to overload the beginning of the rite with music.

THE LITURGY OF THE WORD

1. The Liturgy of the Word proceeds as usual. If, however, it seems pastorally helpful, then "one or more of the Lessons provided for Baptism (page 928) may be substituted for the Proper of the Day" (BCP 312). This is allowed even on Sundays and major feasts. The preacher, for example, may decide that the use of a reading more directly related to baptism would contribute to a more effective sermon.

2. The baptismal sponsors may serve as readers (BCP 312), though only sponsors who regularly attend public worship and have the skills required of any lector are suitable.

3. The sermon should refer directly to the baptisms that are to follow, even if none of the baptismal readings was proclaimed.

THE PRESENTATION AND EXAMINATION OF THE CANDIDATES

1. During the Liturgy of the Word, after the silence following the sermon or immediately after the sermon, the presider, along with the deacon and the acolyte who bears the book of texts, moves to the central axis of the room. The rest of the assembly remains seated.

2. An acolyte holds the book open before the presider throughout the entire rite up to the Peace. Since this rite is not frequently celebrated, the presider may need to refer to the book regularly. It should be noted that the musical setting for the Thanksgiving over the Water is printed only in the Altar Book, which does not contain all the other texts. Therefore, if the Thanksgiving is to be sung:

   ◆ texts not contained in the Altar Book may be printed and inserted into it; or

◆ copies of material gathered from the Altar Book and the Prayer Book may be compiled in a suitable binder; or

◆ the Book of Common Prayer and the Altar Book may both be used, with the acolyte taking responsibility for gracefully shifting from one to the other.

3. The presider invites the presentation of the candidate or candidates, looking all the while at the assembly. The first candidate moves with the sponsors into a central location, and the sponsors present the candidate.

4. The presider asks candidates who are old enough to speak for themselves if they desire baptism. The presider does not look away until the candidates have each responded. For candidates who are not old enough to speak for themselves, the presider looks at each child's sponsors—child by child—and questions their willingness to facilitate the Christian formation of the child and to model the Christian life. Each child's parents and sponsors answer as a unit.

5. Ideally, the baptismal party should stand in a place within the room that allows the presider to look at them while speaking to them, but also relates them to the assembly as a whole. This will be accomplished in different ways in differently configured rooms. For example, if a number of persons are to be baptized in a traditionally arranged space, each baptismal group might first come before the presider, who stands at the edge of the chancel. After they have answered the presider's questions, they move westward, down the center aisle, and turn again toward the east. Then the next candidate and the sponsors move out of the assembly, the presentation is made, and the process continues. This brings each group into close contact with the presider but also with the assembly as a whole.

6. The presider questions the candidates and sponsors as a group about their willingness to undergo Christian conversion. They respond to each question. The members of the baptismal party will need the entire text, although the members of the assembly will not. It is better that the members of the assembly look at the candidates rather than at their orders of worship.

7. The last question to be asked of the baptismal party is: "Do you promise to follow and obey him as your Lord?" They respond that they do. Until this point, the rest of the assembly will have been seated. They must now stand. A printed rubric could direct, "The presider asks the candidates if they promise to follow and obey Christ as their Lord. After the candidates respond, 'I do,' the entire assembly stands." The master of ceremonies, verger, or deacon may also gesture for the assembly to stand. The assembly may need more help and direction to participate in this rite than they would in a normal Sunday Eucharist.

8. The presider, looking at the assembly, asks if they will support the Christian life of the baptismal candidates. This is a genuine query that demands an honest response. The presider continues looking at the assembly until they have responded. Then, still looking at the assembly, the presider bids them to join the candidates as they profess the Baptismal Covenant. The presider may  read the bidding exactly as it is given in the Prayer Book or may use "similar words." If other words are chosen, however, they should be brief and not expand into a second sermon.

THE BAPTISMAL COVENANT AND PRAYERS FOR THE CANDIDATES

1. The presider, by questions, leads the assembly through the Apostles' Creed and continues with further questions and responses (BCP 304). Because these questions are directed to the assembly, the presider looks at them during each question, and continues to look at them as they respond. The acolyte holds the book of texts before the presider for reference, but the presider looks at the assembly when speaking to them, and continues to look at them while they are responding. Maintaining eye contact suggests that the questions are genuine and that the responses matter.

2. At the end of the dialogue, the presider bids the people to pray for the candidates, saying, "Let us now pray for these persons who are to receive the Sacrament of new birth" (BCP 305). The people remain standing for the prayers.

♦ As the presider is speaking, a prayer leader moves to the place from which the Prayers of the People are usually bid. If the baptismal parties are stationed there, the leader stands in another place among the people.

♦ The rite allows that these petitions may be led by one of the sponsors (BCP 312). As with the reading of lessons, however, only a person with public speaking skills and who regularly participates in corporate worship should be given this role.

♦ The prayers, as they are given in the Prayer Book, do not each end with a phrase cuing the assembly to respond. By adding the phrase "we pray" to the end of each prayer, the leader cues the assembly to respond and frees them from needing to look at the text. They can then look at those for whom they are praying.

3. The Prayer Book directs that the ministers, candidates, parents, and sponsors move to the font either before or during these prayers (BCP 312). To stand at an empty font, however (since the Prayer Book directs that it is to be filled only at the time of the Thanksgiving over the Water), seems pointless. To move during the petitions seems distracting. Although it is not what the Prayer Book directs, it would be better to move just before the filling of the font.

4. After these prayers, the presider opens the arms in the *orans* and prays the collect beginning "Grant, O Lord, that all who are baptized," joining the hands just as the assembly adds its "Amen."

THANKSGIVING OVER THE WATER

1. If the font is designed for immersion, acolytes help the presider to remove the chasuble and stole (and cincture) and the deacon to remove the dalmatic and stole (and cincture). These may be neatly draped over the presider's and deacon's chairs or stalls. Either at the chair or upon reaching the font, the presider must also remove the shoes and socks or stockings. Perhaps this is an occasion when the presider might wear sandals.

2. The presider leads the baptismal party to the font. The acolytes accompany the presider to the font and prepare for their various tasks. If the font is at a distance or the baptismal party is large, instrumental music, a congregational hymn, or a psalm provides a context for the procession. It should coincide as closely as possible with the procession. A responsorial psalm is ideal, since it can be ended as soon as the group has reached the font and taken the appropriate places.

3. The presider takes a place behind the font or, if it is an immersion font, the presider descends into the water with the deacon and/or the acolyte who holds the texts. Those to be baptized with their sponsors stand near the font, arrayed so the rest of the assembly can see them. Ideally, the assembly should see the face of each candidate, now and throughout the rite.

4. The font is filled, unless the sacrament will be administered in an already full immersion pool or a natural body of water. Water in a very large ewer or in a number of smaller matching vessels is solemnly carried to the font. Acolytes or parish leaders should bear the water. It should be carried at a height and at a pace so that all in the assembly can see it and attend to it. The water should be warm. If the vessels are filled with hot water before the liturgy, the water will have reached a suitable temperature by this point.

◆ The water is poured into the font slowly and from such a height that the assembly can both see and hear it. A bit of the water may splash out of the font. Far from being an inconvenience, this can stir insights and images of what water is and what it does. *The Companion to the Book of Common Worship* of the Presbyterian Church USA states that "the minister pours water from a ewer, or large pitcher, held high enough above the font so that the falling water is visible and audible to all." In the Prayer Book rite, a minister other than the presider should pour the water.

5. When the water has been prepared, the acolyte opens the book of texts before the presider. The book is held at a height that allows the presider to see the text but does not block the assembly's view of the font. If an immersion pool or a natural body of water

is being used, the acolyte holds the book as for any other prayer. The presider, looking at the assembly, begins the Thanksgiving over the Water with the introductory dialogue, the *Sursum corda*. The presider looks at the assembly throughout the dialogue, including the assembly's responses.

6. The presider opens the arms in the *orans* position and prays the prayer of thanksgiving, keeping the eyes on the text. When the prayer mentions the font or pool to be

blessed (BCP 307), the presider looks at the water. The presider brings the hands together over it and lowers them into it, asking God to send the Spirit upon the water. Like the *epiclesis* of the elements in the Eucharistic Prayer, this is a laying-on of hands. In an immersion pool in which the water reaches only to the knees or just above, it would be difficult to bend over and touch the water gracefully. Through experimentation and rehearsal, the presider may find otherwise. If not, the presider may simply extend the hands over the water. The presider keeps the hands in the water or over it until the prayer is complete and the assembly has added its "Amen."

THE BAPTISM
1. The first candidate, with the sponsors, moves toward the font.

◆   *For pouring over the head:* If the presider will not lower the person into the water but will pour water over the person, an acolyte brings the presider a

pitcher as the candidate approaches. A tiny shell, whether real or imitation, is hardly sufficient to collect enough water to have any visual or aural impact on the assembly, or any tactile impact on the baptismal candidate. Baptismal shells attempt to link the current baptism to Jesus' baptism by John in the Jordan. Historical imitation, however, is generally not helpful in the liturgy. Even if it were, John certainly would not have dribbled a tiny bit of water from a shell onto Jesus. The two predominant images associated with baptismal water—amniotic fluid and a watery grave—call for water enough to gush and, potentially, drown.

◆   *For an immersion font:* If the candidate is a child who can walk or an adult, the person descends into the water. If the candidate is an infant, the infant is given into the arms of the presider.

◆   *For a shallow font or bowl:* The person being baptized is brought to the water by the sponsors. If the candidate is an infant or a very small child, the parents, not the sponsors, hold the child so its head is over the font. The sponsors may lay a hand upon the shoulders of the parents as they hold the baby over the font. If the candidate is a child of sufficient height or an adult, the person stands next to the font with the head bowed over it. The sponsors may lay a hand directly upon the person. It is helpful in the rehearsal to instruct the person to look directly down into the water. This ensures that the head is in the proper position. If it seems appropriate, the person can also be asked, after having looked into the water, to turn the head toward the assembly so that the entire group can see the person's face. As with most other things, this is at the discretion of the presider in consultation with other groups.

2. The presider addresses the person, not including the surname, and then says, "I baptize you in the Name of the Father, and of the Son, and of the Holy Spirit." While naming the Trinity, the presider pours water three times over the person, once at the name of each Person of the Trinity. This can be done by pouring one-third of the vessel each time or by refilling it and pouring three entire vessels of water over each person. Alternatively, the presider can lower the person into the water at the naming of each of the Persons. In any case, the person's contact with the water should have an aural and visual impact on the entire assembly, and a tactile impact on the person being baptized.

3. The Prayer Book allows that the chrismation (or the marking with the cross without chrism) may be done immediately after the water bath. If a tiny bit of water was used so that the newly baptized does not need to be dried, or if the vesting in the baptismal garment is to be omitted, the signing (and chrismation) can be done at this point and the next three steps can be omitted.

4. If the neophytes are significantly wet, each one is taken out of the assembly immediately after baptism to be dried. Those who have been immersed or have stood in a pool of water may be covered with a (white) blanket as they emerge from the font to absorb excess water and provide warmth. A large towel may be draped over the shoulders of those who, though not immersed, have long hair that is holding a significant volume of water.

5. In the place where they are being dried, the newly baptized are each vested in an alb or, if the neophyte is an infant, in a baptismal dress. Private dressing areas must be provided for the newly baptized. While the neophytes are being dried and vested, the assembly may sing a baptismal hymn. Otherwise, a purposeless silence is left in the middle of the rite. Especially appropriate is "We know that Christ is raised and dies no more" (Hymn 296 in *The Hymnal 1982*) because of its strong baptismal language, its reference to the church being clothed in the Father's splendor, and its allusion to baptism as the Body of Christ taking on new flesh and blood. This hymn and others like it situate the sacrament of Baptism and the particular baptisms being celebrated in an ecclesial context. They recognize that this is an event in the life of the church, not just in the life of the neophytes and their families.

6. If the presider and other ministers stood in an immersion pool to administer baptism, they also leave the assembly to put on dry albs. Acolytes bring the presidential and diaconal vestments to the font while the ministers are absent, and the presider and deacon vest in them again upon returning.

7. As the hymn ends (and when the presider and deacon have returned and vested), the neophytes, dressed in white, are brought back into the assembly, ideally with instrumental accompaniment, and take their places near the font, standing where they were before the baptisms.

8. An acolyte brings the vessel of chrism to the presider, if it is to be used. The neophytes are now marked with the cross (and chrismated). They come one by one with their sponsors to the font to receive the seal, in the order in which they were baptized. If chrism is to be used, the anointing may be done in either of two ways.

◆ If the anointing is to be only the marking of a cross on the forehead, the neophyte stands or is held facing the presider. The assembly must be able to see the face of the neophyte in order to witness the chrismation. The presider dips the right thumb in the chrism and, tracing the cross on the forehead of the neophyte, calls the person by name and says, "You are sealed by the Holy Spirit in Baptism and marked as Christ's own forever."

◆ If the chrism is to be used more liberally, the head of the neophyte is held over the font as for the baptism. The presider pours the chrism onto the neophyte's head, near the front. Excess chrism will fall into the baptismal water. The presider then spreads the oil across the person's head and, finally, traces a cross with it upon the forehead while saying the formula. An acolyte or the deacon takes the vessel of chrism from the presider after each chrismation to free up the presider's hands.

9. In the meantime, an acolyte lights a candle from the paschal candle and gives it to the presider, who hands it to the neophyte or, for infants and very young children, to the parents or sponsors. That group moves back to their place near the font and the next neophyte, with parents and sponsors, approaches. This pattern is repeated for each of the newly baptized.

10. The acolyte bearing the book of texts comes before the presider who, looking at the people, says, "Let us pray." Then, opening the arms in the *orans*, the presider prays the text "Heavenly Father, we thank you" (BCP 308).

11. The presider then invites the entire assembly to welcome the newly baptized. The Prayer Book provides a text for this, but many assemblies simply break into applause. At the rehearsal, the ministers and the baptismal party should be instructed to begin the text immediately and forcefully, as soon as the presider invites it. This will cue the assembly to join in the text. Then, invariably, and as it should, the assembly will applaud.

◆ Immediately, an acolyte brings to the presider a large bowl of soapy water and a substantial towel. As the applause continues, the presider, with haste, dips the hands into the soapy water, washes off the chrism, and dries the hands. In order not to stain the clothing of other members of the assembly, or even to stain the presidential vestments, the presider must cleanse the chrism off the hands before extending the Peace to anyone.

THE PEACE AND OFFERTORY

1. The presider, looking at the people, bids the Peace. The presider greets the newly baptized before greeting other members of the assembly. The neophytes may move or be carried throughout the church so that the people may greet them, but this should not be allowed to overpower the rest of the rite. The sponsors move with the neophytes during the Peace, holding the candles so the neophytes' hands are free. The members of the baptismal party then take their seats in the assembly and extinguish the baptismal candles.

2. The Prayer Book allows that the Prayers of the People may follow (BCP 310). This, however, would seem an intrusion. Intentions for which prayers would otherwise be asked could be printed in the order of worship, or the deacon or another representative of the parish leadership could briefly mention them at the time of the announcements. At least needs that arose after the printing of the leaflet should be mentioned.

3. A great many visitors from other Christian traditions and other religions often attend baptisms, and they may not know the eucharistic practices of the Episcopal Church. The presider should use the announcements before the Offertory to welcome visitors in the name of the church, to encourage everyone to approach the Lord's Table, and to explain that even those who will not receive Communion may ask a blessing.

AT THE EUCHARIST

1. "The oblations of bread and wine at the baptismal Eucharist may be presented by the newly baptized or their godparents" (BCP 313).

2. The newly baptized should be the first to receive Communion. The ministers who coordinate the Communion procession should facilitate this. If the newly baptized come forward alone, the rest of the assembly can witness them receiving the Sacrament.

DURING THE CONCLUDING RITES

◆ If the liturgy concludes with a formal recession, the newly initiated, along with the parents and sponsors, may walk just in front of the presider and deacon.

◆ If the presider customarily stands at the door of the church or the door into the social hall to greet the members of the assembly individually, the neophytes and their sponsors (and their parents) should stand with the presider. This will allow all the members of the assembly personally to welcome and congratulate them. Knowing that this opportunity will be given, the members of the assembly may be less likely to use the Peace to do it.